RUNNING AMERICA

5,500 MILES ACROSS THE USA
AND BREAKING ONE OF THE
WORLD'S TOUGHEST RECORDS

D1494175

JAMIE McDONALD

summersdale

ADVENTUREMAN: RUNNING AMERICA

An Hachette UK Company
www.hachette.co.uk

Summersdale Publishers Ltd
Part of Octopus Publishing Group Limited
Carmelite House
50 Victoria Embankment
LONDON
EC4Y 0DZ
UK

www.summersdale.com

Printed and bound by CPI Group (UK) Ltd, Croydon, CR0 4YY

ISBN: 978-1-78783-693-8

Substantial discounts on bulk quantities of Summersdale books are available to corporations, professional associations and other organizations. For details contact general enquiries: telephone: +44 (0) 1243 771107 or email: enquiries@summersdale.com.

Praise for *Adventureman*:

"The fact that you do all of this and don't get any medals at the end of it, and you raise money for sick kids is just so inspiring... a remarkable story!"
Greg Rutherford, Olympian

"Just thinking about what you've achieved blows my mind... incredible!"
Dina Asher-Smith, Olympian

"Power to you, Adventureman; you make such a difference to the world"
Carol Vorderman, TV presenter

"Jamie McDonald proves that the ordinary can be extraordinary. Adventureman is an uplifting story of grit and stick-to-it-iveness that both superheroes and everyday heroes will find fascinating."
Dean Karnazes

"Jamie is extremely tough. What he has put his body through both physically and mentally takes a tremendous amount of determination. Not many people could even attempt these challenges. Whether you're 3 years old or 93 years old, we all dream of and long for adventure, but the way Jamie's managed to combine it with fundraising and helping the world is inspirational. His book is a must-read for all!"
Sir Ranulph Fiennes, OBE

"Having run many marathons, the last thing I'd do is run across Canada. Jamie, you are proof that grit and determination are what you need to succeed."
Paula Radcliffe, MBE

For my big brother, Lee Little. For leading me astray through childhood, constantly seeking out mischief, and paving the way for a lifetime of adventure.

(PS I'm still not going to forgive you for locking me in the shed with three of your worst stink bombs ever!)

CONTENTS

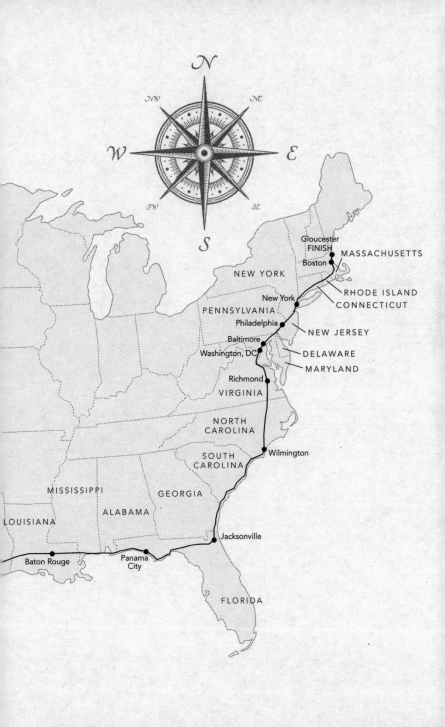

PROLOGUE

It's mid-August and I'm in the Arizona desert – one of the hottest places on earth. I'm 15 minutes into today's run, which is 26 miles from a middle-of-nowhere firefighter's station to the next tiny outpost of Wickenburg. I'm existing in a topsy-turvy world at the moment, sleeping through the day and running at night so that I can avoid the worst of the desert heat. That was the plan anyway. It's now 6 p.m., but still the heat feels off-the-scale brutal. Sweat is pouring down my forehead, dripping from my brow, and I'm struggling to keep my eyes open. I squint at my phone to check the temperature. It's 48°C. Oh dear. I've set off too soon; there is no way I can carry on in this heat. I pass a roadside Mexican restaurant and decide to sit it out for the next few hours, indulging in their air conditioning and swigging down icy tea. When the restaurant closes for the night, it still feels too hot to run, so I move to a bench outside, where I'm joined by one million mosquitoes (slight exaggeration, but there were a lot). I sit still for a minute, slapping at them on my legs and squishing them into bloody blobs on my neck. It's no good. If I'm going to avoid being supper for these bugs, I have to crack on.

It's now 10 p.m. and I'm grateful that the sun has gone down. I set off again, but this time I'm more focused. I flick my head torch on and settle into my "dark bubble" – listening to the sound of my feet pattering on the warm tarmac and letting my thoughts run free. My legs soon warm to the task and I settle into a rhythm, striding strong. Before I know it, I've covered 10 miles through the inky black and it's midnight. It's then that I see a set of headlights heading towards me. It's the first car I've seen all night.

At first it just drives past, but then I watch it brake, slow down and turn around. "Ah, nice, a bit of company, somebody wants to say hi to this lonely runner," I think. The black station wagon pulls up alongside me and the window slowly rolls down. In the driver's seat is a middle-aged woman. I'm beaming at her, ready for a chat to break up my night of slogging, but she isn't smiling. Instead she has a concerned look on her face. "Uh. Um. Are you travelling that way?" she says, pointing in the direction I'm headed and stumbling over her words.

"Yes, I'm hoping to make it to Wickenburg by the morning," I say confidently.

"Right," the woman replies. And now the look of concern on her face deepens. "The thing is... and I'm not sure whether to tell you this or not, but..." She pauses.

"Go for it, whatever it is, I can handle it," I say, wiping the sweat from my face with the dusty sleeve of my Adventureman suit.

"Okay, so you're running that way, yeah?" the woman continues, clearly reluctant to spill the beans. I nod, smiling.

"Well, I think it's best I let you know that, erm, a mile down the road we just saw a... err, mmm... a mountain lion."

There is a silence. I still have a smile fixed on my face, but now the cogs in my brain are whirring, trying to process what she's just said. Then, my brain catches up. My face drops, my heart rate goes through the roof and the first words that fall from my mouth thankfully aren't a string of swear words, but instead are, "So what does that actually mean?"

The lady shrugs her shoulders. "Well, I'm not really sure."

"Well, I'm definitely not sure either," I reply, as my heart thuds harder still and threatens to burst through my chest.

"I just thought it was best to let you know."

"Thanks. It's um... I mean... I..." I stutter.

"Okay, so, good luck. Take care," she says, winding up her window and driving off.

I am in shock. I just stand there with my mouth open, watching the station wagon move off into the distance until its lights are swallowed by the night. My brain is scrambled. I try to clear my mind, but all I can think of is me being a midnight snack for the lion. What do I do? After a few minutes, I manage to calm myself and logic takes over. My choices are fairly clear. Either I run 10 miles back to the Mexican restaurant, where everyone is sleeping and there's nowhere for me to stay. Or, I hope for the best and run onwards into the dark night, into the gaping jaws of a mountain lion. There's only one thing for it. I readjust my head torch, take a deep breath and set off. Kitty cat, here I come.

PART 1

THE US OF A RUNNING START

I was watching the rain bounce off the Pacific Ocean. Large droplets hit the surface of the water and pounded down on the ragged limestone rocks that were scattered among the waves. Beyond the thick rain, through a haze of grey, I could just about make out an island and the silhouette of fir trees springing from its peak. An onshore wind blew and – stood at Cape Alava, the most western point in the continental United States – I was the first to feel it against my skin. I was wearing my brand new green, yellow and red "Adventureman" suit, but the cape of the suit was so wet and heavy that it couldn't peel itself from my back and do what capes should do – take flight. Feeling less than superhero-like, I looked down at my feet slowly sinking into the soggy sand and shivered. "This is tough," I grumbled under my breath, wishing I'd worn something more than a thin layer of fancy dress. But it was my own fault. Anyone else who'd decided to start a 6,000-mile run across America in the middle of Washington state's rainy season would have seen this coming. Let's just say, I'm not much of a planner.

Perhaps my naivety would be understandable, but I need to fess up that this wasn't my first adventure-running rodeo. In 2014 I'd run 5,500 miles across Canada dressed as a superhero and raised money for children's hospitals. At the time, I thought that was the end of my adventures. But I soon realised that everything is a journey – and when one finishes, another begins. It wasn't long before I decided that I wanted to continue what I'd started in Canada and do another trip in North America. This time, I was going to run 6,000 miles (the equivalent of 230 marathons) from Cape Alava, in Washington – the most western point in the continental United States – all the way to the most eastern point, West Quoddy Head Lighthouse in Maine. I had a year on my visa and my mission was to raise as much awareness as possible about the journey and take in as many donations as I could. And, just as I'd done in Canada, aside from raising a load of money, my mission was to connect with as many children's hospitals as I could within a year.

In an attempt to maximise the chances for fundraising, I decided on a route that was a "U" shape, or as I liked to describe it – a smile. It would mean I was going coast to coast but passing through America's deep south, running through 24 states in total. To say that I'd bitten off more than I could chew was an understatement. That morning by the ocean was the first time I'd donned my brand new Adventureman costume – cape and all – and I was feeling slightly guilty about cheating on "The Flash", my old superhero suit I had worn on my previous adventure running across Canada. But I thought, "I'm probably living every little kid's dream right now, dressed as my very own superhero." And I was going to need every ounce of my superhero powers to complete this challenge.

Cape Alava had made its own power known, but perhaps noticing the grimace on my face it had one last trick up its sleeve. Out of the corner of my eye I saw a glimmer of light. The sun was fighting back, pushing the clouds away, as if to say, "Not today." Mist began rising from the beach, as the island offshore now revealed itself in shades of green and I felt a golden light warm my face. This was it. This was the moment. I pulled out my camera, pressed record and poured out all my emotions: the pressure of expectations, wondering whether I was physically capable of doing this run and the fear of letting people down. I went to stop recording and realised I hadn't actually pressed record in the first place. Not the best start.

I was nervous as hell. Fortunately, I was still supercharged with emotion, so I hit record – yep, it was actually recording this time – and went again. This time I was even more emotional; fears, hopes and worries pouring out with even more intensity, I looked around at the amber light spreading across the beach and signed off the video with a promise, "I'll just try my best."

It was now or never. I stepped forwards and put my hand in the Pacific Ocean, the salty water dancing around my fingers as if to say, "I'll be right behind you." A jolt of adrenaline rippled through my body and my only thought was that it was time to run. And run like a lunatic I did! I took off from the water's edge and sprinted as hard as I could for 30 metres, letting out all my nervous energy, until... I blew my engine, could hardly breathe and had to stop. As I was doubled over trying to catch my breath, cool sea air filled my lungs and I thought, "Yeah, brilliant fitness, Jamie! You're totally ready to run 6,000 miles across freakin' America."

On the plus side, after my beach sprint, I only had 5,999.9 miles to go. And as I settled into my pace, it felt like I was "up and running" for real. I strode away from the Pacific Ocean and left the beach behind to join 3 miles of rugged trail, which led back towards the main road. The trail bobbed and weaved through lush rainforest, and I tried my best to enjoy the fresh scent of the trees. But even being surrounded by all that green couldn't keep me calm. I was feeling completely overwhelmed.

Three miles later, I left the trail and I spotted a familiar face stood at the side of the road. It was my friend Ted Eisele – who of course I'd nicknamed "SuperTed".

"Hey there, superhero – how's it going?" asked Ted.

"Well, SuperTed, it's going and that's about it," I grinned.

I'd first met SuperTed six months earlier in London, when I'd been invited to speak at a conference for Microsoft. Ted's official title in the company was director of business development at Microsoft, but to my non-corporate brain that just meant he held the position of: Pretty Big Deal. Ted lives in Seattle. He had really connected with my story after I took to the stage, so when he found out that my next adventure was going to be running across the US, he offered to support me at the beginning of the run and had gone one step further to say he wanted to join me and run a portion of the first day of the journey.

SuperTed let me run the first few miles alone from the beach and was waiting with Caesar in the car park. For those of you who don't know, Caesar is a baby stroller, kind of my "Wilson", my running buddy – a constant companion, but instead of having a baby in it, it was filled with all of the things I needed to keep me going, like my tent, sleeping bag, clothes, water and of course... peanut butter. I felt bad about Caesar not accompanying me on to the beach, but, hey, he was just too fat to lug over the steps and rocks.

"I'm gonna run a half-marathon with you today, thirteen miles," said SuperTed as we unloaded Caesar from the car and set his wheels down on the road. "I've only ever run nine miles before, so it's gonna hurt," he continued. I was impressed that SuperTed had decided to set himself his own challenge, but I was just glad that he was there at all. In the midst of the nerves and the tornado of emotion swirling in my mind, it was nice not to be alone.

As we set off together, I was now pushing Caesar for the first time and running down an open road, surrounded by evergreens, and memories of Canada came flooding back. Unfortunately, my fitness from that journey hadn't flooded back too. Everything felt forced, a struggle. I'd forgotten how heavy Caesar was and how brutal it was to shove him along. It was like pushing a freight train and the shock to my lungs was so big it had me panting like a dog. I began to feel ashamed of myself. I was supposed to be a "superhero adventurer", I had a cape to prove it, but in that moment I felt far from that – I felt as if I was running for the first time in my life. Somehow, I'd forgotten how uncomfortable being on an adventure really was – both mentally and physically. I was struggling to believe I could even make it through the next mile. My legs chipped in and began wailing. "Bloody hell, Jamie. Not again!" they cried. So, I chatted back to them. "Afraid so, legs. Quit moaning. You're back on duty."

Ted seemed to be struggling too, but we were soon distracted by the wall of green that directed us away from the ocean. The fir trees were packed so tightly you could barely see more than a few metres into the woods. All we could hear was the tippy tapping of our footsteps and the remnants of that morning's rain dripping from the branches. When SuperTed had clocked up 6.5 miles from the car (enough to make it part way towards his half-marathon), he packed me off with a giant hug and headed back. It had been great having some early company, but after SuperTed left, the rainforest of the Pacific Northwest unleashed its rainy season fury. It had lulled me into a false sense of security with the sunshine, but now the voice of the rain god was booming. "Buckle up, son," it said, "there are a lot of miles ahead." I gripped Caesar tightly. My body felt tense. My brain was catastrophising with every stride. I looked manically from side to side, noticing that most of the scattered houses had signs out front that read "No trespassing!" It felt like people out here didn't have many visitors, nor did they want any.

Time whizzed by as fast as my thoughts and I realised that somehow I'd hit 20 miles. It was all downhill from here, not for the road, but for my tiring body. Fortunately, SuperTed had caught up in his car and seeing my shattered expression asked, "Where you sleeping tonight, Jamie?" To be honest, I hadn't thought too much about it. I had my tent packed away in Caesar and that was going to be my boudoir most nights, so I just shrugged. SuperTed wasn't having that. On the way to Cape Alava we'd seen a house selling jelly jam which had us both licking our lips. It wasn't far from where I was on the road at that moment, so Ted suggested the jelly jam house could be a good spot to try and spend the night. It sounded good to me – and tasty.

Stumbling towards the house, my legs were so tired that in the last few steps it felt like my feet were actually stuck in jam. I was exhausted. It was my first long run in years. As I approached the house, SuperTed was already wooing Wanda, the storekeeper. I noticed he'd even given her my first book, *Adventureman: Anyone Can Be a Superhero*, in a bid to win her over – well, that and to let her know that I wasn't a complete lunatic. It seemed to work, Wanda smiled and said, "You can pitch your tent in my garden." I looked outside, the drizzle had now turned to hard grey rain. My heart sank at the thought of having to put up a tent, but with no other option, I said awkwardly, "Okay, thanks, Wanda."

SuperTed hugged me goodbye again and wished me "good luck", before heading back home to Seattle. For the first time, I was flying solo. As I set to the task of setting up the tent, I noticed Wanda had an open garage with two cars and, more importantly, a roof. Anything was better than putting my tent up in the pouring rain. I thought I could just roll my sleeping mat next to the cars and sleep outside, it wasn't ideal, but I'd stay dry.

At that point, Wanda's husband Darryl came outside and said, "I'd rather you slept at the front of the house."

I thought, "Oh no, he probably thinks I'm going to steal his man tools."

"Oh, is it a better sleeping spot?" I said, trying to put his mind at ease, but also thinking, "Bugger, I was just getting excited about the idea of the garage!"

Darryl walked me around the front and pointed to a vintage caravan and said, "My son used to sleep in this twenty years ago. You can sleep in it if you like, it's a pretty nice caravan."

"A caravan?" I gasped. "That would be lovely, Darryl!"

Darryl went inside, connected up the electrics and put the heaters on. I'd completed my first marathon *and* nailed a caravan – it was better than anything I could have imagined. As I cosied up inside while the rain battered on the roof, I set about tucking into my rations. But as I cracked open a can of tinned fish, I realised I'd forgotten to bring a spoon. A SPOON!? Caesar weighs 80 kilograms – a large proportion of that was my tinned food – and there wasn't even a tiny spoon in there. More top-notch planning, Jamie.

I sheepishly trudged through the rain to ask Wanda and Darryl for one.

Wanda laughed at me and said, "Here, kid, here's a spoon, a bowl of pasta and a hot sandwich to go with it." Then added, "Fancy a gin?"

I didn't need asking twice and after downing it in a flash, my first-day nerves evaporated. As my tired body sank into their armchair, thinking I needed to get to bed, I looked at Darryl and said, "Thank you, this is so kind."

He replied with a smile, "This isn't kind. It's human."

PART 2

THE FIRST WEEK

The adventure had truly begun. Outside, the rain was drumming on the caravan's roof, the rainforest living up to its name, again. My body grumbled as I forced myself out of bed, slowly packed Caesar and hit the road. As I ran that morning, my brain was a jumble of thoughts: "What are you thinking trying to attempt something this big? Running around America is just too far." My hands had started to freeze too, but with the rain belting down I didn't want to unpack Caesar looking for my gloves in case everything got wet. I didn't feel quite right, I hadn't quite found my groove. After a few miles of running, with nothing but the sound of rain against my jacket and sodden fir trees swaying either side of me in the ocean breeze, I calmed a little.

I tried to make sense of things. Over the past few years my life had been pretty comfortable, and I guess I just wasn't used to it being uncomfortable again. It was tough running, footstep after footstep, mile after mile, but I couldn't stop;

to keep warm I had to keep moving. After 13 miles, my foot began to feel sore and a restaurant named "Breakwater" came into view – it was literally a sign.

I got chatting to the chef, Luke, and began sharing my story as rain dripped off me on to the restaurant floor. I told him I'd started the day before at the westernmost point of the US, Cape Alava. He seemed confused until he came back a few minutes later with a waitress called Shelby and said, "You do know that Cape Alava isn't the most westernmost mainland point in the States, right? It's Cape Flattery. Not Cape Alava."

I'd planned this run to start at the most westerly point, so I could finish at the most easterly. Shelby sensed my confusion and said, "Here, I'll show you on your computer."

I didn't want it to be true so I said, "Oh no, don't start GOOGLING it. Please STOP!"

Too late. Shelby pulled up Google Maps and showed me. It looked true, I was proper gutted. They laughed their butts off at me while saying "Sooorry" repeatedly. Which did soften the blow and, well, made me chuckle too. A whole year of planning and I had still got it completely wrong! After 10 minutes, I thought, "What the heck, this is my adventure, I make the rules and if you look on Google, it's a pretty close call between each point anyway."

After some more giggles, Shelby telephoned the Winter Summer Inn half a mile ahead in Clallam Bay and got me a spot to sleep. I ran on, becoming more and more aware of the aggravation in my foot. I just put it down to "breaking myself in", but it was pretty damn sore. The next morning, the first step on the floor was agony. There was something wrong with the bottom of my foot, perhaps my plantar fascia. I must have overdone it yesterday. This wasn't ideal. My vague plan was to run for six days (or six marathons) and then take a day off. I was only on the third day, I wasn't running marathon distances and already I needed a day off. Needless to say, with 230 marathons to complete in less than a year before my US visa ran out I was feeling a bit sorry for myself.

I spent the day icing my foot, then heating it back up by soaking it in hot water and repeating. A bit of light yoga broke the boredom. The owner of the inn, Sandy, happened to be driving into the town of Forks, an hour away, and said she'd stop at the nearest pharmacy. She picked me up some arnica gel, a natural inflammatory derived from a mountainous North American plant. It helped immediately. Later on, I was lying in bed trying to sleep, but my brain was going at full speed, "You're injured already? You're never going to run across America – what are you thinking attempting this?" I couldn't sleep and, knowing sleep is the number-one healer, I was getting even more wound up.

Then, out of nowhere, I thought of my grandad. A year ago, I was sat with him in his final moments. I transported myself back to that very moment, remembering his breathing was really slow. So, I started synchronising my breathing with his, slowing mine to the same speed and, after a calming hour, I drifted off to sleep. I woke at 6 a.m. and immediately wanted to test my foot. I did a trail walk with my shoes to test the injury. After 40 metres I had shooting pains and was limping. I was starting to think this was pretty serious.

In a panic, I called the nearest hospital 100 miles away and explained my symptoms to the nurse. He concluded it was almost certainly, as I'd worried it was, either plantar fasciitis or a tear of the plantar fascia. He said it would need three to four weeks' rest, at least. My mood darkened, I thought the run was all over before it had even begun. I was going to have to restart this whole thing in a month's time. I decided I was going to travel back to SuperTed's to heal.

I called Anna, my girlfriend and partner in crime, who was used to adventures going wrong. Her response was: "Sit tight. You know these things work themselves out. Just give it another day. You'll find a solution."

I wasn't so sure, replying, "Not this time, Anna. My foot is completely buggered!"

With nothing else to do, I took Anna's advice to sit tight. I didn't last long – an hour later I was pacing around barefoot thinking, "How do I speed up the healing process?" I looked down and realised I wasn't getting pain at all while walking barefoot. A light-bulb moment. I went outside in the pouring rain to run with no shoes on. I couldn't feel a thing, NOTHING! All pumped up, I started to think, "I'll just run across America barefoot, then, shall I?" Although I was eager to get going again, was this simply a terrible idea? I decided to call Ed Archer. I nickname Ed "Arch", he's a South African friend who's a movement and strength expert, and is always sensible with decision-making.

After giving him the low-down he said, "Get something under your feet to protect your skin – and get running. If that means barefoot, do it. You'll only be able to run a few miles, but you'll run the injury off while getting stronger."

In my last adventure, Arch was always super sensible with a kind of mantra that said: "Rest, heal, get moving." So, for him to say, "You'll run the injury off", he must have known something I didn't. Ed and I have always had a theory that having a plan to achieve an adventure is important, but he has always complimented me on having a bit of "naivety" too, where I seem to go with the flow and be able to change plans while on the move.

A few hours later, he sent me a message: "Success in uncharted territory – like your adventures – requires that balance of routine/discipline with the ability to adapt and innovate. That is your mastery. I think we should change your mindset of 'planner' and 'naïve' to 'planner' and 'innovator'. Big love from all the Archers."

It was a great message to receive, it calmed my mind and sent me on a mission to find myself some barefoot-ish footwear. I phoned at least 15 running stores within a 100-mile radius and they either didn't sell any, or no one would post them to me as I was in the rainforest boonies (the middle of nowhere). My frustration grew, after each call I kept thinking, "Didn't you hear the part of my story where I said I'm in a race against time?!"

I thought it best to head to the nearest town, Port Angeles, to look around some stores. Sandy kindly came with me, although as I walked around town barefoot, I think she was embarrassed to be seen walking alongside me. Just when we were almost out of options we went into Swains, a proper old-fashioned American "general store" that sold everything. As we walked around the shoe section Sandy said, "What about swim shoes, they'd have a thin sole and would feel barefoot-like." Genius! We found some shoes that were made for walking in the ocean – and I can honestly say, we discovered the best darn barefoot running shoes known to man or woman. I even ran up and down the aisle wearing them shouting, "These are perfect!"

Back at the inn, I packed my bags and pushed Caesar on to the road. I was buzzing, really excited to don the Adventureman suit and get going again. As I left Sandy's waving goodbye, I began running "barefoot" – and there was no pain. My feet felt so light, instead of pounding the concrete road, I was now pattering the ground like a pussy cat. After 100 metres I began laughing in disbelief. I was now back RUNNING! I pumped my fists hysterically at passing cars.

After 3 miles of pitter-pattering, my feet did become pretty tired from running on concrete. I had never run barefoot in my life. I quickly realised I wasn't actually superhuman, rather just very human. With each mile, the houses became more dispersed, there was nothing but country road and damp, thick green bush either side. Then, 6 miles in it started raining. I longed for a roof over my head, but no more houses popped up and after nine tough, barefoot miles it was time to set up my tent for the first time.

I was slightly anxious. I hadn't tried the tent out yet and I hadn't slept outside for quite some time. Just off-road, I slogged around in the wet grass between tall trees, feet soaked to the bone, and started to set up the tent. I grabbed poles, looked for holes and filled them. I stood to wonder at my handiwork and was rather proud of my quick turnaround. That night, I opened up a tin of sardines to celebrate and gulped them down in three spoonfuls. It crossed my mind that bears might smell the fish, Sandy had warned me about them, but I had to compartmentalise those thoughts. Eventually, I drifted off to sleep, listening to the sound of rain tapping on the tent.

Waking up to the sound of birds was lovely, but I quickly caught sight of my aqua shoes – they were soaking wet. The thought of putting them back on made me cringe. I know I'm supposed to be an adventurer, but I hate wet feet! It's like my kryptonite. I slipped my feet inside and squirmed. As I put the rest of my soaking gear on the sunlit roadside to dry, a sheriff pulled in. He pulled out a pen and paper and took my details. "What's your name, kid?" He seemed to like it when I called myself "Adventureman". After a warm chat, he said he'd mention to the local residents that I was in town.

I got going once more, running barefoot in my wet aqua shoes. Listening to each step "squeege" and "squooge" I felt like a frog who had left his pond and was in soggy search for another. I managed three measly miles before my feet were exhausted again. I flopped down, sitting on the roadside and spooned more tinned fish and butter into my mouth. Still a little damp, I got cold quickly. I had to keep moving, but then, out of nowhere, the sheriff turned up again.

"You're back?" I said.

"I forgot to get a selfie with you!" he replied.

"Me too," I said.

We both took pictures, fascinated by each other's appearance. I may have been dressed as a superhero, but to a Brit his policeman outfit made it look like he was in fancy dress too. It gave me a little kick in my step that someone was looking out for me and I managed to get another mile done. That's when a car pulled up, and the driver wound down their window and handed me $20. "This is for the children's hospital. I think it's amazing what you're doing," said the woman in the car.

That first donation felt great. I wondered if this was down to the sheriff spreading the word. The plan was, as people donated in each state we would give those donations to their local children's hospital, this one being Seattle Children's Hospital. My vision was that if we all support local together, we can have a huge impact on the whole world.

When I was a kid, my mum was told by a doctor, "Your son may end up in a wheelchair." And at seven years old, after spending much of my life in and out of hospital, I was diagnosed with a rare spinal condition called syringomyelia. I had epilepsy, a weak immune deficiency and sometimes I couldn't move my legs. I'd wake up and it would feel like a ton of bricks were weighing down on them. The outlook for my health was grim but, when I was nine, miraculously, I got better. No one could understand why as most people with the condition continue to deteriorate. But I put it down to the kindness of the doctors and nurses who had helped me, and my love for movement. I was always trying to move, even trying to do so when I didn't feel well enough. I'd never forgotten the care I received and the help from Gloucestershire Royal Children's Hospital and Great Ormond Street Hospital. So much so that I went on to found my own charity called Superhero Foundation, which supports kids' hospitals and individual families who have a sick or disabled child. Now as a healthy adult, I'm not just walking, but running, and not just running, but running across countries. I have the ability to run across continents. I never thought I'd say that, ever, and what I've realised is that if I can do it, anyone can.

And if there was anything I'd learned from my adventures, it was that on any journey you're never alone; from the nature around you, to the wildlife that crosses your path, to the brilliant people you meet. Just like the donation that I received from the woman in the car.

I pushed on, a spring in my step, more like a prowling panther than a house cat. But after 6 or 7 miles, my right foot started to flare up again. I called it a day – and stopped at a couple of homes to ask for a camping spot. They both directed me towards the lonely trees of the Pacific Northwest.

As I nosed around the damp treeline I eventually stumbled upon a run-down recreation campground. It would have to do. I piled all my stuff into the outdoor kitchen. Although I was outside, at least I would have a roof over my head – and I knew a roof was a luxury in the rainforest. The constant damp had made things a little chilly so I began to bundle wood together to make a fire, pulling out two big weapons that Bear Grylls would be proud of:

1. A lighter
2. Some firelighters

Still, I did feel manly as I got the fire roaring. In the pitch black I stared at the flames and then did an hour of yoga, stretching out my injury, battling insecure thoughts. I repeated to myself, "This may be the biggest challenge of your life, and there's a heck of a long way to go, but you can do it. Day by day, mile by mile."

PART 3

THE POWER OF CONNECTION

I'd reached a milestone. One week on the road. I looked at last night's fire and saw it was out, not even smoking. Although we were on the cusp of spring, it was still pretty cold and I thought about lighting it again, but decided it would take too long. My breakfast was a drink of iced tea given to me by a well-wisher the day before. As I supped the sweet drink, the fire lit up again all on its own. It was so freaky, but I loved it. It warmed my bones as rain began to pour. As I watched it tumble down, bouncing back off the ground, I procrastinated – a lot. I didn't want to leave the warm fire and roof that was keeping me dry. So, I put each item away in Caesar, one by one, very, very slowly.

I decided to put my normal shoes on instead of the barefoot ones. After two days of running barefoot for the first time they felt tired, so I thought I'd give them a little support for the day. Amazingly, as I ran the first few miles, there was no pain. I giggled and felt slightly emotional, I knew I wasn't out of the woods with the injury yet, but felt like I was defying the odds.

As I neared Forks, I had my surprise goody bag at the ready from SuperTed. He'd said, "You can only open this up when you get to Forks." Bizarrely, as I looked inside it was jam-packed with garlic, holy water, stakes and a picture of the vampires from the *Twilight* movies. It put a big smile on my face because Forks was the spot where they had been filmed.

I had an idea, I grabbed my camera and began filming while holding one of the stakes and shouting, "If I see that hunk of an actor (who knows his name, the famous British one!) I'm gonna kill him!"

I'm sure drivers were passing by thinking, "What is that crazy-ass person doing?!"

It was clear, one week on the road, not seeing many people, I was starting to lose my marbles. But after my little vampire-slaying session, I was pleasantly surprised to see I'd covered 10 miles. It wasn't a great distance, but it was another day of getting my body and my feet stronger. The constant rain meant Caesar and I were soaked to the bone. I needed something to warm me up, so I stopped at a local restaurant and wolfed down a huge plate of pancakes, sausages, eggs and syrup. As I mopped the last bits from my plate, a local fisherman came over, and we got chatting about the human body and what it can withstand.

"When you're injured, it's best to take a rest and not push on," he said.

I didn't have the heart to tell him I was injured and I'd been running barefoot for the past few days.

As I left *Twilight* town, I began building my confidence by alternating between the barefoot shoes (which I nicknamed my "cat shoes" because I felt I ran like a cat, pitter-pattering away) and my normal runners, which with their extra support felt like running on bouncy castles. It was working. I began to feel all the things I loved about running again: endorphins were flowing, I was on a natural high, working my body and feeling confident.

With the running going smoothly, I built up the courage to ask a lady in her car if she would be willing to share my fundraising story with the local people.

I finished by saying, "I've spent the last week with people looking at me like I'm a complete weirdo in this superhero costume. Well, I kinda am, but you know?!"

She laughed and said, "Everyone has their quirks, huh? I'll definitely share your story."

As I ran on, I thought, "That was easy, I just needed to ask."

Five minutes later, I turned around and the lady in the car was back. She wound down her window and shouted, "How about I take a picture with you? That way I can show my friends you're a good human and not a weirdo!"

What a great idea. I asked her name. "Eden," she said, "like the Garden of Eden." She drove off with a grin.

As I reached the half-marathon distance of 13 miles, I felt pretty chuffed with the ground I'd covered. I turned off the main road into Hoh Oxbow Campground just as the rain began to hit again. I had two sleeping options: a toilet or my tent. I went into the toilet to see if it was suitable for sleeping, but it wasn't (don't ask) so I went for the tent. While lying snugly inside, I thought I was getting into a rhythm: soggy feet, soggy tent and a soggy dinner of butter and nuts, and was beginning to feel fairly relaxed about it all. I was now settling into the adventure and for the first time I began feeling like a strong gladiator. That was when a giant bee flew into my tent and I wailed out noises I've never in my life made before like, "WURGH" and "OH-WOAH-NO". Once I had shooed away the bee, I let out a deep breath, put my head on to my clothes, acting as a pillow, and drifted off into the land of nod thinking, "Hmmm, maybe not such a gladiator after all."

The next morning, I packed up and headed south towards the coast. When I hit the ocean my jaw dropped. It was rugged and raw. Tall trees dared to get as close to the swash of seawater as they could, while a purple sky pushed against a wash of white ocean and the sunlight burned against the jagged rocks and virgin sand. It was one of the most beautiful coastlines I'd ever seen.

I felt blessed by nature and then moments later by technology, as I managed to get a signal on my phone at a nearby garage. It'd been a long time since I'd had one so strong and it happened to be my dad's birthday. I FaceTimed him and sang happy birthday. After I'd damaged his ears with my awful singing, I explained my worries about not doing enough miles because of everything that had happened. Dad instantly put my fears to rest.

"J, you're doing brilliant, but it looks to me like you're trying too hard. You're barefoot, for bloody sake! Relax. Take it easy and don't overdo it. You've got a whole year to overdo it!"

Feeling reinvigorated by Dad's words, I clocked up some miles on a very long and straight road with a whole lot of nothing, until I hit a half-marathon and called it a day. I was looking for somewhere to sleep, when just off the road I spotted a quarry. I quickly set up my tent only to find it was all wet on the inside. Argh! It made me so mad. I hate wet tents. I didn't have a towel, so I used my Adventureman cape to dry it out. The wetness continued though. At 3 a.m., I woke with a start. It was pouring so hard with rain I began panicking, wondering if I'd camped in the middle of a floodplain – I kept checking the floor to see if there was a raging current about to flow through at any point.

After a wobbly sleep, I was back pounding the tarmac the next morning. My body felt its heaviest yet – soooo heavy. I just put one foot in front of the other, like I was trudging through thick mud. At about mile 8, I seemed to be getting slower and slower when the Inty boys, Craig Joseph and Aaron Watts, showed up. A year ago, I was asked by Craig to give a motivational talk on the power of connection for Inty – a Bristol-based company that sells cloud-technology products – at their company conference. I had organised all my human connection stories from my previous adventures into a 45-minute talk. While I was on stage, I dropped a hint, "I'm running America soon!" And before I knew it Craig introduced me to Ted Eisele – aka SuperTed. The power of connection was coming true in front of my eyes. And now, here were Craig and his work colleague Aaron, who had tracked me down to a rainforest in the middle of nowhere.

"We've got a surprise for you!" said Craig.

"Go on then!" I said, intrigued.

"A few of us at Inty are going to fundraise for you," said Craig, "but before we start we'd like to make a contribution of £12,000 to get your campaign going. Is that alright?"

I couldn't believe it. It was one of the biggest donations I'd ever received, if not the biggest single donation ever. I smiled from ear to ear and said jokingly, "Well, just because you've donated, it doesn't mean you're getting away with it that easy, come on, come for a run with me."

"We can't! I'm wearing jeans and Aaron is too," Craig said pleadingly.

"That's not an excuse," I said.

Moments later they were running their hearts out in jeans. As the three of us ran, Craig, now panting, shared a story.

"So, an hour ago we got pulled over by the police for speeding. I told the police officer that I was speeding to come and see you. I thought for sure I'd get away with the fine. I told her all about you; wearing a superhero suit, running across America for sick kids. Guess what? She didn't believe me. Still got the fine."

We all laughed and after a few more miles of chuckles we hugged and I ran on alone. An hour ago, I felt like I was running through mud, now I was flying as high as a kite. I'd clocked up 19 miles, my longest run so far. I was creeping towards that marathon distance, which was what I needed to be hitting if I was going finish the run by the end of my one-year visa.

A day later though, I was heading back to Seattle. SuperTed had created some big fundraising opportunities for me – a party at his house and a talk at Microsoft's HQ. In order to make it, I'd have to get a lift and go back on myself. Getting in a car to go to events wasn't part of my adventure rules, but it was such a great fundraising opportunity I couldn't turn it down. I quickly decided that every time I got a lift to an event, I'd simply just go right back to the spot where I finished the last run. That meant I'd still run every inch of the chosen route and at the same time really make the most of every single fundraising opportunity.

It was amazing to be back with SuperTed and his family, they'd looked after me so much the week before the run had begun. As I walked into his house, I saw a big sign that read, "Go Jamie Go" that was made by their kids, Andre, Aidan and Saya. They even had Adventureman cakes on the kitchen table. This was the result of Ted's wife Tamami and her Japanese baking skills. It wasn't part of my diet, but I scoffed one anyway. Then two. And then three. I had to, you know, for Tamami's sake.

Over 30 people had shown up, so I gave a little talk. I could see eyes beginning to well up as I said, "And this is where I need your help. I find it hard to ask, but if you can donate, it would make such a difference." It was the first time I had asked people for donations face to face. Amazingly, every person kindly donated and so I gave them signed books in return. In all, we'd raised nearly $3,000. We couldn't believe it! It also helped that most of the people were from Microsoft, as they were matching everyone's donations. DOUBLE donations. Double boom!

The next day, I had to give the biggest talk of my life – at the Microsoft HQ. I couldn't help but think, "How did I ever end up here? Boy from Glawsterr done good!" Outside the conference room and watching online, there were more than 200 people waiting for me. I was nervous. Not because of the size of the audience, I've done thousands before, but that I really wanted them on board to support my US fundraising journey. I knew I had to create a good impression.

Behind the scenes, all of a sudden I heard Gavriella Schuster, the corporate vice president of Microsoft, say, "Right everyone, stand up, are you ready to cheer Jamie in for his big talk?"

HOLY HELL, WHAT? I wasn't supposed to be on for another 30 minutes. I didn't even have my Adventureman costume on! In sheer panic, I ran out of the room and started getting into my costume as quickly as possible, saying, "Please STOP! NOT NOW!"

With the costume half on, I then heard Gavriella say, "False alarm, that's how we're going to welcome him in 30 minutes."

My heart was pumping out of my chest. Phewwww.

Eventually it was time to speak. As I walked in, I heard screaming and cheering, it felt like a crowd at an American football game – they were ultra-enthusiastic and full of that American positivity – which I just love. I shared stories about challenges, tying in my story with Gavriella's amazing talk just before mine, hitting Microsoft's message that "every person on the planet can achieve more". At the end I said, "Find more within", and to my surprise I was given a standing ovation – I was blown away.

It was worth the nerves and the time spent not running. Gavriella's right-hand man, Jeff Dubois, got me my first local media coverage with Fox News and global coverage with GeekWire. The word was out.

Now it was time to visit a place that made all the running worthwhile, Seattle Children's Hospital. This was the first hospital we were raising money for and the building looked amazing. Craig, Aaron and I walked around the play area, and could see how comfortable, colourful and entertaining they had made it for the kids. I saw one kid, who was so shy he hid behind his dad as soon as I said hello.

As we left the hospital, I said to Craig and Aaron, "I'm keeping my fingers crossed that I'm going to meet more families and kids like that. It's obviously amazing having corporates like Microsoft giving their energy, it's just really important I connect with families and sick kids too – that's where my heart is."

PART 4

LET'S GET IT OREG-ON!

After the fundraising shenanigans, Craig managed to get an Uber driver to give me a lift back to my starting point, over 100 miles away. Jim was ex-military, with a big bold frame and a big bald head, but more importantly an even bigger heart. He was so intrigued by my adventure he took me for pancakes to find out more.

"Maaaan, when you get to the Arizona desert, you're gonna need some night lights as it'll be too hot to run in the day," he said

"That's months away, Jim! I can't think about that now," I said.

"Okay, maaaan," he replied, with his warm, calming energy.

Jim dropped me where I'd stopped running a few days previously. I had left an American flag tied to a street sign to make sure it was the right spot. Sure enough, it was still flapping in the wind when we arrived. As I got back on the road, something weird happened – I was now feeling completely at home running in the wilderness of the rainforest, which was odd because a few weeks ago my comfort zone had stretched to sitting on a sofa drinking coffee. After 10 miles, I took a break and as I did the sun made a rare appearance. I didn't waste a second, whipping off my trousers so I was wearing just my Adventureman shorts. It felt amazing to get my chicken legs out and give them a bit of sun.

Eighteen miles in, I was in the zone and my running was strong. Much to my surprise, Jim turned up again to give me a new camera stand and some freshly cooked tuna made by his wife Joanie. By 19 miles, the thought of a tasty fish dinner was too much so I stopped at a house to ask if they knew of a good camping spot. I was greeted by a crazy dog who wanted blood, and the owner didn't seem too intent on stopping him, so I apologised and walked away. It was getting dark, but I found a spot off the side of the road. As I got settled, I realised I had chafed my "down below". It was time for the manuka honey! This type of honey is from New Zealand and contains an antibiotic to stop infections. As I spread it on, it stung like crazy, but I convinced myself the burning was healing it.

I was back to it the next day, my muscles creaking and groaning as they slowly warmed to their task. By the time they were nicely loosened, a car pulled over in front of me. Daniel, the driver, had seen me on the news the night before and offered to buy me an "Al's Humdinger burger" in Hoquiam, 4 miles ahead. That certainly put a spring in my step and set the saliva in my mouth going. With the promise of the best burger in town, I cracked out those remaining miles with ease.

When I arrived, Daniel was already there with his wife. He wistfully said, "Thirty years ago I cycled across America and people were so kind, I'd like to pay it forward and help you out!"

I bit down into the big, juicy Humdinger burger, thinking the juice was fuel for my running tank, and Daniel donated $60 for the Seattle Children's Hospital. Sadly, I didn't get to stay too long as I had a radio interview that Jim had arranged up ahead in Aberdeen at Sunny 102.1.

Jim had also arranged for me to stay with a friend of his, so I ran on to meet Chris and her daughter, Sarah. It was a mile off my route, with a steep painful hill to finish it off. I called Jim to let him know I was safe and said, "You kept the hill part quiet, didn't ya?"

Chris and Sarah let me set up my tent in their garden as they fired up the barbecue for more burgers. It was a real burger kind of day.

It was also "Wednesday ladies' night" where the local women come around for a game of cards and some giggles. At one point, Chris grabbed her gun, which totally looked like a real gun – but was actually a pellet gun – gave her best James Bond pose and said, "If anyone comes in my house, I'll point this at them and shoot." It was kind of serious, but at the same time said with a laugh. I was getting used to all kinds of American hospitality.

With Chris protecting me with her "gun", I woke up after a whopping 9.5 hours' sleep. I think sleeping in someone's backyard had made me feel more secure than sleeping in the wilderness. It was everything I needed; I felt so refreshed. Chris and Sarah let me help myself to coffee. And a coffee in the morning is one of my favourite things in the world. I'd been depriving myself of it while sleeping in the bush, so it tasted even better today. Sarah made breakfast of sausages and eggs, while Jim turned up with more jars of home-cooked tuna. I was feeling nurtured. As I went to start the day's running, Jim pulled out my first book and said, "Can you sign it for me, my man?" After I signed the book, I thought, "I may have a man crush on Jim."

I fled Aberdeen with a mile-wide smile, especially as it was mostly downhill. My feet were pounding hard on the concrete, so I moved to the side, pushing Caesar on the pathway with my feet on the soft grass. It was so spongy and for a mile it felt like I was running on the moon. I thought, "If only the surface could be this soft all the way across America."

After seven miles and two mini mountains, I took my midday break. I wrote my blog for the previous day and began my strength training. Although I was running on tired legs most of the time, I needed to try and maintain some all-round strength to keep the injuries at bay. I used the trees for chin-ups and a big log for overhead squats – any form of nature that would help. If Rocky Balboa had seen me, I'd have made him proud.

Continuing on, there were a couple more tough hills to climb, but after the extra strength training my legs were empty. On the final mini mountain I leaned into Caesar and muscled my way up, questioning whether I'd make it to the top. Eventually I did and found a camping spot. Although I was exhausted, I knew I needed to do some yoga later and if I was going to do yoga, I needed a fire for motivation. I scrabbled around for tree branches and got the fire going. Then it was dinner time, I took my second mouthful of tuna and the spoon snapped. Animal instinct took over, I began spooning butter and tuna into my mouth with my fingers – and when appropriate, my hands. It was messy, but you gotta do what you gotta do – and no one was here to judge me.

Climbing out of my wet tent the next morning, I warmed up at the side of the road with my yoga stretches (I probably looked like a right plonker in front of the cars) and then ran on. During the first few miles I became really insecure about my body breaking down. In the back of my mind I had the feeling my left knee was going to give in, or my right foot was suddenly going to break. It's odd how you can get into this mindset so easily.

I completed an uneasy 10 miles arriving in Raymond, a small riverside fishing and logging town, absolutely starving. After scoffing some food at the Pitchwood Alehouse Inn, a barman gave me advice on which route to take. My choices were an unsafe busy road towards Portland or staying on Route 101 and sticking to the coastline, which would take a little longer.

I went for the coast for safety, but also because it looked like there were a few towns on the 101 that might be able to help with fundraising.

It wasn't long before I was proved right. Towards the end of my second shift of the day, my mind was focused on where I'd stay. But some wheels were already in motion, as a woman stopped at the side of the road and yelled from her window, "OH MY GOD, are you that guy? You stayed at my friend's the other night. Chris?" I nodded my head. She carried on excitedly, "This is going to sound too good to be true, but my mom lives a hundred metres away, right over there. I can call and get you a couch at hers tonight – that and the best oysters you'll ever eat!"

While the lady was chatting, I filmed our whole conversation including the directions to her mother's house. The filming was for social media, I love to show people the kindness of strangers. I ran the 100 metres in a flash, but hadn't been listening properly to the directions – I couldn't remember the house number, or the road. My goldfish brain was in full force. I stood there for 5 minutes in the pouring rain until I figured it out, I'd call Chris who I stayed with two nights ago. Chris had no idea who the woman was, even after I described what she looked like – although I'm sure it was a case of my description being rubbish.

Fifteen minutes went by. More rain and, seemingly, no brain. Anger started to boil inside me until I remembered – all I needed to do was look at my film footage! This lady had said everything I needed to know when I filmed her. With damp fingers I looked at the footage on my iPhone, I'd filmed the lady and my feet for about 5 seconds and then it must have turned itself off. I couldn't believe it. Twenty-five minutes went by. More rain and, yup, zero brain. I was just wishing someone would come out of the house and wave me in. But there was no one and no cosy couch or oysters either. I lost it. I ran on through the neighbourhood shouting wildly, "Why do you have such a goldfish brain, you %$#^?" Four miles later, I was somehow even wetter and realised I'd just called myself every name under the sun for as long as it took to run those miles. But it wasn't all bad news, that was probably the fastest ground I'd covered throughout the whole trip. And, magically, I found a metal fork by the side of the road to use for dinner that night.

I found a campground at Bruceport County Park. I put my wet shoes and clothes in the toilet to dry off as there was a heater in there. My tent was soaked from the night before and I couldn't face it, so I rolled my sleeping mat out on the picnic table where there was a wooden roof overhead and climbed into my sleeping bag. Laid on the table, I couldn't help but think that the woman, a big plate of oysters in front of her, probably now thought I was a horrible person, or even worse, she was probably thinking, "What the hell happened to him!?"

All I could hope was that she saw my social media posts, knew that I was okay and that I had a dreadful memory! Fortunately for me, the next day I could remember how to run. But as I got going so did the rain, sweeping across the road in mini torrents. It felt like I was running through a river. I let the splashing of my feet soothe me, feeling at one – if in a very wet way – with nature.

This river running was new to me and after 9 miles of rolling hills and mini rapids the sun eventually clocked on. I took a break and set about some more tinned fish, remembering the stash of manuka honey at the bottom of Caesar. This time I wasn't going to smother it on my nether regions, I was going to eat it. As I spooned it into my mouth I felt like a bear. After the honey, I gave myself a soothing leg massage with a tennis ball I'd brought with me. Fuelled by honey and fuzzy tennis balls I felt incredible. The afternoon run was a buzz too. I seemed to glide down the road, my body at one with the road beneath it.

After clocking up 18 miles, I noticed I was running low on essential supplies, so I stopped at a house to ask for water. I knocked gently on the door, dogs barked and eventually a guy poked his head out. He had a skinhead and a black shirt with a skeleton face on it. His face was smiling, but he seemed preoccupied. As we chatted, he warned me to be careful round here as, "Recently, someone had answered their door and was shot and killed on the spot. That's why we got the dogs and while we were chatting I had a gun behind the door pointing at your head."

I gulped, thanked him and went on my way. I couldn't believe he had a gun to my head while I was waiting behind the door. I felt nervous as I ran on, but found a cosy spot to camp and continued to believe most people are inherently good and more importantly there wouldn't be any more shootings tonight. That evening, I received an amazing message from Heather Davisson Runyon, the lady who had offered me a couch and oysters with her mum the day before, until I got lost and had to run on. Luckily, my Facebook post had popped up on her feed.

"Jamie! Thinking of you, wishing you all the best! I want to let you know just how thankful I am we met. You gave this single mom a short but exciting adventure that I have desperately needed! I was so worried about you, but I drove around and saw that you were headed to Bruceport campground. I called and left them a message to not charge you a fee as I would run up and pay for it. Please save my number and reach out if you are ever in need. Hugs to you, my friend!"

I was so glad she found me and got in touch. It definitely made me sleep a lot easier. The next morning was a little different though – as I got back to running I felt my body growling at me. Even the pretty evergreen trees and the gentle sound of a slow-moving river couldn't soothe it. Eventually, I loosened up and ran well, but my brain was exhausted, so I was delighted when I saw a drive-through coffee shop in Naselle. I pushed Caesar to the window. The woman at the counter instantly passed me a coffee and said, "That woman in the car before wanted to buy your coffee."

Another lady came up and we got chatting. She was called Denise. I naturally told her what I was doing – it's kind of hard not to when you're wearing a cape – and thought I'd pay for her coffee to "pay it forward", but she said, "Oh no, you're not!" then paid for her own coffee and made a $10 donation.

The coffee and the donations did the trick. Running on with a buzzy coffee brain, it felt like my feet were on fire with speed. A little later, I checked my Facebook messages and noticed one that read: "Jamie, where are you? We want to track you down! John and Patty."

I sent them a Google Maps screenshot of where I was because my live tracker was still being built by Microsoft and ZeroSixZero. They turned up an hour later with a warm hug and a bag full of Trader Joe's food, including nuts and energy bars. It was easily worth over $100. They were the first couple to track me down and had driven over an hour to do so. There are times to love social media and this was one of them.

We gasbagged for an hour while I scoffed down their food, nearly choking at one point, until John passed me a $100 bill and said, "This is for you."

I was so humbled, but insisted I'd put the money in the charity pot.

He said, "But it's to keep your spirits up, so you can keep doing what you're doing."

I said, "Seriously, John, that's so lovely, but I've saved up my own money for this trip. It makes me feel so much better to know that donations go to help kids that need it. I really don't need much money for this adventure, especially with all this Trader Joe's food. This will feed me for the next year!"

We laughed and hugged. I got moving again and felt like I was running on air. People's unfaltering generosity was giving me the energy I needed. I felt like there was a wind beneath my feet and I was gliding along the road with every step. Ten miles flew by when I spotted a long bridge in the distance.

My mind whirred, "Is that the border bridge into the next state?"

I spotted a fisherman by the rolling river and shouted over to ask. He said, "Yeah, that's Oregon right over that water."

I couldn't believe it. Was I crossing the border from Washington into Oregon today? Now that I was living day by day, hour by hour, step by step – everything seemed to be a surprise.

It was starting to get dark and the bridge was 4 miles long. In fact, the Astoria-Megler Bridge is the longest truss bridge in America. On my side of the river there was nothing and on the Oregon side it was full of bright lights.

I thought, "I need a hotel – it's now or never, let's do this!"

I pumped my legs, increasing my speed as a driver went by and shouted, "You're not heading over that bridge, are you?"

"Yes, I am," I smiled and shouted at the same time.

The man's face looked a little worried, but then he fist-pumped the air and shouted back, "I believe in you!"

The bridge was so narrow Caesar could barely fit on the hard shoulder. Cars were whizzing past and the grey Columbia River was rolling steadily below. Caesar's lights had stopped working a week or so ago, so I draped a fluorescent rainproof jacket over him and faced the traffic. I do pretty much all of my running during the day so hadn't thought to get the lights sorted. I was annoyed at myself, big time! The road felt dangerous, but the speed I was running at I would have given Usain Bolt a run for his money. It was now almost completely dark so I ran even harder. Halfway across, Canadian geese flew over, a majestic sight, I felt like their quacks were cheering me on. On the final hill, I was pushing Caesar with all my might, swearing my little head off, when I saw a siren pop up ahead. A police truck! It pulled in, a man got out and said rather urgently in a deep voice, "You do realise this bridge isn't for pedestrians?!"

"Uh. Oh. I didn't."

"Okay, well hurry up and reach the other side."

"Sure thing!"

Surviving the long bridge and making it into Oregon was a relief and boosted my confidence massively. Only a week or so ago I had thought the adventure was all over, now after 21 days I had completed my first state. Only 23 more or so to go! To celebrate I treated myself to a night at the Atomic Motel and gave all my devices – the tracker, Fitbit watch, power battery, laptop, iPhone – a good charging.

The next morning, handing my key into reception before checking out, a lady looked at me laughing and said, "You must be that guy I heard about on the police scanner last night. They said there was a crazy person wearing a cape running along the bridge!"

Today, my target was to get some strong miles in and make it to another scary bridge. However, this bridge was legal to cross on foot. But that morning I ran straight into trouble. I was running on Route 101 and it was heaving with traffic – I was terrified. I faced the cars and waved frantically with my left arm to warn the drivers I was there. Halfway across another long bridge, I conceded. I'd never lost my bottle before, but I realised if two trucks passed each other there wouldn't be any room for me and Caesar and I'd be dead meat. I waved at a guy sat in a tower on the bridge and explained I couldn't go any further because I was too scared. He said, "I'm closing the bridge to let a boat pass and I'd recommend you run as fast as you can until you reach the other side!" The sirens went on, cars stopped and I did as I was told. While running, all the cars waiting in a long queue cheered me on out of their windows, one man even handed me a bottle of water, which made me feel like I was in the London Marathon!

Eventually, I escaped the bridge of doom and left the 101, finding a quiet road that snaked along the Oregon coastline. I hit the town of Sunset Beach where the huge houses were like nothing I'd seen before. I thought I was going to see the likes of Tiger Woods walking out of his home. I couldn't help but think, "It's a shame no one knows I'm here, it's probably a hotspot for big donations." I continued on, enjoying the cool sea breeze and the relaxed environment. No one had signs that read, "No trespassing!", or "Private property do not enter", which I had experienced in the boonies. It felt so welcoming, I could knock on someone's door and ask for a glass of milk. Trying to stick to the coast, I got slightly lost (nothing unusual) and called it a day after running 11 miles.

It always made me slightly anxious not hitting bigger miles, as I knew I'd have to make them up down the road. I knocked on the door of the first house I saw, a man answered and said it was okay to camp on his front lawn. I gave him a slip of paper with my website written on it – adventureman.org – and said, "Just in case you think I'm a weirdo – this might help."

After setting up my tent, the man, Rene, came back out to say, "My wife is going bananas in there, she says you've got your own Wikipedia page." Then, his wife, Suzeanne came out. "Let me get a picture of you and your tent!" It turned out Rene was half Canadian, so I told him I had run across Canada for my last adventure. That was good enough for Rene, 20 minutes later he came out with half a roast chicken, salad and a glass of red wine. A further 10 minutes later he reappeared with a $60 donation and said, "Here, this is for the kids."

With warm, fuzzy feelings going on, I polished off the chicken in minutes. I normally nibble on the end of the bones to get part of the cartilage (apparently, it's healthy for you), but this time I ate the cartilage and the bones. BONES, DAMN IT. I've never eaten bones in all my life. Day by day, I think I'm turning more and more into an animal, but worryingly, I think I like it.

PART 5

COASTING THE OREGON COAST

After packing up the tent on day 22, Rene and Suzeanne invited me in for breakfast. Rene was intrigued. He said, "I've been thinking all night, can I ask you personally, what have you learned most about yourself after all your adventures?"

I didn't need long to think about it. "I discovered I had the 'keep going' gene, whatever that is, but I didn't know I had it until I cycled in China and it got really tough. Then, when it really mattered – I had no choice but to discover it. It always makes me think, who else has this type of gene, but hasn't discovered it yet?"

Leaving their house, they asked if I needed anything and with the sun beating down I said, "An American hat would be nice!"

Running on, 3 miles later, Rene and Suzeanne turned up with an American cap to replace my Canadian cap I loved so much. I thanked them and said, "Boom. I'm practically an American now!"

That morning I had another plan too. Heading into the town of Seaside I was in search of The Freedom Shop which was going to print some extra messages to put on my Adventureman suit to help with fundraising. A few days ago, a couple stopped me by the side of the road after seeing me on the news. They didn't know what to type into Google to follow the journey and donate. I wasn't sure myself, so before I went into the shop I called Anna for some advice. She's really good at this stuff. We agreed on a "Jamie McDonald" crest where my heart was, my website on the cape – "adventureman.org" in the colour white – and the genius idea of putting "Adventureman" along my sleeve in red.

It turned out Chandler, who was helping me with the prints, had spent a fair bit of time in hospital as a kid and couldn't have been more helpful. Fully branded up, I ran to the beachfront and 5 minutes later a lady stopped me. We chatted for a few minutes and a guy joined us and said, "Hello, Jamie McDonald." I was like, "Oooo, hello, how do I know you?" The man said, "I just went to your website after seeing your cape and made a donation too." It was working already.

Running my afternoon stint was a breeze, I was floating on a wave of goodwill. Me and Caesar on the open road with the Pacific Ocean to my right, the evergreen trees behind, beautiful low-rise towns to the left and the wind flowing gently through our hair. Well, okay, my hair. Soon the ocean road ran out and I was back on the 101. I had to climb a small mountain and within a few miles my legs powered down to empty. But I was never far from inspiration as I entered the lovely town of Cannon Beach where some of *The Goonies* was filmed. I just kept running, even on empty. A kid pointed at me and said, "Look, Mom, Superman!" I felt like saying, "I wish I could fly right now."

My destination that evening was Wright's campsite, but it was closed and the man next door didn't look impressed when I asked to camp on his lawn. I carried on until sunset, reaching nearly a marathon distance. Eventually, I found a good bit of bush in the woods that I could crawl into. Setting up my tent, I was rewarded for my extra miles with a blissful sunset that created an ethereal orange halo above my tent – it seemed Mother Nature was looking after me today.

The next day, I was hauling Caesar up a mountain, alongside Oswald West State Park, lost in thought, pushing harder than I'd had to at any point so far. I was ranting at Caesar a LOT because it was his weight causing the burning in my legs. This only stopped when I paused to take in the view: a sprawl of emerald forest and red cliff stone that tumbled all the way down to the small beach town of Manzanita and the depths of the Pacific Ocean. When I reached the top, I discovered I wasn't the only one marvelling at the vista. A British couple introduced themselves.

"Hey, Jamie, how are you?" the man said.

"Oh, hey, yeah, good thank you. This is beautiful, isn't it?" I peered over the lookout to distract them.

I needed to take a breather because it was really weird, I felt like the couple were planted here just to talk to me. How did they know who I was? Was I in my own version of *The Truman Show*? I wondered if I was having a psychotic episode.

The lady turned to me and said, "We saw what you were doing on BBC News back home and have been following you ever since. It's amazing what you're doing, can we take a picture with you?"

It was like I knew exactly what she was going to say, before she said it. I was seriously weirded out.

"Sure you can," I said, trying to look calm. As soon as the picture was taken, I ran on thinking maybe I was spending too much time on my own.

After bolting downhill making big strides with bounce into Manzanita, an older couple stopped me. The woman, Karen, asked, "What are you doing?"

This time it didn't feel like *The Truman Show*. "I'm running around America for kids' hospitals."

She burst into tears. "My six-year-old granddaughter is at Disneyland in Florida right now on her very last holiday. She has a brain tumour. It's terminal and she doesn't have long left to live."

Karen and her husband, Bob, invited me for lunch. I mentioned that my parents had taken me to Disneyland when I was eight years old, saying, "At that time, my parents feared I'd end up in a wheelchair, or possibly worse."

I didn't want to say to Karen and Bob they thought I might "die". Although it was true, it didn't feel right.

I continued, "It was the most magical time and without a doubt my best holiday EVER, especially meeting Mickey Mouse."

Although they were enjoying the story, I felt like nothing I could say was getting around the fact they were going to lose their granddaughter. My heart sank with theirs as I felt their pain.

After lunch with the loveliest grandparents alive, I had to get going to make an interview at a radio station. The station was owned by a local man, Gary McIntosh. He walked me around his house and showed me his studio, in his bedroom. Then he walked me to the window showing the one and only road running through Manzanita with its population of 350 people.

He said, "So here's where I do the traffic report."

Right at that moment, a solitary car drove along the road.

I said, "Wow, Gary, there seems to be a big traffic jam out there today!"

After we wrapped up, I knew I had to get some hardcore miles in. I ran along rolling coastal hills and tackled each one with force, enjoying the deep blues of my constant companion to the right. I clocked 21 miles and made it to Paradise Cove RV Resort and Marina campsite. It cost $27 and had the added bonus of showers and toilets, but the campsite was so spread out and my legs so tired I didn't even think about using them. I set up my tent, looked at the ground and thought, "This is some seriously expensive grass."

The next day, I started out emotionally flat, thinking maybe it was the expensive grass that was irritating me. That was until I saw a sign for a motel that read, "Sleep with us and get crabs". I spent the next hour smiling, thinking that my sleeping spot could have been a lot worse. A runner's life isn't just running and jokes about STDs though. Seven miles in, I stopped at Offshore Grill for lunch and to do my social media.

A woman burst through the door. "Hi, I'm Liz, I kinda know your girlfriend Anna and I was hoping to catch you. When I saw Caesar outside, I knew it had to be you!"

Liz Dodd was a travel journalist cycling over 18,000 miles around the world. She was a brave and bright spark and joined me for lunch. Two 19-year-old blokes who knew Liz and were also on a very long ride, over 10,000 miles, joined us for a chinwag. It was fascinating to hear how Liz was leisurely cycling her way around, while the two 19-year-olds were all about speed. One thing was for sure, I was impressed with what the young lads were doing at 19 years old – my mum was still doing my washing at that age!

I went to pay for everyone's lunch but the waitress said, "The owner has already paid for it, his son is battling leukaemia and he loves what you're doing."

As we all got prepped to leave, the owner came over to say thank you. We had a heart-to-heart and I turned around and saw Liz welling up.

She said, "I've been following your journey and to suddenly be a part of it, even just for an hour, and see what you see brings a tear to my eye."

After hugs with everyone, I left all fired up and ready to get going. That afternoon, I ran strongly. I sucked up my belly, brought my shoulders as far back as possible and strutted along like a peacock. It felt like a strong pose. As I burned through the miles, up to 19, I felt my shoulders slump and had to grit my teeth until I hit the town of Tillamook at 22 miles. It was one of my biggest days of running so far.

I was desperate for a bed and a proper night's sleep so I headed for the Western Royal Inn. The ladies behind the counter gave me a "fisherman's discount" when they discovered why I was dressed as a superhero. A month ago, when I crossed the border into the US from Canada, I met an extremely serious and sceptical man at customs who said he didn't like Americans. I put him right and told him they were lovely people and that I'd look forward to meeting more of them – and it was certainly true. That night at 3 a.m., I awoke to some incredibly loud noises. The walls were shaking, and... well, let's just say the Americans in the room above me making the noise were being very lovely to each other too.

The next day, after a sleepless night, I decided that I deserved a treat. Outside the motel, I stared at a sign for the Blue Heron French Cheese Company that read, "We give free cheese tastings". I'd heard Tillamook was the spot for world-famous cheese and wanted to try it so badly, but I'd already passed it and with my tired legs couldn't face going back on myself. I ran on knowing I'd missed out on a treat and regretted not being kinder to myself.

Just before I left town, I bumped into a man who said, "We've been trying to get a hold of you. I'm from the *Tillamook Headlight Herald* and we'd love to share your story." We both agreed that Tillamook is a pretty big town, and this was a pretty neat coincidence – so I did an interview there and then.

Four miles of running later I did finally treat myself by stopping at a fried-chicken restaurant. The superhero cape was like a magnet and two blokes with sports caps and baggy T-shirts were keen to find out what I was up to.

As I finished my story, one of the guys said, "Yeah, we've got challenges of our own. We're both recovering addicts."

Now they'd said it, I had that vibe.

"What drugs did you use?" I asked.

I didn't mind asking these questions growing up, my mum and dad had tried to support people with drug addictions by letting them live with us. My mum was always trying to help people, sometimes to the detriment of her own needs. She was a foster parent for years, but her attempts to help people extended way beyond the kids in her care. I'd been lucky enough to be part of my mum's drive to help addicts by bringing them into our home. It led to some heartbreaking moments, with my cousin dying from an overdose, to amazing moments of helping people choose a better path through life.

Doug and Kyle were really open about their struggles. They had been crystal meth addicts.

I asked, "What does crystal meth feel like when you take it?"

Doug said, "You feel like Superman, like you can do anything."

It must have been so tough to get clean, I could see it in their faces.

"When did you get off it?" I asked.

Doug replied, "I've been clean eleven years now, Kyle has been clean a year."

I asked them both, "When I'm running on my own in the wilderness, should I have been worried about bumping into the likes of you when you were on crystal meth?"

He paused, then said with a smile, "Nah, I still had a moral compass when I was high."

I found out Doug was now a foster parent too, helping kids in his own way. He put it down to his own life experiences that he wanted to give something back now he was out the other side of his struggle. The conversation was warm and open and, as I ran on, I thought about how freely they'd chatted about their problems. I was grateful they'd been so honest and that I'd got to hear their story. In years gone by, speaking about struggles with addiction would have been taboo, but I know from first-hand experience there's so much more to a person with an addiction than the addiction itself. There's always a beautiful soul somewhere beneath the haze of drugs or alcohol. The battle to get that beautiful soul to the surface over the course of a lifetime is one that some win and others sadly lose.

I felt uplifted after connecting with Doug and Kyle, but as I continued along the busy Route 101 my body just wasn't in tune. I'm not sure whether the chicken I'd eaten was salty, but I had an incredible thirst, much more than normal, and I had no water. I stopped at the nearest house.

A young woman came out holding her camera and the first thing she said was, "I'm Facebook Live streaming you right now."

I replied, "Cool. That's okay!"

I couldn't tell whether she was scared out of her wits, or if I should start asking for donations? Fortunately, she let me have some water and I headed for a quieter road, but my legs were empty and, in all honesty, had been all day.

Regardless, I kept shuffling along wondering how many miles I could run like this for. After clocking up over half a marathon, I grabbed the camera, feeling as if my eyes were shutting, and explained, "I'm completely spent and I'm going to jump into the next bush I see to camp."

Then, out of nowhere, a boy came on to the road and said, "Would you like to have dinner with us tonight? We're eating spaghetti and elk."

I felt my eyes spring open and said, "WOULD I?"

The little boy was called Jacob Whittles and we ran to his home where I met his sister, Rachel, and his parents. His mum, Tracy, explained they'd seen me on the side of the road three times that day and wondered if I'd run past their house. Jonathan, the dad, showed me around their patch of land. They had chickens and bees, and everything looked entirely self-sustainable.

I asked about the sheep. "What's he for?"

"Oh, that's a ram. He cuts our grass," said Jonathan.

"Huh!? You have a sheep to mow your grass?"

"Yup," he replied casually.

"Well, that is the best thing I've ever heard of. I'm never going to mow a single patch of grass ever again, when I go back home, I'm going to buy myself a sheep!"

For dinner, I ate two platefuls of elk and spaghetti.

Then Jonathan said, "Have you had tried Tillamook cheese yet?"

I just smiled and thought about those extra few metres that I didn't want to run back to the Tillamook cheese factory. They brought out a huge plate of the stuff with honey on the side. I was sceptical at first, thinking cheese and honey was a poor combination, but I didn't want to be a rude guest, so I got to work dipping lumps of cheese into the gooey honey. Wow. My mouth burst with saliva, revelling in every single ounce of sugary and fatty goodness. The family stared at my face while I made pleasurable noises. I'd finally got to taste the famous Tillamook cheese and I don't think I could've experienced it in any better way.

After dinner, Jonathan said, "Would you like a bed tonight?"

I said, "WOULD I?" for the second time to these kind people and slept brilliantly on a full belly in a warm, cosy bed.

The next day, I left the Whittles family loaded up with cheese, honey and elk. I ran on in my barefoot shoes just pitter-pattering away. Eventually, I passed through the beautiful town of Pacific City where a giant slab of rock known as Haystack Rock sat proudly in the rippling ocean as trees sprung up from sandbanks at the end of beach. With so many amazing spots to have a holiday out here, it was a shame I was blasting through so quickly.

After I ground out half a marathon, it started to get physically and emotionally rough. I noticed this was becoming a daily ritual after 13 miles. As I faded, I thought coffee would be a good solution, so I walked into a cafe and sat down to do social media posts and get a caffeine hit. It didn't help. My vision was blurry and I couldn't see what I was writing. I couldn't recall the day. I couldn't even remember where I had woken up. What I did realise was I'd run for 14 days on the trot. The original plan was to have at least one day off a week, but with the injury on day two of the adventure, I had catching up to do. Slightly worried, I necked 2 pints of water, nailed some strawberries and pancakes, and my vision came flooding back.

This was a good thing as there was someone I was definitely looking forward to seeing, my superhero, Anna. We've been together for five years and, although she doesn't have a ring on her finger, she's my one and only life partner. Anna is a bit of an adventurer herself. She's run the length of New Zealand, cycled all the toughest peaks in South America and even cycled the 50 states of America. I've definitely met my match.

It'd been three months since I'd seen her and normally we spend every single day together. Three months felt like years and I was bursting with excitement and nerves. When I first saw her, we beamed at each other.

"Helloooo," I said.

"Well, hello," Anna replied.

As much as I wanted to see her, I was a little weirded out. We touched each other, but she felt like a stranger. Now I knew what it's like in the film *Castaway* when Tom Hanks finally sees his wife again after all those years and they're like strangers. Anna and I gazed into each other's eyes trying to suss each other out. We kept at it, hugging, kissing, then 10 minutes later something clicked emotionally and it felt like she had been with me only yesterday. I had missed her like crazy.

PART 6

WONDER WOMAN AND ADVENTUREMAN UNITE

Anna was joining me for a week of running – which I was so excited about. There aren't too many partners you can take on an adventure like this so I was a very lucky boy.

While we were outside a coffee stall near Lincoln City getting set for our first run together, Anna said, "I have a surprise for you! Wait here."

Two minutes later she was back from behind the coffee stand, frolicking in slow motion singing the *Superman* theme tune but wearing a bright Wonder Woman outfit. I couldn't stop smiling.

Anna mapped out our route for the day. She's the planner in our relationship and secretly I was happy to have one less job to do. This was a good thing, as running along the coastal backstreets the hills were absolutely ridiculous. Although Anna's a pretty minimalist kind of woman who doesn't need to bring make-up or a hair dryer with her, Caesar was still a lot heavier with her gear, so I was either pushing him uphill at a snail's pace or trying to hold him back from racing back down the other side. There was no rhythm to our running, but it didn't matter, we beamed at each other the whole time. It'd been a long time since I'd had my soulmate by my side.

After 7 miles, Katie and Jeremy from *The News Guard* turned up to do an interview. Katie told us that she lived up ahead in Depoe Bay so we could stay with her if we liked. Knowing we had a place to stay, we finally found our running rhythm and knocked out a good number of miles.

Halfway along, with Anna pushing Caesar she turned to me and said, "What must these cars think? A woman pushing a baby buggy down the highway, they probably think I'm an irresponsible mother!"

If I was still in any doubt that one day Anna might be motherhood material... I was even more convinced when a few miles down the road she ran into the bush to go to the loo and I thought, "That's my girl!"

Hitting 15 miles, the inside of my left knee had become sore and Anna was a little tired as well.

She turned and said, "You know, I was a bit anxious about wearing a costume like this in public, but now I think I'm too tired to care!"

Wearing one myself I completely understood. Finally, we arrived at Katie's house where a feast of salad, ravioli, sausages and red wine was waiting for us. We had dinner with her friends, Eric and Josh, and a comfy bed for the night. It was a tough-ass day, but one to be proud of. Just having a helping hand in pushing Caesar was like being given some extra superhero powers.

The day after, we were treated to free cups of coffee at the Pirate Coffee Company while we caught up on our social media duties. Running along with Anna for the first few miles there was soooo much honking from the cars. I think two capes flapping in the ocean breeze meant double the amount of honking! As we got into our superhero rhythm, we bumped into a walker called Dave. He advised us to go on a quiet road, which would take us away from the 101 and the hills. A piece of advice that meant I would never trust a man called Dave ever again.

The road he mentioned along the ocean was pretty – pretty hilly. It went up and up and up, like, so far up that Anna and I had to take a break at the brilliantly named Cape Foulweather. As we slumped over its wind-blown edge, Dave caught up and confessed with a smile, "I thought it would be better to not tell you about the mountain you had to climb…"

With 10 miles down, we grabbed lunch before it was time for another 10-mile run. A mile in, I stopped to look out over the ocean.

Anna took a picture and said, "You look like you're saving the world! No big deal."

A few miles later, Anna spotted a road that had split in two as if an earthquake had opened it up.

I took a picture of her air-punching the road and said, "Just breaking roads with your fist. No big deal."

By 16 miles, my engine was empty. I tried to focus on the positives of the day so far and that running a half-marathon had started to become somewhat normal. I reasoned now I just needed to make a 20-mile run somewhat normal too. I carried on trudging along, but Anna was in great shape with fresh legs. Or maybe she actually just is Wonder Woman. At 20 miles, we were starting to discuss stopping for the day when a beach trail appeared. We wheeled Caesar along hoping to find somewhere to camp when a firepit popped up – as did a wind-sheltered sleeping spot in the middle of pine trees and a spongy ground as good as a mattress. It was like someone had made the camping spot especially for us. As I collected wood for a fire, I gathered way more than usual – to impress Anna with my caveman skills, of course. Three years ago, on one our first dates together, I was trying to impress her by building a fire, but I couldn't get it going – so I'm still making up for my failed attempt all those years ago.

After a fire that crackled and sparked to celebrate our reunion with a dinner of tinned fish and chocolate-covered strawberries, we climbed into my tent and, blissfully content, drifted off into the land of nod.

By morning, I woke to hear Anna saying, "Is that black spot up there a slug?" She poked it and was like, "Yuk! Slimy. Definitely a slug."

We got running, but I was feeling pretty sluggish myself.

Anna said, "Are you okay?"

I said "Nah, my body feels awful and I feel miserable."

Anna sweetly replied, "That's alright, looking at your face, you're doing a very good job of being miserable."

At mile 10 we took a break – a big meal of tacos with all the trimmings. I was enjoying the break. Anna wasn't.

She was getting itchy feet. "Come on, let's go!"

I complained, "But I've got social media to do, I need to do yoga and I need more rest."

Anna didn't say much, but ploughed her energy into a nap on the grass outside instead.

Just before we set off, we chatted things through and Anna explained, "I just wanna get the job done for the day so we can have more time later – but I know you like your rest in the middle of the day, so we'll do it that way."

We both agreed we adventure slightly differently and that it was hard for one of us to adjust to the other's routine. Our first little disagreement. But it was a sign of our respect for one another to "sort it out" and remind ourselves we're individuals and independent people.

It wouldn't have been a normal day without someone pulling us over. This time the cops were back in town. A sheriff pulled in and put his blue lights on.

Anna turned to me and with a mock-guilty face said, "Oh noooo, what have we done?"

As it turned out, the deputy sheriff of Lincoln City just wanted to wish us luck and pass on a special coin that read, "In the service of mankind". By clocking 20 miles, I felt like I'd turned the day around from not even having enough energy to smile to seeing the best in mankind and feeling so alive.

The next day it was Anna's turn to be tired. As we ate breakfast, she looked at her body and then at me and winced. I knew she was sore after running 80 miles in the past four days – and I liked it! I liked knowing I wasn't the only one suffering.

I thanked her for the look of pain and she said, "Glad to be of service."

Anna wasn't done yet though. As we got going she turned it up a notch and said, "Here, give me Caesar. I wanna fire him up these mountains. It's my final day so let me damage myself. I get to rest after this and you don't."

I watched as Anna tore ahead with Caesar, she was running like a rhinoceros. It was so funny to watch her bum stick out as she charged up the hills like a wild animal. I couldn't resist telling her and she kept saying, "Give me Caesar, it's rhino time!"

On a sharp bend in Lincoln County we hit the Devil's Churn, a frothing mass of water running in from the ocean that battered everything in its path. Feeling in need of some froth ourselves we spotted a coffee stall.

"Espresso time?" said Anna.

"Espresso time," I replied.

A lady in the queue loved our outfits so much she wanted to buy our coffees. The lady who owned the shop threw in a free brownie too. We drank our frothy coffees next to the frothing Pacific – it was a million-dollar view for sure.

We were rolling with the punches, and the ocean. The roads were long, straight and the tarmac was smooth like it had just been freshly laid. We ran down, along, up and over them, glancing at the ocean as often as possible and enjoying its blissfully cool moisture. We drifted into a runner's paradise for the next few hours revelling in each other's company. One minute we'd be looking at a lighthouse in the distance with rolling turquoise sea waves brushing up the red rocks, the next we'd look at each other like, "Is this really happening?"

After 9 miles floating along the ocean road, Anna turned to me and said, "I think this is the best day running with you, EVER!"

I turned to say, "This has been the best day of the run and I'm so glad I got to share it with you."

We camped near the ocean and the next morning Anna went to hitch-hike from the town of Florence back to Seattle to fly to Mexico and give a keynote speech. That's how we both make our living, motivational speaking.

After a long hug, Anna's eyes welled up and she said, "I love you, I'll miss you... and don't get hit by a car."

I said the same back, except the getting-hit-by-a-car bit. As sad as it was, I knew I'd be seeing her again in a few months and I'd have to continue the adventure on my own.

PART 7

COUNTDOWN TO CALIFORNIA

After Anna left, a man named Steve turned up having found me via my live tracker. As he shook my hand, I looked at his face and thought, "I know that face!" Steve was Canadian and had run with me on the final day of my 5,000-mile run across Canada. He was here on holiday and thought he'd track me down. As he'd come all the way from Canada, I thought I'd spend some quality time with him, so we ate lunch together. While eating, a family overheard our conversation and wanted to buy us lunch, which was a lovely gesture, but I was a bit cheeky and slipped it into the fundraising pot instead.

Anna had left me feeling stronger. I was running with confidence and that evening I set up camp and a fire near Dunes City. It was pretty lonely without her, although I did have a few mosquitoes to keep me company, and I was eating leftover dates too – so you could say it was a different kind of date night. There was another thing to wrap my head around,

I realised I was now over 500 miles into the run, still heading south, and nearing my third State, California. With 5,500 miles to go, I was going to have to run the equivalent of over 210 marathons in less than 300 days. Oh dear.

I spent the day covering the ground slowly and fairly effortlessly, until I reached 20 miles. This seemed to be the new goal – 20 miles a day. I was nearing that marathon distance, 26 miles, day by day. That night I reached Winchester Bay, a small town with rippling sand dunes on its beaches. I entered a little grocery store to stock up on rations and asked the checkout lady, "Are there any restaurants in town?" She shook her head. I was pretty gutted as I was craving a hot sit-down meal, so instead I bought all the hot food from the store – fried horrible stuff that had probably been sitting there for days. As I left, having spent over $40, I saw that there were a couple of lovely restaurants in town. I got so angry. All I wanted was a good meal. I started thinking, "I should go back and tell that woman I want a refund on all the dog food I just bought." I calmed myself and thought it through, perhaps she genuinely didn't know there were restaurants in town. I did this all while scoffing the fried dog food and went to the restaurant anyway and scoffed down some delicious calamari, chips and salad as well as a beer to chill the heck out.

The next day, my right Achilles tendon was flaring up again, but I just set off anyway hoping the running would cure it. I ground through my gears and after 10 miles my legs were loose and I hit a new kind of rhythm. With barely a thought, my legs just seemed to go round and round. My breathing was light and I felt I could just keep going and going.

For my second run of the day, an older man on the street shot me a look and said, "Who do you think you are, Superman?"

I was trying to work out whether he was joking or not. I honestly couldn't tell, so I said, "Actually, I'm Adventureman and he's better than Superman."

The man seemed to nod in agreement and, quite satisfied, went on his grumpy way.

I bustled onwards through North Bay and Coos Bay. The towns were getting bigger and busier, so I tried a few backstreets as shortcuts. Every corner I took seemed to lead to steep hills until, much to my horror, I came to a dead end. My frustration grew. My supposed "shortcut" was hillier and longer. Hitting the 101 again after backtracking for a couple of miles, my mind was wobbling. I kept having intrusive thoughts, sentences forming like, "People don't care what you're doing, or why you're running." My anger boiled and boiled until I cracked and blew my top. I grabbed my camera and let out a foul-mouthed scream like Gordon Ramsay after a tough shift in the kitchen. I often find it better to film when I'm feeling sad, angry or particularly low. It's comforting, like having somebody with me to regulate my emotions.

Luckily, as my mood was dropping, a car pulled up and a familiar voice called out, "Hey Jamie! How you doing, maaaan?"

It was Jim, the Uber driver who had helped me in Washington state a month ago.

"What the heck are you doing here, Jim?"

"I got you some new lights for Caesar. Remember I said you need some lights for the desert?" he said, grinning

"What?! We must be 300 miles away from where you live."

"400 miles actually," replied Jim with a smile.

"You drove 400 miles to give me some lights?! That's an 800-mile round trip. You're insane!"

"I've also got you a new indestructible selfie stick that's hand-built by my friends to help with your filming too," he said.

"Well that definitely warrants an 800-mile drive," I said, smiling. "You do realise you've covered the distance of the UK to deliver me lights and a selfie stick. You're the craziest American I know, Jim!"

Jim casually replied, "I just love to drive, maaaaaan."

He checked us into a hotel and began attaching the new lights on Caesar.

"These should help keep you safe when you're running at night," he said as Caesar lit up like a Christmas tree. "And, man, you're going to have to run at night in the desert. Seriously, maaaan, it's so hot there it's not even funny."

I wasn't sure about how I felt about the desert or what it was going to feel like, but right now all I could think was, "Everyone needs a Jim in their life."

The next morning Jim looked at me and said, "I'm sorry, maaaan, I'm taking up all your time."

I was like, "Jim, shhhhh, will ya? I think driving 800 miles to keep me alive warrants a little more time with you!"

In truth, I was a little sad when he left me to it.

That afternoon I decided to call my dad using my wireless Apple AirPods for a little bit of company. I hadn't spoken to him for a few weeks and he'd just finished doing some running himself, raising money for Superhero Foundation by doing four marathons in four days on the Cotswold Way.

Dad said, "To motivate the other runners, J, I just kept telling them our hundred miles is way harder than your puny six thousand. I told 'em the truth, that you're a wussy compared to what we're all doing!"

I laughed as I ran. An hour after our chat, I got a message from him that read: "Hi Jamie, it was so great to hear your voice! I can tell from your voice you're absolutely buzzing again!! Love everything you're posting and all the wonderful people you're meeting!! This journey you're doing and the selflessness you're showing for all the sick children not only in America, but the rest of the world is just phenomenal!!! This is what you were born to do and as a father it makes me the proudest dad in the whole world!!! Keep doing what you're doing!!! Stay safe!!! I'm with you every step of the way, especially the ones that hurt and are so painful!!! I know in my heart there are still unbelievably great things to come on this journey!!! Love you!!! Speak to you soon!!!"

It filled me up inside, I was buzzing, rocketing along the roads all day. That afternoon while running along in a meditative state, my brain went all dreamy. I thought about creating a kids' book that taught values on movement, purpose, giving back and killing a big arch-enemy at the end of the story. Miles and miles later, I realised I'd been in another world, thinking big. It was my dream place. Of course, putting dreams into action to make them happen is the difficult part, but for now I was loving the idea of having a series of Adventureman kids' books. I find movement does that, it makes you think big and believe in the wildest of dreams and believe that they can come true.

After my dreamlike run, finding a camping spot was tricky with no wild bush by the roadside. All I could see were signs everywhere saying, "DO NOT TRESPASS". Eventually, I knocked on someone's door and a lady agreed to let me camp in her garden. I gave her a slip of paper and said my usual, "Here's my website, check it out, just so you know I'm not a weirdo."

She took the paper out of my hand and said, "Well, just so you know... you look like a weirdo."

She squinted at me, looked towards where I'd be camping, closed the door and that was the end of the conversation. Climbing into my tent, I gobbled some home-baked tuna from Jim's wife with my Irish butter, then complemented it with a dessert of apple and honey before drifting off back into my dream world.

The next day, I woke with a busy mind. I had deadlines and fundraising tasks going on in my brain: "I gotta write that blog, post that video, edit the second YouTube video, share a news clip – I gotta tweak the fundraising page." As I ran, the to-do list felt overwhelming. While I was going through the list my pace got really fast. I felt like I was in a weird "hunting mode" and if I didn't make it to the next destination quickly,

I wouldn't survive. By the time I'd run 20 miles and reached the town of Port Orford my legs were blown out. I don't really enjoy being so task-oriented as I feel much better when I can stay "in the moment", but at least I got the miles done quickly. That evening, I visited a restaurant called The Crazy Norwegian's Fish & Chips. I piled some of their famous clam chowder – made up of clams, a milky broth and onions – into my belly. I licked my lips at its creamy goodness. After eating, I started chatting to the restaurant owner Dianne, I shared the story about the woman who let me camp on her lawn but said I looked like a weirdo. She laughed so much and said, "I love what you're doing. Dinner is on me tonight!"

It was back to the to-do list, I worked late into the evening on fundraising, but barely made a dent, so I woke at 6 a.m. and continued on until 9 a.m. Sometimes running is only half the battle in this challenge, but I'm not complaining, fundraising is what it's all about so they were hours well spent. To treat myself, I went to Tj's Cafe for breakfast and wolfed down two pancake meals. Who knew that syrup poured over eggs and sausages worked so well? If you put sweet and savoury together in the UK it would be considered a crime.

During the run that morning my calf muscles began to burn with pain again. They seemed to be getting worse. The pain became so bad I slowed to a snail's pace. I came across an incredible ocean view, but couldn't enjoy it as my brain wouldn't stop thinking about my pathetic calves. My thoughts lurched into disaster mode: "What if your calf muscles NEVER EVER recover – the whole journey is dooooomed!"

I knew these were irrational thoughts, so for the first time on this trip, I put my headphones into my ears, signed into Spotify and clicked on Robbie Williams' *Greatest Hits*. I know, I know – but Robbie's my dirty musical secret. The first song that came on was "Rock DJ". Oh yeeeeah! Within a few minutes, Robbie had changed my world view. I was now looking at the stunning ocean, singing my heart out. I plodded along until my break where I rolled out my mat, put my head under Caesar so I was out of the sun and put Robbie on loudspeaker. A policeman promptly showed up. Was he investigating crimes against music? No, he was just inquisitive and making sure I wasn't crazy.

At the end of our conversation he said, "You'd be surprised how many people I've found here in the sticks pushing strollers who are really strange."

I looked at him proudly and said, "I'm glad I'm not one of them."

He smiled, before giving me that famous American line, "Have a nice day!"

Running on, still very slowly, I was readying myself to camp in the bush, to camp anywhere really. But just then I saw a sign that read, "Honey Bear Campground up ahead". Any sign with the word "honey" wins me over. At mile 17, I saw the sign again, this time it read "3/4 mile – Honey Bear Campground" with an arrow heading off-road. I started to lose the plot. "Nooooooo, that's too far off my running route to go there and back!" After a 1-minute meltdown, I checked Google Maps and it turned out the campground was only just off the highway and wouldn't actually add any mileage to my run – Honey Bear, here we come!

As I arrived, it got even better. Another sign said, "Bar & Grill". I could hear music playing in the distance, so I quickly set my tent up and headed over. I got myself a pint of dark stout beer, half a chicken and listened to the live music. I was now in Gold Beach, Oregon, and had truly struck gold. The first song was Simon and Garfunkel's "Homeward Bound". Though a little too soon for the words to be meaningful for my journey – I loved every single second of it. While I enjoyed the music, a kid came over holding a $20 bill and said, "This is a donation." He said he was here with his family, so I walked over to meet them. The Kudlacs had seen something about me on Facebook the other week and wanted to donate. I loved how unplanned and bonkers this day had been. One minute I was planning on sleeping in a bush and the next minute I was drinking beer, eating hot chicken, listening to live music and seeing yet more incredible kindness from the local people. I drifted off to sleep in a state of peace and harmony.

In the morning, as usual, my calves and Achilles tendons felt like they'd been beaten with a baseball bat. Grunting with pain, I stretched them out, but couldn't help feel gloomy about the start of the day. I grumbled my way through the morning run and around lunchtime knocked on a random door to ask for some water. It was a friendly door that also scored me some food as I was invited in for lunch. The couple who lived there were called Jarek, who had big fuzzy black hair and one front tooth missing, and Angie, who told me they used to own a cannabis field.

"You really did that?" I whispered, forgetting cannabis was legal in Oregon.

Jarek said, "Hell yeah, we had 15 employees. We helped people for medical purposes and eventually sold up to live here in Pistol River."

It blew my mind. I had plenty to think about as I cruised towards the end of my second American state; above me the sky was a mix of blue and grey flanked by a crop of rocks to my left and banks of tall trees that ran away up the hillside. To my right, the Pacific frothed towards the shore and as ever the road ploughed on endlessly ahead. I felt calm and completely in the zone as if I didn't have a worry in the world, that was until I stopped to check my social media. As I scrolled through my messages, someone had sent me a BBC News link reporting a cougar attack. The headline read, "Cougar shot dead after killing US cyclist and mauling another". I couldn't help but click the link. Just to make it a little scarier, it was right near where I was now running. I must've been told a hundred times over the past 40 days, "Watch out for cougars", and I'd always thought, cockily, "Yeah yeah – they don't really exist, it's a myth." This naivety had probably helped when I'd camped in the wilderness, but reading this story it really hit home they were in fact very, very real.

Trying to push away the fear of what I'd just read, I quickened my pace and focused on the ocean with its distant crashing waves providing a soothing sound that had me dreaming about what the next state would be like. In fact, I was definitely California dreaming when the border came into view. I saw a giant blue sign that read "Welcome to California" in big yellow letters ahead. I smiled, pumped my legs a little faster, crossed the state line and punched the air with a big, "'Ave it!"

PART 8

CALIFORNIA DREAMIN'

As I strode across the border I brought up Google Maps on my phone and zoomed out to look at the size of California – and had a slight panic attack. This new state had me in a state – it was enormous. Like, nearly twice the size of England. I made some quick calculations; 700 miles down, 5,300 to go. After the shock, I ran on and noticed that, true to its name, golden light was shining down on me. With the sun on my face, I started to relax and enjoy the fact I was now running in CALIFORNIA!

By the day's end I'd made it to the Redwood Hills where I was met with a huge final mountain climb. I pushed Caesar with all my might for 2 miles, wheezing and woozing like an old accordion, until I crested the mountain and saw everything was drowned in mist. It was super eerie, nothing like the California I'd experienced earlier. I moved off-road and explored the thick dark-green forest where I spotted a gap in a tree trunk and decided that would make a good camping spot.

Nearby, I lit a fire and went to grab my food bag – and that's when I heard a CRACK in the woods.

It was about 20–30 metres away, deep in the thick, foggy forest. A shiver shot down my spine. The entire scene was like something from a horror movie. Then, another crack. This time much louder and much closer to me. My heart began to race – my mind went straight to the BBC News report of the killer cougar. I went into fight-or-flight mode, although I couldn't tell you which I was in. First I screamed, "COME ON THEN – I'LL 'AVE YA!" then I went into sheer, "I NEED TO RUN AND GET THE HELL OUT OF HERE" panic mode. My hands began to tremble. I had no phone signal. So, I went and grabbed my knife. I tried to control my thoughts, telling myself it was probably an elk. Another crack. It seemed to be circling me, like a big cat stalking their prey.

After what felt like an eternity, the cracks seemed to stop and now I was the one who needed to hunt for some food. The adrenaline and shock to my body had stripped me of all my food reserves and my hunger shot through the roof. I didn't want to crack open Jim's home-made tuna because I thought the cougars would love that – along with a nice slice of British meat. My next thought was to crawl into my tent to eat it, but I knew a thin layer of canvas wasn't going to save me, so I popped open the can there and then and threw the tuna down my neck. No chewing, just swallowing it all in one gulp. As it got darker and darker, I was on red alert, listening to the sound of the forest. I needed to keep my energy up, so I grabbed two packets of Walkers shortbread biscuits and sugar-binged like never before – gobbling 18 biscuits in quick succession. The biscuits weren't enough so I grabbed an energy bar and my honey and scoffed that as well. I felt a bit better. With a full belly, I started to think about sleep until I realised I'd left my sleeping bag in Caesar 40 metres away. Cougars, bears, PAH! I'd have to walk in the pitch black to get it. I knew I wouldn't sleep without it, so I had no choice. I grabbed my head torch and walked the trail listening to every inch of the forest on the verge of pooing my pants the entire time. I kept telling myself, "You're going to be okay, this is all in your head", but it didn't help, I was waiting to be pounced upon. I made it back to the tent but sleep was impossible. Instead, I lay on my back all night, eyes open, knife next to me and tried to relax. I know – relax?! Right?! Day 43 had scared the hell out of me.

Come the morning, the Redwood forest was still as misty as the night before, so I packed up quickly and ran the hell out of there! I was alive and hadn't been mauled by a cougar – though I felt like I'd slept with one. Getting to the bottom of the misty mountain I stopped to chat to a road worker, I poured my heart out about the night I'd just experienced.

He said rather casually, even perkily, "It was probably a cougar, or a bear," which made me feel precisely 0 per cent better.

I ran on, a dribbling wreck, through to Crescent City, my legs just going round and round in slow motion. I was completely sleep-deprived, but soldiered on, dreaming of a bed – and a lockable door. By mile 10, I stopped at the Woodland Villa restaurant. I forced down a burger with my eyes half shut and discovered they had a room I could sleep in. I took it.

Just before I drifted off, there was a knock on my door. "Sir, if you hear banging on your bedroom wall tonight, don't worry, it's a bear coming for the garbage. He's harmless enough, but I'd probably suggest not taking a selfie with him."

"Right. Okay. Don't worry, I won't be popping out for a selfie, I promise," I replied.

Luckily, there were no more knocks on the door and by morning I wasn't feeling *grizzly* but refreshed after a good night's sleep. The next morning I was just happy to be back running. I had my barefoot shoes on and was bouncing with every single step. After my brush with nature, I thought I'd reacquaint myself with it by visiting a local tourist attraction – Klamath's Tour-Thru Tree. This was a giant redwood tree that you could drive through. That's right, drive *through* a tree. I had to do it. It was a tight squeeze, especially for Caesar, but we snuck through.

After 9 miles I saw a scenic route that ran parallel to the highway and, oh my, I had never seen trees like the redwoods. They are the tallest trees in the world, as big as skyscrapers and obviously wide enough to drive a car through. Apparently, some are over 2,000 years old. I'd never seen anything like it. I tilted my head backwards to see them climb into the clouds, but they went so far up I almost lost my balance and toppled over. There was another treat in store for me too. The road was all slightly downhill, so Caesar pushed himself and I just gaped at the redwoods. It was a really quiet route, but every once in a while you'd see a tourist taking a picture of a tree. I'd never seen people taking pictures of trees before.

After 7 miles, a car pulled over and a lady handed me a $10 donation.

She said, "A week ago, I saw you on TV in Alaska at my grandma's house. It's amazing what you're doing!"

I thought it was pretty odd, but cool that my story was being shared so far away.

"That's awesome, thank you! Where are you headed now?" I replied.

"Back to Alaska!"

"But we're in California!? Surely you can't drive that far?!"

"Yeah, we drove 2,000 miles to see these trees!"

They were pretty good trees.

It cracks me up how willing Americans are to drive and drive and drive. Minutes later, more drivers. Kathy and Steve showed up. I'd been exchanging messages with Kathy for the past month after Glenn Mann, a lovely Gloucester man, had tagged Kathy in a Facebook post asking her to help. She turned up with enough protein bars to feed an army.

After lots of excited chinwagging Kathy said, "Right, I hope you don't mind, I've been calling the news stations, I've got a running club ahead that would like to run with you, a restaurant that would like to feed you and in about a hundred miles a motel that would like to put you up for the night. Sorry, is this too much? Tell me if I'm stepping on your toes?"

I said, "Kathy, this is exactly what the adventure needs. All I can do is run. It's people like you that make the difference!"

She was a proper nurturing mama bear, that's for sure.

After a 20-mile run, I set my tent up next to a big tree and nodded off listening to the rain pitter-patter on the tent. The next morning, all was still as I left Prairie Creek Redwoods State Park, nothing but the scent of incoming rain and, wait, an elk. There was one on the roadside just metres away from me. He seemed to be flaunting his perky bum as our eyes met. He didn't blink, just stared, probably thinking, "There's that Adventureman fella." A magical moment.

As I ran, it did start to rain. A thin film that wasn't falling hard, but soon had me soaked to the bone. My body grimaced. I tried to push positive thoughts to the front of my mind, but I just couldn't. After nine miserable miles, a car pulled in.

The door opened and I heard, "Duuuuude! I'm been trying to track you down! My name is Dru from Redwood News."

Dru was young and had such enthusiasm it perked me right up. I told him I'd been struggling and after the interview we agreed to eat breakfast down the road at the Palm Cafe. While eating pancakes, sausages and eggs, a couple came over to ask some questions.

After I mentioned I was doing the run for kids' hospitals, the woman, Mary, said: "We lost our son, Scott, at four years old. He was born with a heart defect. The hospital was amazing during those years and even though it was thirty years ago that Scott passed, you never get over it."

She welled up. I could see it was really hitting home to Dru as he watched our conversation. When it came to the bill for our food, the waitress Tasha said, "It's on the house, I got this."

Dru and I were dumbstruck by the cycle of pain and generosity we'd witnessed in the space of just 20 minutes. Then her husband Steven pulled out $5 and handed it to me saying, "Here, that's all I have."

To psyche myself up for the afternoon run and leave the comfort of the cafe, I had to give myself a talking to: "Those miles ain't going to run themselves." But hitting the rain and wet road again, I was back to misery. Everything hurt and everything I looked at was gloomy. I was in the worst mood. The clouds looked terrible. The mountains looked ugly. I genuinely couldn't help but think every tiny part of my world was miserable. I was even getting annoyed at myself for being so damn miserable. I tried to think of Mary, Steven and their boy Scott, but I just felt sad. I just kept running, clocking up the miles. There was nothing else to do but run.

As it started to get dark, the roads began to bend and narrow, I needed to pay attention to keep myself safe. If anything, focusing on my safety was a good distraction for my mind. I hauled Caesar from one side of the road to the other on each narrow bend and then charged up hills as quickly as I could to give cars as much time as possible to see me and keep everyone on the road safe.

I was looking for a sign, anything to cheer myself up, when I literally saw one – "San Fran 297 miles". That meant if I kept heading south, I'd be hitting the big city in just two weeks.

At mile 19, I saw another sign – "Big Lagoon State Park Campground". I'd have to stay there as I was out of water. I was happy the day was about to end, although the road to the campground itself was never ending. I ran 100 metres, then 200 – where was this freaking campground? It was another mile until I arrived. I was done. Well, almost. I went to get water – another 100 metres away.

On top of a day like today, adding another 1.1 miles on to my trip and knowing I'd have to cover an extra 1.1 miles tomorrow was just the icing on the cake of such a miserable day. Yep, today I made miserable look gooooood. If my mum could've seen my grumpy face she'd have said, "If the wind changes, you'll look like that forever."

Having battled through one of my most miserable runs yet, the next day I made it to Arcata. A Canadian mama bear and therapist, Anne Solo, who had treated me to a massage on my last adventure – had used her networking magic to get me a meeting with a lady called Sylvia. Sylvia had long black hair with big brown eyes and a ring piercing the bit in between her nostrils. She looked like your typical quirky Californian girl. She was a trigger-point therapist. I'd never heard of one before.

As I lay on her bed, she said, "Now, I'm going to push real hard on certain points in your muscles and I'll continue to push until the muscle 'lets go'. Oh, and it's going to hurt."

I thought, I'm used to pain, I'll be fine. Then she pushed and squeezed her fingers into my calf muscle.

"RAAAAHHHHHH!" I screamed.

Sweat rushed from all over my body. Tears rolled down my face.

Sylvia said, "Just breathe."

After 30 seconds the muscle tension eased and she let go.

"What just happened, Sylvia?!" I said in disbelief.

"Welcome to trigger-point therapy," she said, smiling. "I put your muscle under so much strain it sent a signal to your brain to 'let go' of the muscle. Look at your calf now."

As she wobbled it, it was completely loose, compared to my other one which was as stiff as a board.

Sylvia carried on, pushing every muscle in a magical spot. I screamed in pain, every time.

"Sorry, Sylvia," I said.

"Nothing to be sorry about here," she said in a caring, soft Californian tone while pushing another trigger point.

I'd never had a session like this. I'd been in so much pain day in, day out, and as painful as this was I felt her energy healing me as my tears flowed. It was sadistic and cathartic. Afterwards, even though I felt like I'd gone a few rounds with Mike Tyson everything felt loose. I had my body back again.

As I left, I said to Sylvia, "If only I could take you on the road with me!"

She replied, "Any troubles, WhatsApp me. I'll show you how to trigger yourself. No worries."

What a star.

"I really hope we meet again," I said.

PART 9

DOCTOR, DOCTOR

With every new day of running, I was moving more freely and strongly. There was no pain in my Achilles tendon and I seemed to be clearing more space from the ground up between each stride. Though weirdly, my "down below" wasn't feeling too great. There was a dull ache that seemed to be getting worse and worse. I had to keep going as I'd planned to stay with a British family who'd moved to America 25 years ago and I didn't want to let them down. I slipped my barefoot running shoes on and started pattering away. To make things worse, at mile 10, I needed the loo – a number two to be specific – and this was a moment of "when you gotta go, you gotta go". Of course, now I was on a road that was totally fenced off on both sides with nowhere to go, or hide. Nowhere!

I kept running, and clenching and running, and clenching, hoping something, actually anything would come up! Then I saw it, a ditch with a bush. The bush had just enough greenery that people wouldn't see me. I threw myself in – big mistake –

I found myself squatting over a rotting possum. It smelt so bad I considered running on, but it was too late, I'd mentally "let go".

After nearly evacuating from both ends, I was glad to be back on the road in the fresh air. Each mile felt like an achievement. I stopped in a little shop and bought myself a bottle of sparkling water – San Pellegrino – to celebrate. I poured myself a glass of bubbly. The cool, hydrating sensation of it slipping down my throat was incredible. Five further miles passed with five sparkling celebrations, until I got a surprise. I'd been tracked down by Chip and Kevin from Healdsburg Running Company so they could give me a beer on the side of the road – and a cheesecake. It was supposed to be for their friend's birthday, but they thought I'd make better use of it. We were still hanging out at 10.30 p.m. when Jonika and Steven, the British couple who were hosting me that night, turned up.

Jonika had a worried look on her face. "We found you! Your tracker stopped so we thought we'd come and look for you! Actually, I was really worried about you, that's why we're here!"

You could see Jonika had that worrying thing going on, so she made sure I got back to their house by running the last mile with me.

I'd been running for 40 days straight without a single day off. So, after a late-night feast of marinated Soy Vay flank steak strips and tons of veggies, Jonika said, "You can stay here as long as you like." I thought this would be a good spot to rest up for a day. And my Adventureman suit definitely needed a day off so it could hang out in the washing machine and get clean. For the first time in a long time, I was able to stop and take stock of the country I'd been running through. As well as the Harrison family looking after me, I kinda felt their whole neighbourhood who all lived in a cul-de-sac together were keen to adopt me.

That night we had dinner with a group of them.

Steven began pointing out who they were. "That's our neighbour Fred, he used to be a doctor. You can sit next to him."

Fred looked about 60 years old and had neat silver hair. I thought, what a stroke of luck that I have a doctor sat next to me. Making it through the main course, I was trying to pluck up the courage to tell Fred about my "down below" issue. But every time I was about to tell him someone would start chatting to me. I felt so awkward trying to bring something like that up. I made it to dessert until finally I seized the moment, leaning over and whispering in Fred's ear...

"So, Fred, I've got a problem down below, a dull ache in the two things. You know what I'm talking about. Is there any way you can help?"

He looked up, paused, then looked back at his trifle. He was thinking, like a doctor.

"How do I put this, Jamie. There's really not much I can do, unless I look at them and touch them."

My eyes widened "Okay, okay," I said, trying to gather what he was saying.

Fred was one step ahead of me though. "But do you mind if I finish my dessert first?"

I spat out a piece of my pudding and burst out laughing as Fred dissolved into a fit of giggles too. Everyone looked over as we sniggered away like a couple of naughty schoolkids. With the trifle polished off, Fred and I went to the toilet where he diagnosed a hernia in my abdominal area.

"A hernia? That doesn't sound good?!" I said.

"Well, it's muscle losing its place and going weak, it may end up falling out from your body, but you can get it surgically poked back in. But if you do have surgery, you'll need weeks to recover."

"Weeks off, Fred? No chance!" I groaned.

"I normally wouldn't say this," he said, "but under the circumstances I'd say just keep going and hopefully the pain isn't so bad that it stops you from running. You could maybe then have the operation when it's all over."

As we rejoined the dinner table, Fred said, "It's not overly glamorous being a superhero, is it?"

I replied, "Nah, but after what you've just seen, I don't think it's overly glamorous being a doctor either."

Having had such a warm welcome, taking the decision to rest for a few days was an easy one. Although midway through the second day, my feet were getting fidgety and there was a tension beginning to build in my belly telling me it was time to get running again. On an adventure as big as this one, there was no such thing as a day off. Even if my body was resting, my emotions were still racing on the mission at hand.

After 48 hours with the Harrison family and their lovely neighbours we'd formed a really strong bond, so their hugs, well wishes and goodbyes were everything I needed to drive me forwards. I also knew I had to step up my miles and start running marathons if I was going to visit as many hospitals and communities as I could before my visa ran out – and there was no better inspiration than what was to come next.

PART 10

DEAN'S ON THE SCENE

A few months back, I managed to get the email address of one of the most famous ultrarunners in the world, Dean Karnazes. When I was 16, I read his book, *Ultramarathon Man: Confessions of an All-Night Runner*. It was the first time I realised you could run more than a single marathon in one go. It had a huge impact on my life. Dean would often run up to 350 miles in one go and had won some of the biggest and toughest ultramarathons in the world, so I sent him an email. With his celeb status I wasn't really expecting a reply, but sure enough, I got one:

Sir Jamie!

You are amazing and I hope and plan to join you. I'm tracking your progress and hopefully will be around when you cross the Golden Gate Bridge. That would be a dream. Can't wait to hear the stories. You've now collected several lifetimes worth of them. Bravo.

Wishing you ongoing strength and endurance,

Dean

He called me "Sir" – I couldn't quite believe it.

With a few more days of solid running under my belt, I made it to the town of San Rafael near the Golden Gate Bridge where I had arranged to meet Dean the next morning. That night, I was thinking of all the questions I'd ask him. "Why do you love running so much? What do you eat to run so well? What about this? What about that?" I had a million questions stored up. Dean wasn't an adventurer as such, more an athlete who enters in long-distance organised endurance races and wins them.

By morning, I was like a kid at Christmas. Some people might like to meet Brad Pitt, some might like to play football with Lionel Messi, I had always wanted to run with Dean Karnazes and today that dream was finally going to come true. Packing up my tent, I spotted a man running along the pathway towards me. He was wearing a bright top, he was muscly as hell and I thought, "That's Dean for sure!" I went in for a giant man hug right away. It reminded me of how people say how much they like meeting me in the flesh having read my book, and here I was doing the same with Dean. I felt a little star-struck and was probably staring at him a bit weirdly, for a little too long.

After our hug, the first thing Dean said to me in a really chilled way was, "How are you doing?"

It felt like he genuinely cared and really wanted to know the answer. If there was anyone in the world who would understand how I was "doing" after running hundreds of miles, it was Dean. I felt a connection straight away. So, what do two runners do? They run! We set off from the park, chatting about how sleep is so vital and how we both have to wear eye masks to rest properly at night. Dean was having a good go at convincing me to use earplugs too.

"Have you noticed your hearing gets hypersensitive to noise? There's been so many occasions in the middle of a long race when it's been a struggle to sleep. I always wear earplugs," Dean said.

As I soaked up the knowledge, I wanted to send a WhatsApp voice message to Anna so she could hear Dean's voice. She's a big fan too and has Dean with us in our bed – for reading, that is. Dean was game.

"Anna, we need you," he pleaded into the phone. "We need another presence with us. Also, I'm telling Jamie to wear his eye mask at all times. And I'm encouraging him to wear earplugs too."

Anna responded in 30 seconds with a message that read, "YOU'RE WITH DEAN! He's wiser than Buddha – EARPLUGS are where the party's at. Enjoy you crazy kids!! Quite possibly two of the most awesome men on the planet in one place. MAGIC."

Dean and I ran together with me throwing a billion questions at him, but he was too kind and kept turning the attention back to me to give some love for what I was doing. I wasn't having any of it, I really wanted this to be about him, knowing what an impact he'd had on my life and the lives of others too.

"What do you eat?" I eagerly asked.

"Anything to do with fat. That seems to keep my engine going," he fired back.

"There was this one time, I was racing the Italians and every time we hit the feeding stations, I'd look over and they were passing a bottle of olive oil and downing it between them. I mean, I couldn't do it, but those guys were tough, maaan!"

We ran rhythmically alongside each other, soaking up the sunshine and sharing our knowledge. After my eleven-billionth question we'd chalked up 11 miles and were now pacing alongside a sparkling sea with a prime view of the Golden Gate Bridge as the tall, metallic buildings of the city reached for the blue skies above. Not that I paid much attention, I was gazing longingly at Dean's legs: tanned and shiny with defined muscles, and perfectly placed veins – they were to die for.

"Bloody Nora, Dean! Your legs are ridiculous," I gasped.

"It's my mother and father I need to thank for that. Just good genes, Jamie," he said, smiling.

We began to hit the heart of the city and all was going well until we set off up a big hill and things started to hurt. As I huffed and puffed pushing Caesar up a 10 per cent gradient, I thought, "Don't slow down now, Jamie. Dean Karnazes is next to you!" I was blowing, gasping for oxygen and Dean slowly pulled ahead until he reached the peak. He then turned around and gave me a "clap, clap" to say let's keep moving.

Dean was the only person on the planet who could get away with telling me to "push on" after 800 miles while shoving 80 kilograms of gear up a hill. Anyone else, I would have stuck my fingers up at, but instead, I pushed harder. My calves felt like they were going to explode. I pushed harder still until I was level with Dean once again. As we neared the Golden

Gate Bridge we were ambushed by a low-hanging mist – the infamous San Francisco fog. It came out of nowhere and glided over our bodies making me shiver and the hairs on my arms stand to attention, but it all added to this surreal and wondrous moment of running with my hero. Knowing we were nearing the end of our time together, I wound up for one big final question. I turned to Dean and said: "So why do you love running so much?"

He replied, "I love running for the freedom and adventure. You meet people. You see things. You experience the world. I mean, tourists wouldn't get to feel that cold fog on their body like we did just now. We ran through it. You don't just see the sights; you feel the wind on your skin. It's just a more immersive experience, it's beautiful."

As we stood under the famous bridge, mist enveloping our bodies, a fleeting thought ran through my mind, I thought they said you should never meet your heroes, but I say what a load of rubbish. Today was one of the best days of my life.

We hugged and when I let go, I said, "Dean, you're a massive inspiration and you've had a huge impact on my life, so keep doing what you're doing."

He replied, "I'll strike you a deal. I'll keep doing what I'm doing. If you keep doing what you're doing."

Without a moment's hesitation, I said, "Deal."

PART 11

SO LONG, SAN FRAN

As I was leaving San Francisco people were kindly offering me places to stay "down the road", but because the city sprawled in so many different directions none of them really worked out. Feeling fresh after my run with Dean I also didn't want to stop. I had juice in my legs and I wanted to run. I kept on going and going, my legs feeling strong as the sun began to set. Even the sky was in a positive mood and seemed to stay a constant light blue as golden light bounced off the glass-fronted buildings. I was experiencing San Fran in all its glory.

I pushed Caesar along mile after mile of pathway, running up and down wave after wave of hills. I pushed hard, taking control of Caesar and pumped my legs until nearly 10 p.m. Eventually, I looked at my watch – it read 27.3 miles. Wow, it had happened without me even realising – I'd run my first marathon. Well, more than a marathon. I allowed myself a smile and thought, "You're doing it. You're really doing it." That night, I climbed into a bush in a city park, settled down as proud as punch and thought my American dream was just beginning.

The next few days seemed to go on forever, the city limits stretched for miles and it was hard getting away from built-up areas. Every morning after pitching my tent in a park, I woke to someone shaking it saying, "Get out of here!" I was treated like a homeless person and it didn't feel good. Eventually, I began to hit more sparsely populated areas along the coast with lots of inviting thickets and bush to camp down in. Now that I was covering greater distances I could run on later into the evenings and on one of the following nights I pushed on near to a town named Salinas, the biggest in Monterey County.

While checking Google Maps, I spotted a green patch that looked good for camping. At 3 a.m., I found it, pitched my tent and I was pretty certain that this time I wouldn't be upsetting anyone.

As I nodded off, I heard a harsh voice. "Grab your s**t and get out of here otherwise I'm calling the cops."

My heart rate jolted and I thought I should explain what I was doing so I said "Hello" but heard nothing back. I convinced myself it was a dream and nodded back off to sleep.

The next voice I heard was much louder. "Get out of the tent. I haven't got all day. And come out with your hands first."

I knew I wasn't dreaming this time. And "Come out with your hands first" I'd heard many times in America on the TV series *Police Camera Action!* and it's never a pretty scene. It sounded like a policeman, a policeman holding a gun.

I unzipped the tent with trembling hands and peered around the corner. It was a cop, his hand resting on his holstered gun.

"What's your name?" he shouted.

It felt unnatural to be so tired, yet so scared, knowing I was quite literally in the firing line. I couldn't gather my thoughts or what was going on, so I said, "Ugh. Ah. Ummmm..." then took a deep breath and shouted, "I'VE GOT A WEBSITE!!!"

A few seconds went by, I thought, "Did I really just say that?" Once I explained to the copper I was running and raising money for charity he was nice enough, but still looked at me like I was completely stupid. It turned out I was camped near a house, although I couldn't see it.

He asked, "What if some weirdo was camped outside your house? You'd be like, 'What the f**k?' Wouldn't you?"

That's when I was about to say, "Not really, I'd ask them if they fancied a cup of tea," but thought he probably wasn't after any British wit right now.

"I'll be on my way," I said.

As I pushed into the cool morning air, I began to cry. Was it from that guy? No, I think it had to do with running 1,000 miles. Something had to give. Mile by mile, tears continued to flow, flushing out the hardship and pain of all the challenging days of running. I trudged forwards alone, running into a big headwind that battered my face and brushed away the tears, until, suddenly, a lady showed up. Her name was Mary. She was tall and kind.

"Jamie, let's get in my car and out of this wind."

She showered me with nuts, bananas and sparkling water, which seemed to heal my emotions somewhat.

Running on, a little lighter having spilled all my tears, I stopped at a fruit and veg shop. The woman working there was called Rachel and she asked what I was doing.

Realising I always needed to be honest, I told her the story and added, "You know, I'm having a really off day. I've been crying all morning."

She looked at me sympathetically and said, "I'm glad you told me and sure you feel much better for getting it out of your system."

I nodded in agreement.

As I fuelled up on strawberries and got ready to leave she came over and said, "Say, do you know what the word 'trudging' means?"

I wasn't sure what she was getting at so I said, "Like when you're running through treacle type of thing?"

She smiled and said, "Yes, that's true, but it's a little deeper than that. The real meaning is that you're trudging through with a meaningful purpose."

Leaving the shop, I trudged on happily. Almost like I was supposed to be trudging through treacle. After all, this was never meant to be easy. With 6 meaningful miles under my belt, thinking about Rachel got me thinking about all the other people who had helped over the past few days. There had been so many small acts of kindness and warm, smiling faces that had seemed irrelevant at the time, but I now realised were such a big part of my energy. At the side of the road, I pulled out my iPhone and scrolled through my pictures. As I thumbed through them, each image told a story about how they had helped me. There was surfer dude Antony who ran 6 miles with me and must have used the words "amazing bro" at least a hundred times; Mary who brought me tons of healthy food; the waitress who bought me a beer; the guy who had fallen down an elevator and had brain damage who said I was amazing (I kept thinking how amazing he was!); as well as a couple named Suzy and Dave who gave me a bed for the night in Santa Cruz. Then there was Natasha and her daughter Lydia who painted a sign that read "Jamie & Caesar"; Tessa and Ima who bought me breakfast at Country Kitchen; Duane who sorted out a night's stay in a Marriott Residence; and the final picture I looked at was a woman called Kim and her kids who took me for dinner and then donated $100 to the Superhero Foundation. I remembered Kim looking me straight in the eyes and saying, "You are making a difference and you better believe it."

As I put my phone down I couldn't help but think how incredible the world was and before I knew it I was back in my "love bubble". It was time to get back running. My legs had a newfound lift and I ran through the streets of Salinas ramping up kerbs and waving gleefully at as many cars as I could. As the sun started to go down, the road out of town became flat. There were mountains either side and a huge tailwind funnelling me along. As we passed between the mountains the wind's energy was squeezed into such a small space it blew even harder – so much so Caesar was pushing himself. The sky dissolved from light to a deep purple and then a fiery red. My eyes were glued to the scenery. Amid the beauty of it all, a text popped up from a man named Dave, "Go to Soledad Fire Department, there's a piece of grass you can camp on. Captain Tardifs is expecting you."

Six weeks ago on a beach in Washington state, I met Dave and his wife Jeanette. They had been following me on Facebook since and saw the video with the cop who pulled a gun on me. They decided to take action. It turned out Dave was a firefighter and Jeanette had come up with the idea of getting the fire stations on board for safe spots to sleep. Knowing I had somewhere to sleep for the night, I ran on even more strongly. I'd spotted a nice, quiet route through some vineyard roads that ran parallel to Route 101.

I started pushing Caesar through bumpy vineyard fields, passing signs that said "No trespassing". I was well and truly lost. Yep, I couldn't google my way out of this one because Google Maps had it completely wrong. It was 11.30 p.m., I was 19 miles in and had no idea how to get back on track. I started to head cross-country back in the direction of the 101. I pushed Caesar across dirt tracks that kicked up dust towards a well-lit building which, in the middle of nowhere, struck me as pretty odd! That was until I saw a sign that read "Salinas Valley State Prison". Of all the places to be lost, I was currently running alongside a prison.

My mind raced, I thought if a guard spots me right now, he'd be certain to think I was a prisoner "breaking out"! I ran fast – really fast – eventually making it to Soledad's Fire Department at 2 a.m. Obviously, no one was up, although there was a sign that read "WELCOME JAMES" on the gate with a map showing me where to camp. Getting my name wrong had me chuckling and I quickly set up my tent and crawled in, exhausted. I'd run 31 miles – my longest distance so far. I felt proud. Both for the miles I'd covered, and for not being shot at by a prison guard. But even more than that, for being back in my love bubble thinking amazing thoughts about the world and all the kind people in it.

The next few days were bliss, every single night I was scoring a sleeping spot in a fire station, getting a bed, a shower, even their protein bars. Waking up one morning with the King City firefighters they warned me it was going to be a really hot day, but I don't think I realised how hot they meant. Americans use Fahrenheit and as a Brit, I'm more of a Celsius man. I set out early at 9 a.m to try and beat the heat. With each mile my mouth got drier and drier, but I just kept trucking, trying to do as many miles as I could. If I was going to make it to the town of Bradley, I was looking at a loooong 35-mile day to the next California fire station "hotel".

At noon, the heat went up to a whole new level, something I'd never experienced before. I instinctively knew it was time to stop, the problem was there was no shade. Nothing. Just field after field without a single tree to shelter under. In the distance, the mountains looked small against the endless blue sky which the sun ruled the roost over. It beat down relentlessly, nothing could escape its wrath. The earth was bone dry, where only the toughest shrub could survive.

I felt like I was under attack, that the sun was bringing me down from every angle. I craved shade and looked to every nook and cranny in the sun-baked earth thinking, "Can I crawl under that?" At one point, I convinced myself that some cabbages planted in the ground would do the job if I laid down and squeezed under them tightly. It was, of course, a ridiculous thought. It wouldn't let up, another 3 miles down and I was panting like a man who'd fallen asleep in a sauna. Finally, I spotted some wooden pallets in a field. They were stacked just tall enough to create shade the size for one body to fit in – mine. I ripped my top off and laid down, sweating. I piled a litre of water down my neck and half a jar of almond butter. I grabbed my phone to check the temperature – it was 42°C.

Out of nowhere, a young man with short dark hair and brown eyes appeared, peering around the pallets and said with a Mexican accent, "You can't lie here, bro. Our crops and food are growing right there and it doesn't look good having you here. Can you go over there behind those pallets, away from the food?"

He pointed across the field.

I agreed, but while moving my stuff over he seemed to change his mind. "Nah, you can't stay here, bro."

I thought he didn't trust me and I was going to have to run on in the scorching heat.

I looked ahead, the road blurry from the heat, but he said, "It's too hot, bro. I can't leave you here like this, it's inhumane. You have to come with me!"

We walked over to his farmhouse in the distance. When we got there, he opened up a barn and said, "Here you go, this is a better spot for you."

The temperature inside was drastically cooler. He wandered off, returning a few minutes later with some bottles.

"Do you drink beer?"

"Yeah, why not? It'll be good for hydration," I replied with a smile.

Of course, I knew it wasn't good for hydration, but when I'm in someone else's territory I always try and say yes to everything as it helps build a connection quicker. Plus, with all this heat I actually really fancied a beer. We chatted away. Vince was 27 and had lived on the farm his whole life. He'd never left and knew the land like the back of his hand. He was really looking out for me.

"Here, jump on the tractor, I'll take you to an even better place to cool off."

After bumping along in his tractor, we stopped and climbed some barbed-wire fence, then I saw what he meant. In front of me was a huge river.

"It's Friday afternoon. It's part of my routine to come here. You've timed it well. Shall we take a dip!?" said Vince, breaking into hysterical laughter.

We waded in together and sat there cooling off for a good 10 minutes. It felt so sweet, I kept dunking my head in as Vince laughed at this weird running man he'd found in his field.

Around 5 p.m. my body was back to a normal temperature. I had stopped panting for the first time in 6 hours. Sadly, it was time to say goodbye to Vince.

He offered his hand. "I've loved the past few hours. I don't know what it was, I just had a good feeling about you. I felt like I was in a Harry Potter movie listening to your accent." Then he laughed his head off again. Vince wasn't done yet though, he reached into his pocket and pulled out a $100 bill and said, "Here, man. This is a donation to the kids," and put his hand over his heart.

I muscled on through the afternoon heat smiling at Vince's kindness and his infectious laugh. I'd clocked up 21 miles as I ran through a valley with grey, sun-scorched mountains either side. In the farmers' fields, sprinklers were trying to get some moisture into the ground, jetting off in hundreds of different directions and as they mixed with the slipping sun creating a field of infinite rainbows that stretched away towards the horizon.

As I paused on a dirt track road I checked Google Maps and it seemed fine to get back on the highway. One thing Google Maps didn't show, however, was the enormous barbed-wire fence blocking my way. Having to go around would add another 5 miles. I could've just about squeezed through, but Caesar, no way. I zigzagged back and forth, but there just wasn't a gap in the fence. In the end, after a few extra miles I found a road that got me back to the highway.

The hottest road in America had a few more surprises up its sleeve. Lining the hard shoulder were these huge hammer-head machines moving up and down into the ground, literally hundreds of them, but there was no one in sight. I later learned these were big old oil pumps digging down for a fossil fuel reward. It reminded me of that film *War of the Worlds*, starring Tom Cruise, where aliens try to take over the world with enormous machines. After fleeing the film set, I glanced down at my watch – 9 p.m. I'd now shot past the marathon distance of 26.2 miles and my feet were letting me know in no uncertain terms. I changed shoes to make them feel better, but it didn't help – they'd had enough. Even seeing my first sign for LA – "243 miles" – provided only a moment's respite. At 10 p.m. a policeman pulled in. I thought, "Please, not again, I don't want guns pointing at me!" But he had this huge beaming smile on his face and said, "What you doing? Can I help you?" It was the warmest greeting ever for a Friday night on a busy highway.

After a quick selfie, I ran on to finish my day in Bradley. There was a fire station there, but I wasn't sure they were expecting me as everything had been organised at the last minute. Running through the tiny town as lights were being switched off, I saw the fire engines and a couple of people standing outside. I blinked my eyes in disbelief. Then I heard clapping, then more hands clapping. I ran towards it, like a music fan running towards their idol. In total, there were seven firefighters clapping me in. One said, "We've been following you on your tracker! We could see you getting lost in the oil fields – running back and forth! We all fell about with laughter."

It was the hottest and longest run so far, 34 miles, and had been packed with adventure. I sometimes forget how much I love it, searching for shade, meeting random lovely strangers.

As the firefighters showed me around the station – the kitchen, the shower and my already made bed – and said, "Make yourself at home," I couldn't think of a better place to rest after a day under the blazing hot skies of golden Californian sun.

PART 12

PARTY TIME

The days seemed to roll by quickly as I was fixated on reaching LA. Usually, I'd be telling myself to stop thinking of the goal and to soak up the surroundings. I was also ignoring the cough that seemed to be forming. The roads were dry and sun-drenched, a long way from the Washington and Oregon rain, and I couldn't help but wonder if the cough had something to do with it.

There was no time to dwell on those thoughts, as I had another surprise visit from Norma and Chad. Norma was the sister of my friend Ed Archer from back home. They had a sign for Caesar! They'd heard about my run-ins with the police and thought a sign with my face on it, along with a map of my route, would help.

It read:

RUNNING ACROSS USA

Don't worry, I am not a squatter.

My name is Jamie McDonald, aka Adventureman, and I am in the process of running 6,000 miles across the United States as part of a charity event to raise money for US children's hospitals.

My adventure started in Cape Alava, Washington, and I'm running a marathon each day until I reach my finish line at West Quoddy Head Lighthouse in Maine.

Please visit my website for more information:

www.adventureman.org.

As well as that sign, they gave me another to hang on Caesar that read: "No baby on board".

Five minutes after the signs were attached, a girl with a shaved head noticed and came over for a chat. Her name was Pierce.

"I love what you're doing!" she said.

Pierce was 21 years old and was already a cancer survivor. What were the chances the very first person to see the signs would be someone like Pierce?

"I'll be following you," she said with a lovely smile.

As I appreciated Norma and Chad's artwork, a second person came along and asked, "Would you like a picture of me?"

Norma, Chad and I looked at each other, slightly confused.

He then said, "You don't know who I am, do you?"

Norma shouted, "You're Memoryman!" – although I suspect this was because she'd seen his T-shirt that had "Memoryman" written on it.

He seemed pretty chuffed at someone recognising him and proceeded to show us a video of him in the 1980s breaking the world record for remembering 50 digits in a row.

Then, Memoryman remembered more things. "I'm the creator of the Memoryman comic book too!" he said.

We all looked at each other on the verge of laughter.

"This is hilarious," said Chad, "Memoryman meets Adventureman! You couldn't write this stuff."

As Memoryman read Caesar's sign he said, "I'll donate one of my comic paintings. It's probably worth ten million dollars."

Norma and Chad looked at each other like, "This guy can't be for real?"

Memoryman said, "You don't believe me, do you?"

He then walked over to a shop, grabbed a paper, opened it up and the first thing we saw was a headline that said, "Invest in Memoryman Art", and sure enough the article was saying his art was valued at $10 million.

He beckoned us over. "Come to the car," he said. "I'll let you know which painting I'm going to give you and you can meet my wife too."

He gave us a piece of paper with the name of the painting, "Oh dear," he said, "this one is actually worth fifteen million dollars and if I die, will probably be worth twenty-five million dollars."

A moment later we were being introduced to his wife. "She's the girl who wrote most of Barbara Streisand's music," said Memoryman with a satisfied smile. He then gave me his mobile number and said to call to arrange collection of the painting, although he did stumble on his mobile number, which considering he was Memoryman gave us all a laugh, but I was definitely going to be calling him about getting a painting donated.

In a few weeks' time I was going to stay at Norma and Chad's as I'd be running past their house, so it was only goodbye for now. The immediate plan was to run through Los Angeles and make it to a house in Venice Beach to celebrate Independence Day. I ate up the last few miles with a spring in my step. As I neared Venice Beach, Hilary – whose party I was going to – turned up on a bicycle to escort me back to his house. Hilary was an Englishman, with a shaved head and a nice tan who used to work with my Anna. As I ran, he cycled. We whooshed past lanky palm trees hanging lazily by the shore as Hilary gave me the history of Venice Beach. We hit Muscle Beach and Hilary said, "And yes, Arnold Schwarzenegger has trained here."

It was still really busy as we whizzed in and around people in tight workout gear, some with star-spangled headbands on. At one point I saw a dog balancing on a woman's shoulders as she did the squats – it was all pretty surreal.

"Welcome to LA, Jamie. If you wanted to show off your athletic prowess this is the place to do it, although you might need to borrow a dog," Hilary said with a smile.

Hilary's house was incredible. It sat on a lazy-flowing canal where big, boat-sized fake pink flamingos cruised elegantly by. I met his husband, Mark, who was lovely too. I was surveying the scene when a friend of Hilary's introduced herself: "Hi, nice to meet you!" Her energy was beautiful. Hilary walked over and said, "Meet my friend, Mindy – she's got a story, I tell you!" That's when Mindy, casual as you like, said, "Oh, yeah, I used to be an adult-movie star."

I sat there, smiling at the casualness of it all, and asked, "Oh, so... how was that then, Mindy?"

"Yeah, it was alright. It served its purpose, but I'm done with that and now I make jewellery."

I nodded my head like it was a totally natural step. I loved this woman's openness – she was clearly an independent, intelligent lady.

Hilary had made it a Spice Girls themed party and called it "Make America Britain again". British banners, booze and posters were splashed all around the house. I really couldn't have picked a wackier spot to be in. Guests began to arrive, men wearing sparkling hot pants and nothing else. I did wonder where they were going to keep their donations!?

But as the party got going, Hilary hadn't forgotten and gathered everyone around for a little speech, finishing by shouting, "Now you are going to donate, aren't you? Cause if you make Jamie happy, you make me happy!" I was quickly falling in love with Hilary.

Even after running a marathon, I danced the night away. It felt great to let go, drink beers, some extravagant gin cocktails and act normal for once. Well, as normal as it is to dance with lots of men in hot pants. The next day, I felt a bit gross – I was dehydrated and nauseous. I think with my body being so clean, the alcohol was a shock to the system. I wasn't quite sure how I was going to make it through a day of running, but luckily I had some support. Today, I was being joined by an old school friend called Gez who was going to attempt his first marathon.

It had been over 12 years since I'd seen Gez, but that was okay because we had 26.2 miles to catch up. Starting at Venice Beach among the palm trees, sun-beaten paths and surfers, we started jabbering away. Even though Gez lives in LA, we had got so distracted by each other's stories we soon realised we were lost. Fortunately, we bumped into Mindy who pointed us in the right direction.

After Mindy's helpful directions, Gez and I began comparing injuries – my Achilles, my knee, my hernia and now Gez's pinky toe was feeling the burn too. He was short and stocky and built more for rugby than marathons. Even so, he still took Caesar for a few miles. It was quite funny watching him try and control the runaway train as we made our way up and down the hills along the coast. It was crazy hot, so I rewarded him with an ice cream at Manhattan Beach. Fortunately, two sweaty dudes hauling a buggy had caught the locals' attention and we spent the next 15 minutes eating ice cream and talking to the locals who began donating and offering warm words of encouragement.

By the time we reached Hermosa Beach, Gez said, half exhausted, half smiling, "This is the furthest I've ever run, over a half-marathon!"

We stopped for lunch where Beth and Simon, who were friends of friends, wanted to treat us.

Then it was back to it. Gez was flagging a little so I offered him some practical help. "Fancy some Vaseline? It really helps with the chafing downstairs?"

After seeing me apply some he politely declined my sticky, outstretched hand. We plodded on, and although Gez wanted to keep pushing Caesar I could see his breathing was starting to become increasingly laboured.

"You're breathing a bit funny, Gezzer!" I said. He just grinned and grimaced and raised a thumb as if to say, "I'm good, but never, ever again."

With the sun fading we spied Long Beach in the distance. I encouraged Gez. "Nearly there, keep going."

I looked down at my watch and saw we'd reached marathon distance. As I let Gez know, he collapsed into my arms, giving me a giant bear hug. I think he was elated he'd completed a marathon for the first time and even more elated it was all over. The miles weren't over for me though. As we said our goodbyes, thinking what a great way a marathon was to catch up with an old friend, I still had 6 miles to run to my next destination.

PART 13

CURIOSITY KILLED CAESAR (ALMOST)

I made it to Jennifer Robin's house. She followed me on social media and had reached out to offer me a bed for the night so I'd be well rested to visit Miller Children's Hospital in the morning. Jennifer was going to join me at the hospital, which I loved, as I always want people to see what I see. Though for me, this was my most difficult hospital visit yet. Maybe after 59 marathons I was weak and emotionally vulnerable, but what I witnessed that day put the weight of the world on my shoulders.

The first family we saw were in the cancer ward. That's where I met the first kid fighting for his life. As I looked at his parents, I could see how much they were struggling. It was simply heartbreaking. With the kids I always try to put a smile on their faces and have fun. We goofed around flexing our muscles at each other. With the parents, I always approach it a little differently. I speak to them and try to get in tune, so I can almost try and absorb some of their pain. This time I just felt helpless. I couldn't even take an inch of their pain away, so we simply hugged.

Leaving the hospital, Jennifer said, "That place is amazing, I'm signing up to volunteer."

I thought that was great, but I felt like the wind had been knocked out of me. Normally I leave hospitals fully motivated and inspired to run more miles, but for whatever reason I just didn't feel like running. There wasn't a choice, I had to keep going.

To make things worse my cough seemed to be getting worse. I decided I'd run along the coastal path to get a little breeze and some sea moisture to make things more bearable. But I was also a sitting duck for idle attention. The beach was packed and I quickly had people waving me down; a Mexican man wanted to feed me, a lady called Tina wanted to buy me a healthy lunch and another lady called Lauren decided she was going to run with me.

Lauren had a stroller too, but hers actually did have a baby in it. We ran together for a bit and even swapped strollers. I felt like I'd been given a Ferrari whereas Lauren said pushing Caesar was like pushing a "truck". Poor old Caesar. I don't think he was too offended though, he's used to taking stick by now. Anyway, I didn't push the baby for too long as I didn't want to get comfortable with the Ferrari feel – sometimes as long as you don't try anything new, the old feels pretty darn fine.

There was more familiarity to come as I reached my sixtieth marathon at Norma and Chad's house in Irvine. It felt like a safe haven as it had a connection with back home in England. As I walked through their front door, my body just gave way. And my mind too. Everything just went floppy, like I'd surrendered to the world. It must have been the homely surroundings. As I flopped on to a sofa, I told Norma and Chad, "Sorry I don't have much energy, I feel emotionally burned out."

While I had physically stopped running, my story was running at its own pace. I got a call from Fox News who wanted to share it on national TV. Even though I was feeling below par I had to summon some energy. Chad gave me a lift to West Los Angeles where I spent the day in a studio, first going on a big breakfast show called *Good Day LA* and then doing back-to-back interviews that would be seen and heard in over 30 states. It was all worth it. My story went "national", reaching millions and millions of people. The donations flew in and we raised over $10,000 in 24 hours.

As I arrived back at Norma and Chad's, I knew I was in exactly the right spot at this point in the trip. They made me feel so comfortable.

Norma said, "I think you should quit running and stay here for the remainder of the run."

Then, Chad told me a story of when he gave his first public speech to a running club, how much stage fright he had and how awkward he felt. He finished by saying "If you're Adventureman then I'm Awkwardman!"

I couldn't stop laughing almost to the point where I stopped breathing, I felt like my body and mind were able to "let go".

That night, they did. I went into a full-blown fever, sweating and aching. The next day I called Dr Fred and gave him my symptoms.

He was quick with his diagnosis. "You've got bronchitis, you're going to need antibiotics."

Fortunately, there were some old ones in Norma and Chad's cupboard. I was grateful I didn't need to see a doctor, it comes at a cost out here, which made my fundraising feel even more important for those families that can't afford medical treatment.

With fundraising on my mind, I decided to call Memoryman to see how he was getting on with donating his $15-million painting. Surprisingly, he answered the phone, although the call didn't last long. He sang Shania Twain's "That Don't Impress Me Much" in full down the phone and that was the last I heard of Memoryman.

While I recovered, Norma and Chad took up the running baton and joined the "Snail's Pace Running Club". This was a community club that any runner, advanced or beginner, could join. I asked Norma if running was something she'd usually do?

She said, "Ummm... no, probably not."

But the connection they made to the club led to its president, Bob, making a donation of $200 and giving me two free pairs of running trainers too. Chad and Norma did their first run and found they loved it.

It was quite the switch-up, me lying around recovering for days on end, while they were the ones out running and spreading the word. We spent most of our days just hanging out near their temperamental coffee machine they'd nicknamed "Roger Federer". Most matches we had with him, he was spluttering and sending water flying, in fact he wet himself on many occasions, but eventually he could come up with the goods and serve a decent coffee. I loved my time here, if there was a good place to catch and recover from bronchitis and to nurture me back to health, this was it.

With my mojo back, it was time to leave Norma and Chad's and break myself back in with an easy run. I needed to prepare myself for the desert; my Adventureman suit couldn't be worn as the material would be too hot, so I improvised with a pair of red shorts and a loose, breathable T-shirt with the letter "A" on the chest drawn on with black permanent marker.

For the first mile, Norma and Chad ran with me until Norma tapped out.

As Norma left she said, "Now, Jamie, I know this is about children's hospitals, but for us, it's even bigger than that. Your ripple effect is magical. Because of you we've got new friends from the running club and we're running! Can you believe that? Seriously, you give us hope."

Norma's eyes welled up like I was one of her kids. I felt like one too. We hugged tightly and said goodbye. A few miles later it was Chad's turn, he tapped out and I said a warm goodbye to "Awkwardman".

I was left to it, just me and the adventure once again. I popped up Google Maps to find the shortest route, but noticed a huge squiggle that meandered its way through Santiago

Oaks Regional Park. Having pounded roads for so much of the trip, I was intrigued by these off-road trails. Well, you know what they say, "Curiosity killed the cat", and today that cat was going to be Caesar.

As soon as I hit the trail, it turned incredibly rocky. So much so, I wasn't sure if Caesar was going to hold out – his wheels were already wobbly enough. He juddered and clattered, wheels flailing at impossible angles, groaning at me to slow down. Up ahead, I saw a gravel mountain rising up to the clouds and I thought, "Wow, there's no way they would've built a trail over that." But the trail did go over it, climbing higher and higher into the sky. I grimaced, forcing Caesar and his protesting wheels upward. I kept saying to myself, "It will descend soon." But every time I reached what I thought was the summit, it simply continued upward. In fact, it was getting worse. Way worse.

I pushed harder, forcing us both up the mountain of dirt, dust coating my costume and Caesar's sides until I realised I couldn't turn back because pushing Caesar back down, with no brakes, could've spelled the end for both of us. Moments later a 15-year-old boy called Tyler skidded to a halt next to me on a mountain bike sending a cloud of dust into the morning air.

"Hey, what you doing up here?" he said, perhaps mistaking me for an ice cream man with his cart.

I looked at his clothes, fit for off-road biking, and knew this route hadn't been earmarked for a wally lugging a cart full of canned fish. The kid knew it too.

"Can I give you a hand?" he asked politely.

I nodded in appreciation as Tyler set to helping me manhandle Caesar up the dirt mountain.

"How heavy is the cart?" Tyler asked.

"The weight of me or you and then some more," I replied.

He gave me a pained look and I thought, "Tell me about it, I've been pushing him for months." As we pushed ever higher I thought we must almost be there, and that was true. According to the map, we were now almost at the next TWO mountains. At that point Tyler thought his was work was done.

"Okay, good luck then," he said, letting go of Caesar.

I took the weight and replied, "So all I need to do is get over those next two mountains and I'll be back on the main road?"

He looked at the mountains and with a half-smile said, "Yeah. You're going to die."

I'd have been happier swimming in a tank full of sharks than being on this mountain, but with two more to get over, I knew I had to keep plugging away. My tactics were this: on the super-steep parts I'd do 10-second power blasts, calves and Caesar's wheels screaming; then pause, breathe for 20 seconds and repeat. With every power blast, my footing sunk into the dirt, causing me to slip and my heart to beat like a bass drum. I kept saying to myself, "You're the worst adventurer, EVER."

Trying to push myself and Caesar was stripping me of my power. I was tiring fast. I ground up the second mountain until I reached the steepest section – and the most dangerous – because if I went off the cliff edge here, it wouldn't be an ambulance coming, it would be a coffin. The sun bore down on me. I was bucketing sweat. I mopped my brow with a filthy sleeve until my footing slipped again. I began to slide, at first a metre or two, but then I was catching speed and my life began flashing before my eyes – all the things I'd seen, all the things I'd done – I thought, "This is it, you gotta let go of Caesar otherwise you're gonna go off the edge with him!"

I slid further, my knees digging into the grit as I tried to slow us and just as I was about to let go my foot caught a small boulder and slowed us. As Caesar's weight leaned into me, eager to carry on I knew what I had to do. I started to grab everything loosely tied to him – my tent and my food bag which was ridiculously heavy. It worked, Caesar no longer wanted to commit stroller suicide, or take me with him. With all the strength I had left, I pushed as hard as I could to the crest of the mountain. As I reached the top, I panted in relief and looked down to see my knee was bleeding badly, although I was so pumped with adrenaline I could barely feel a thing.

After going back for all my stuff, I repacked Caesar and continued on. Luckily, the third mountain was fairly tame and I was over the worst of it. As I set foot back on the flat tarmac, I puffed out some air and vowed never to cheat on it with not one, or two, but three pesky dirt mountains ever again.

PART 14

THE LOVE MILES

If ill-advised mountain climbs were reckless, the next destination had a similar reputation for carefree fun and rash decisions. Craig from Inty wanted to bring me to Las Vegas for the Microsoft Inspire conference where I'd speak and spend time on their stand doing some fundraising. It was too good an opportunity to turn down – plus I'd never been to Vegas before.

To smooth things along, Craig flew out Rich Leigh, one of my friends from back home who helps with my PR. Rich picked me up in a rental car up near Moreno Valley, a 4-hour drive later and we arrived in Las Vegas at 3 a.m. It was like the night was just beginning. We dropped off the car and piled into a taxi. As we hit the strip, buildings rushed towards us like Christmas on a freight train.

I asked the taxi driver how long he'd lived here and he said, "Most of my life. You know, back in my day, this was all mob land run by crooks. It wasn't the kind of place you'd bring your wife and kids on holiday."

When we arrived at the Bellagio Hotel, I immediately recognised its grand appearance from films like *Ocean's Eleven*. This place really was dripping with money. After a few hours' sleep we headed to the conference to try and raise some dollars of our own. I met Craig, whose stand I was going to be on. They were running a campaign where for every selfie someone got with me and posted on social media they would donate a dollar. Plus, they bought 300 copies of my previous book to give away too.

Although I was used to going at a pace, this other side of the run was really important too. I was connecting with tons of people who genuinely wanted to fundraise and help with the rest of the run. With lots of successful networking, Craig continued to go all out on the Vegas experience and invited his employees, Rich and me to meet outside the Bellagio where a flashy limousine was waiting for us. We were off to see Bruno Mars. I was feeling a little guilty and worried about not being on the road running, especially with my visa running out, but sometimes you just have to enjoy what's in front of you. I sank a beer and danced the night away, thrusting as good as Bruno Mars. Well, at least I think I did.

After Vegas, it was time to head back to the spot where I'd finished running near Moreno Valley. Within 48 hours of being in Las Vegas the temperature had risen to nearly 50°C. It was a dry, boiling heat and one of the hottest places on earth right then. This meant it would be impossible to run in the daytime. It was never in the plan, but there was no other option than to switch to night running.

Anna had flown out to join me for another stretch and was now sat in a hotel 50 miles away in Palm Springs. I felt it was crucial to spend as much time as possible with her and as I looked outside into the darkness and the long road ahead, I knew I didn't want to miss a single second with her. I ran into the night thinking, "I've got enough miles in my tank that I should be able to run it in one go." I felt anxious, I'd never run through the night before. I took a quiet road, but was surprised at how bright it was. The stars were out and they lit up the open road as I began pitter-pattering away in a tranquil state of mind.

Three miles in, I felt stupid for even worrying about running at night. I was at one with the desert, it was so quiet. I ran in the middle of the road, bounding along the yellow stripes to keep my eyeline. I felt like I was getting ahead of the world while it slept all around me. The road began to rise and fall and at one point I had red rocks either side of me as I cut through a beautiful starlit valley. A warm wind contributed to the sweat dripping down my back and miles were floating by as I flowed silently through the dead of night. All I could hear was the sound of my footsteps and the occasional swirl of wind. I was so excited at the thought of seeing Anna, I'd already clocked up 30 miles.

By mile 40, I realised I'd now covered my greatest distance so far, but I felt a dull aching pain beginning to nag on the inside of my knee. With Anna only 10 miles away, I had to keep going so I began to think of them as "love miles". Although "love miles" may have been "stupid miles" as my knee was feeling much the worse for wear when I fell into her arms in Palm Springs.

Spending the day with Anna in an air-conditioned room, drifting in and out of sleep, was amazing. While I slept, she cleverly created a route with places where we could stay in the daytime to survive the desert heat. That night we went out for dinner in preparation for our first night run together. After filling our bellies at a Thai restaurant, we loaded up Caesar, Anna donned her Wonder Woman costume and we were ready to run away into the night together.

We were both nervous. Anna because it was night and me because of my sore knee. Still, it felt good to be out on the road together. I liked having Wonder Woman for company and we had lots to catch up on, so the first few hours flew by. We took it in turns to push Caesar as we pounded along the pavement, which was the poshest pavement I'd ever seen. It was laid out in curves and swished its way between patches of neat grass lit by the golden glow of street lights. At 1 a.m. it was still 42°C and insanely humid. As the Palm Springs lights finally faded behind us, the moon became our guide and we ran deeper and deeper into the desert.

We glanced up, two starry-eyed lovers running under them and it dawned on me for the first time since leaving LA – I was now running cross-country, west to east.

With our bodies overheating, we developed a few tactics to keep cool – like kneeling down to dunk our heads in the roadside sprinklers or scoring a cold drink every hour at one of the gas stations. I went for my usual sparkling water, while

Anna gulped down cold chocolate milk. By 2.30 a.m. we'd covered 20 miles but still had unquenchable thirsts. Anna looked exhausted and my knee was giving me gyp. We ran on in silence, crunching out the miles and finally made it to a motel at 4 a.m.

After a big daytime sleep, we woke to do another night of running. Anna was worried that the towns were getting smaller and we were going to run out of pavement and suggested we put on some high-vis vests. She was always the one to worry about things like this. I told her that Caesar had good lights and that I was used to running in the dark, but she was having none of it.

"Please, J – just humour me and put the vest on, will you?"

"Go on then". Anything for an easy life, huh?"

I sighed as I picked up the lightweight piece of fluorescent mesh and pulled it down over my bare chest. I caught sight of myself in the mirror. I looked ridiculous.

"I look like I'm in the Village People! Are we gonna do the YMCA before we leave?"

"No, you don't," said Anna, but she was trying to suppress a smile. "I think you look more like Freddie Mercury. He was a class act, you know."

"Oh, bloody Nora. I do look like Freddie!" I said, checking myself in the mirror again. Considering I'd been wearing a spandex costume for much of the trip, I realised I didn't really have a leg to stand on. "I hope you know this is love, me wearing this," I grumbled, tugging at the vest.

"Well, I'd love for you to be alive and safe out there. And besides, you haven't seen mine yet... it's a DISCO VEST!!

Wahey!" she shouted, flicking a switch on her own high-vis number which had LED light tubes running through it making her light up like a rainbow.

"Woah! Can you run behind me if you're going to wear that thing – I'll have an epileptic fit if I look at it for too long."

Unfortunately, the Village People vest and making sure we could be seen on the dark roads turned out to be the least of my worries. By mile 8 the pain from my dodgy knee was back with a vengeance. As we pierced the black of night, a storm lit up the sky to the south with the distant roll of thunder and white flashes of lightning. It seemed to sync with my discomfort. As the storm got bigger, I began wincing more and more and the tarmac felt harder and harder. By mile 18, I was limping so much that I crashed to the ground in defeat. My "love miles" had caught up with me and this felt like it had the potential to be an adventure-stopping injury.

As dawn broke and the sun rose from behind the mountains casting a warm light over their dark contours, we weren't the romantic cast the scene deserved. I limped to the nearest town – Anna and I looking at each other, our eyes hanging out of our heads, knowing we had to stop. We took sanctuary at the nearest motel and crawled into bed. I was pretty sure I wouldn't be going running again anytime soon. Scared about whether I could complete this adventure before my visa ran out, I began making some quick calculations. So far, I'd run over 1,800 miles, the equivalent of 70 marathons, still with 4,200 miles to go. I was five months into the journey and had 160 marathons left to complete in 210 days.

With a buggered knee, my confidence took a big knock. We spent a few days holed up in the city of Indio in the Coachella Valley. It was a weird place seemingly designed for workers, you either stayed in a motel or ate fast food at a restaurant, that was it. We were stuck, but that was okay. I iced my knee and Anna shifted her focus to researching future destinations like Bombay Beach on the shores of the Salton Sea. It was described as a "barren post-apocalyptic wasteland". Apparently, in the 1960s a flood created a beautiful lake. Naturally, it became a holiday destination, then because of the desert climate there was no rainfall for years and it gradually dried up until fish were left rotting all around it, hence the "barren post-apocalyptic wasteland"! Anna was smitten. "Sounds like a great place for a romantic break."

By our fourth evening in Indio, the pain in my knee had died down a little and we were ready to hit the road again. Bombay Beach was 50 miles south and we calculated it'd take us two days to get there. We'd sorted out staying with some firefighters along the way, but Anna hadn't been able to find any motels in Bombay Beach. I was up for just running into town and going with the flow, but Anna – who is always more of a planner (and probably more sensible) than I am – wasn't so keen.

"I'm all up for winging it, J, but not when there's a chance we could end up with nowhere to sleep in the hottest place on earth!"

"Ah, it'll be alright." I smiled, knowing that would wind her up.

"But what if it's not alright?" she said.

"Okay, you said earlier that there was a bar or something there?" I asked.

"Yeah, there is. It's called the Ski Inn."

"Well, how about I call the inn? Maybe they can help. I'm sure they have people rocking up all the time looking for a place to stay..."

"Probably not two people dressed as superheroes pushing a baby stroller! But yes please, can you call them?"

After dialling the number, I got the surprise of my life when a woman answered with what sounded like a British West Country accent. This was odd, but maybe they had strange American accents similar to mine out here in the desert. As I explained who I was and what I was doing, the woman clocked my accent too and when I told her I was a Glaaawwwster lad she seemed even more eager to help. As it turned out, Sonja was originally from Cirencester in Gloucestershire, where she had lived 30 minutes away from me. Better still, she was true to her hospitable West Country roots and offered to meet us and put us up for the night. Anna couldn't believe it when I told her the woman was a fellow West Country lass.

"See, I told you. I knew it'd be alright," I said, smiling cheekily.

"Of course you did, J," she said, rolling her eyes.

Hitting the road again, I had grown a little nervous. I realised I couldn't really afford any more days off, I just had to hope my knee was fully recovered. I was hoping for an uneventful day running to a fire station on the North Shore of the Salton Sea. Before we set off, I thought it would be a good idea to inflate

Caesar's tyres so he'd roll easier over the ground that night. But as I went to detach the pump nozzle from the tyre it got stuck on the inner-tube valve and ripped off completely. Note: that's not a good sign.

I heard the dreaded noise "Pfffffffftttt" (you know, when a tyre goes completely flat) as green slime spluttered from the inner tube all over the tyre.

"NOOOOOOO! Not now!!!!"

Anna shot me a look that said, "Let's find a solution, immediately", and said, "You do have a spare inner tube, don't you?"

I wasn't sure I did actually.

We rummaged around in Caesar, Anna repeating, "Please tell me you're not on this adventure without a spare inner tube."

It was Anna's worst nightmare, she'd never run without having a spare in her stroller. Continuing to rummage around in Caesar – potentially for the sake of our relationship – I was hoping one would be knocking around. Then, right at the bottom I found one.

"Phewww, I knew it was in there," I said, not entirely convincingly.

A month before, I remembered Handy Howard from Hart Velo Bicycles had given me a spare for free after a woman had been rude and treated me like a homeless person in his town, Nipomo. Back then it had really upset me, but now she'd done me the biggest favour of all. With Caesar's tyre all fixed, we finally got running. We were instantly swallowed by the black of night, the only light that of our head torches tunnelling into the gloom. The warm air was still as we pushed forwards, the only sound the pitter-patter of our feet. Anna was actually running barefoot, training for her next adventure running 100 marathons across Britain for Girlguiding. She's an ambassador for them, helping to empower young girls. I listened to her feet, running just off the road in the sand, and made mine run in rhythm with hers so we had our own little pitter-patter band. That was until Anna screeched, "Oh my god! What was that?!"

"What's the matter?!" I said, panicking.

"Look at that, what is it?!" she said, clearly alarmed.

"Anna, that's a scorpion," I said in disbelief.

It scuttled across the road as our head beams followed, its pincers and curled stinging tail glowing in the light.

"I nearly stepped on that," said Anna.

"Hmm, I think your barefoot training is over."

"Yeah, I think I'll get my shoes on."

Leaving the scorpion to wander into the night, our eyes were firmly fixed on the ground from there on in.

"How're you doing, Anna?" I said.

"Not good," she replied. "That scorpion freaked me out."

"Me too, this is all a little bit too adventurous for me."

We weren't living up to our billing as adventurers right now. And as we continued scanning the road for scorpions there was another sting in the tail, we'd missed our turning a mile back.

After running back the extra mile we eventually found the turning. It was a sand-gravel road that quickly became open fields. We weren't very happy runners, especially when I saw a second scorpion on the ground. Up ahead, a small truck started to flash its lights. We gave each other a look like, "This is going to be the angry farmer whose land we're on, isn't it? But what's he doing out here at 2 a.m.?" The truck drove towards us kicking up dust in its headlights. We froze. It stopped and the window came down.

A Mexican man's face revealed itself and so did an enormous smile, "*Hola!*" he said warmly.

Anna quickly began speaking Spanglish. Then, I showed him the map of my running route, which he seemed to understand. He kept pumping his fist into the air saying "*Bravo!*" and "*Agua, agua*", motioning to the land around us. We didn't understand.

Then he hopped from the truck and walked us over to his little plants in the ground and said, "Peppers!"

We connected the dots.

"Ah! You water the peppers through the night?!"

He nodded. "*Si! Si!*"

The friendly exchange calmed our nerves and we got back into a slick running rhythm. With nothing to see but darkness, my sight took a back seat as all my other senses became heightened. I began to feel subtle changes in the air – an increase in humidity, a slight shift in the wind, Anna's breath. The last couple of miles were run in silence, we were both covered in a thin layer of sweat and sand, our mouths as dry as the desert, until we finally made it to the sanctuary of the CAL FIRE Riverside County Fire Department – Station 41.

On our second night the scorpions were absent as we headed for Bombay Beach – that mystical place on the Salton Sea just 50 miles from the Mexican border. We started to feel like professional night-time runners (if that was a thing) camouflaged by the cover of darkness as if we were a part of the desert itself. The sky was beautifully clear, just the stars and then a full-blown meteor shower.

"Woah! J, did you see that?!" Anna gasped.

"Beautiful!" I replied, in awe of our private performance.

As we gazed at the sky, we willed for more, and in a grand encore a star streaked across the sky for a whole second. It was the biggest shooting star we'd ever seen. We gawped as it left a trail of red light in its wake. Incredible. Back to feeling like adventurers again, we ran on and made it to Bombay Beach. As promised, Sonja from Cirencester was waiting: all smiles, hugs and West Country accents as if greeting two strangers dressed up as Adventureman and Wonder Woman at 3 a.m. in a pub car park was the most normal thing in the world.

After Sonja showed us to her caravan that she was letting us sleep in, Anna and I tumbled into bed exhausted, but deeply satisfied at what we'd accomplished.

I turned to her with a smile and said, "You know, I think this is one of the most romantic breaks we've ever been on," while beaming like the stars we'd just ran under.

We woke in the late afternoon eager to explore Bombay Beach, a town of less than 300 people. We headed to Sonja's Ski Inn pub, a quirky wooden shack where the walls and ceilings were covered in dollar notes. In the corner was an old classic jukebox that looked like it was from 1960s. The energy was electric with all the locals chatting away and drinking beer. The desolate desert outside made it feel like the end of the world and if it was going to end today, this was the place to have a beer and burger – so that's exactly what Anna and I did. After, we left the pub and sat outside on a sandbank watching the sunset, knowing these were our final few hours together.

PART 15

GOING LIVE

Saying goodbye to Anna was sad, as it always is. But she was with me in an organising sense. I still had one more leg on her itinerary, from Bombay Beach to Brawley – just on from the Salton Sea – to a little community called Glamis. Before leaving Brawley, I noticed that one of Caesar's tyres was going down again. I'd already used my only spare and there was no Anna to come to the rescue this time!

I was scratching my head wondering what to do when I spotted a maintenance guy wearing grey overalls. He was Mexican, short, tanned and had a crop of dark hair. It was time to make a new friend.

"Hey! What's your name?" I asked.

"Hector," he said proudly.

I went straight for it. "Hey, Hector, do you have a puncture repair kit at all? The tyre is going down on my buggy."

He looked a little confused, but went on to his hands and knees to check the tyre and realised the problem immediately. I waited for his diagnosis.

"Walmart!" he said.

Walmart? What, the supermarket? I pulled out my map and Hector pointed to it.

He must have seen my face drop when I realised it was 5 miles away, so he pointed to his car and said, "I'll drive."

Hector's kindness didn't stop there, he paid for some spare inner tubes and green slime (to stop any more punctures) and changed my tyres. He refused to take any money.

I pleaded with him. "How can I thank you, Hector?"

He picked up his phone, pulled up a review website for the Brawley Hotel he worked for and said, "Write 'Hector is very helpful!'"

I thought that was a heck of a deal and I was happy to do so.

That night, running on staring at the silver-specked sky, I was craving human connection. Even though Anna and I would run in silence, the fact she was there made it so comforting. When she wasn't, I tended to slip back into mission mode. Nearing the end of the night marathon, with the sun starting to rise, some more light dawned on me, I could do something for the run and get some human interaction. I pulled out my iPhone and began a Facebook Live video for the first time. The thought of going "live" scared me, that I might say or do something wrong, but I really wanted a connection with the world.

As I started to live-stream, followers began to flood in and comment:

Tasoula Kanellakopoulos: Watching from South Africa ? ♥

Michelle Grant Hallam: Watching you from Australia, massive effort, well done.

Amelia Reeves: I am watching in Calgary too!!

Karen Vitale: Watching from Gloucester. X

It was pretty sweet, people were tuning in from all over the world, even my home town of Gloucester. They were really inquisitive, asking what my surroundings looked like, so I spun the camera around so they could see what I could see.

Scotty Travels: Wow. You're in the middle of nowhere!

"Yuuuuuup, nothing but desert. Welcome to my world!" I replied.

It felt incredible that I really was in the middle of nowhere, yet people all across the globe felt as though they were next to me. Even my mum and foster brother from Afghanistan joined in:

Ann McDonald: Me and Shabir are watching.

"Hi, Mum! Love that you're here!" I replied excitedly.

The mum-and-sons love-in didn't go unnoticed either, comments were flying in:

Shane Lehmann: Love that your Mom is able to watch.

I knew my mum would be enjoying the virtual "love" she was getting. As I continued streaming, I reached a small community that had a strange aura about it. There were buildings, but no signs of life. To my left, it looked like a campsite might have been there 30 years before, but had long since been abandoned; on the right, a shop that was clearly closed. It looked like a scene from the post-apocalyptic film *The Road*.

I knew this wasn't good. Anna had mapped out the entire route so there'd be civilisation at the end of each run, but it looked like the final place was deserted. It was 7.30 a.m., there was only one way I was getting out of this potential horror movie and that was to hitch-hike back to the Brawley Hotel before the sun came up. The temperature was rising fast and I knew I didn't have long before I was toast.

Everyone was still watching and when I'm anxious I'm pretty good at disguising everything with humour, so I said, "If someone picks me up and turns out to be a wacko, you've got my back right?!"

A comment popped in immediately:

Nitz Nitz: Oddly entertaining. We've switched off the TV and are watching you...

It made me smile, but inside I was nervous. Nothing ends well being stuck in a desert in 55°C heat. Serious trouble was on the cards unless someone helped. Deep breath. "Okay, Jamie, you got this." I set myself up next to the road and waited for a car. Fifteen minutes passed before one approached, I put my thumb out... and it drove right by.

I went back to my phone to see what people were saying:

Adam Pasquet: Need more leg. It gets 'em every time!

Shane Lehmann: Wish I could send you an Uber.

After a few more cars drove by, it was looking a very real prospect that I might not get picked up. My heart sank and my body began burning.

Another message woke me:

Lauralyn ÓRaghallaigh: In my experience... no one likes to pick up hitch-hikers round there... :-(Call 911

Then my mum started to comment...

Ann McDonald: Put a sign up.

Ann McDonald: Jay, this is really bothering me now, put a sign up.

Ann McDonald: Jay, put a bloody sign up.

"Okay, Mum, I hear you. Though surprisingly I don't have any cardboard or a permanent marker handy to do the job!"

Now I was caught between feeling worried for myself and trying not to worry Mum. Although getting my mum not to worry is like telling a monkey not to eat a banana, it's an impossible task!

Every 15 minutes or so, another vehicle would approach and drive right by. I'd never felt so demoralised.

People started to chip in with advice...

Rebecca Roderick: Wave your bib? xxxx

Kaley Broersen: Hide Caesar!

Chris Murray: Can you write on Caesar that you're not a hobo?

As I looked at rusty, dusty Caesar and myself covered in filth, I realised no one would want to pick me up! Back to the live feed...

Mandi Campbell: Get on your knees

Kevin Dunseath: This is painful.

Wendy Scott: This is better than TV, on the edge of my seat. x

With sweat stinging my eyes, I said to everyone watching, "We're over an hour in now, this is not going well. I'm struggling to keep my eyes open from tiredness and I'm beginning to physically cook."

All of a sudden, people on the feed started to spring into action making calls to surrounding towns...

Gin Riutta: No answer at the Ranger's station.

Catherine Petracek: No answer at the radio stations.

At that moment, a car pulled in across the road. My heart jumped for joy and I shouted, "Yes, one's pulled in!"

Rebecca Roderick: YOU DID IT. XXXXXXXX

As I walked over, I saw three men dressed in overalls who looked like they were off to work (don't ask me what!). I explained I needed to get back to Brawley before I cooked.

"Sorry, man. We're going to a completely different place. Here's some water though."

As I gratefully took the water, they looked pretty worried for me, but I could see that was as good as they could do. I went back to Caesar where the followers could see my disappointment.

Juliet Hodgkinson: He just stopped and won't give u a lift?!

Shane Lehmann: If only these cars knew your story, they'd be lining up to help you.

I sat on the scorching highway, it was nearing 10 a.m. and was only going to get hotter still.

I pulled out my sun cream and splashed it all over, but because I was so sweaty the cream just splashed around like paint and wouldn't soak into my skin.

Rebecca Roderick: GO AWAY SUN – GRRRRR.

Natalie Shelby-James: I can't imagine sitting on the side of the highway after RUNNING A MARATHON!!!!

Lauralyn ÓRaghallaigh: I was hoping you wouldn't be running there in the middle of summer... the hottest recorded temperatures on earth right now...

Clare Janine: What's across the road, worth a look over there???

Out of options, staring at an old shack, I wasn't hopeful.

"Good idea," I said.

As I neared, there seemed to be some movement at one of the windows. I couldn't believe it.

Sandy Jimson: I'm on the phone to someone there, Jamie. Go over to the shop, the lady I spoke to wants to help you...

Boom! Was I saved? I ran towards the shack to find out.

I couldn't believe it, the shop was OPEN! Still live-streaming, I went inside and got chatting to a sturdy-looking lady with short blonde hair called Pamela.

"I just got off the phone with Sandy. She said you needed help?" said Pamela with a smile.

Once I'd explained "everything" she said, "Well, hitch-hiking is tough, that's for sure, but I think someone will pick you up."

Then a useful comment came in:

Teri Tran Magnuson: Jamie, ask her to make a cardboard sign that says, "Need lift to Brawley."

Yes, Teri!

So, we did. Pamela and I created a "Brawley" sign on her checkout desk, much to my mum's delight...

Ann McDonald: Thank god!

As I went to leave the shop and get back to the hitch-hiker's grind, Pamela handed me a bag of Classic Lay's chips and said, "Here, take these to keep you going."

Back on the side of the road, I was hoofing down the chips, sucking the salt between my tongue and the roof of my mouth, replacing the lost salts from my run. Another 30 sweaty minutes, still no lift and the energy of the chips had worn off. My brain craved sleep. Hitch-hiking in 55°C heat was not the way to recover from a marathon. I looked at the live feed, there were now more than 800 comments and it had reached over 100,000 people. I kept tuning in and out of the messages.

James Clay: I finish work in 90 minutes, please don't make me do overtime and keep watching, someone pick Jamie up!

Pauline Briggs: You looked like you enjoyed those chips!

Chris Greener Greening: I've got four other people watching with me now.

John Myatt: You should do this more often, I've got my feet up dunking biscuits in my tea. I'm going to get a sweepstake going on when you get picked up.

Then, a weird one popped up that caught my attention.

Chris Murray: SEE SANDY'S COMMENT, DUDE! Someone's coming! Now get back in the shop and get an ice cream.

I scrolled back through the comments and there it was...

Sandy Jimson: Jamie, someone is coming for you from a hotel in Brawley!

"You have to be kidding me?!" I shouted.

It was like my world had just turned from night to day – the kind of day that's not so hot it kills you. I skipped across the road back to the shop. I thought Chris' idea to get an ice cream was top-notch – it was time to celebrate. I treated myself to a Butterfinger ice cream. Chocolate on the outside, creamy on the inside, with dollops of peanut butter throughout. That was victory right there.

As I devoured it from the shade of the shop, the sun beat down ever harder on the already baked earth. I was saved, but where was my saviour? After 30 minutes, panic started to set in again. I checked the live-stream to see if I'd missed something.

Emma Camps: Come on Hector! I need to do the housework.

Susan Rice: I'd have a stern word with Hector if he wasn't being so lovely helping you.

Tanya Mansell: Does Hector have a cell?

Micheline Gilmore-Hendricks: Waiting for Hector, hope you get picked up soon, it's getting hot out there.

Clare Janine: If Hector is single, I bet he would get lots of dates now for being such a superhero!!!

Hector, huh? *The* Hector?! *My* Hector! I must have missed that when I went to get my ice cream. But as a truck pulled in, like a mirage, there he was. The same Hector who'd helped fix Caesar's tyre the day before. Hector the freaking maintenance guy with the glowing review on the hotel's website. I hugged him warmly.

Comments started to fly in once again...

Tricia Cunningham: Yay Hector!

Mike Jodie Clevett Mercer: Three cheers for Hector!

Clare Janine: That has brought a tear to my eye. x

PA Gordon: What a movie!

As I climbed into the truck with Hector and we headed for Brawley, we exchanged warm smiles and drove off into the desert like Thelma and Louise.

PART 16

THERE'S A STORM COMING

Waking up at the Brawley Inn it was a quick turnaround, I packed all my stuff into Caesar to head back to the spot where I'd finished running in Glamis. At 9 p.m. Hector turned up to drop me back. As we drove, Hector explained I'd have good phone signal all the way across the desert; because it's so flat, I'd pick up cell towers hundreds of miles away. We could see an electrical storm surging in the distance.

Hector's brow furrowed. "Use your phone, check the weather."

I did, and it reported "a little rain" and "dust warnings" – which I thought would be fine. At Glamis we said our goodbyes.

He put his hand on his heart and said, "You'll be in here for the rest of my life."

I thought exactly the same.

After yesterday's fandango it was time to get running again. The air was slightly cooler than usual, which was a relief, but up ahead the night sky was filled with menace. From a distance the lightning flashes across the sky were spectacular, but gave me a slight sense of trepidation.

I filmed the storm and tweeted the video with the comment, "Should I be scared that I'm running into this?"

Almost immediately, Anna called. "Err, J, yesterday I was meant to warn you there was a big monsoon heading your way from Phoenix, two teenagers got struck by lightning. I didn't think you'd be hitting the storm so soon."

I replied, panicking, "Were the kids alright?"

Anna replied, "They were badly burned and had to go to hospital. I'll check the forecast now and see if you're heading right into the storm and will call you back. Bloody hell, J. You're wrecking my nerves, you are!"

As Anna hung up, the headwind grew a little stronger and a lightning bolt rippled down followed by a crack of thunder. I was sure you're supposed to hear the thunder seconds later, not at the same time. My heart was smashing against my ribcage and my adrenaline skyrocketed. Was I already in the eye of the storm? I didn't want to be alone, so I began live-streaming again, hoping I might get some advice on what to do.

I got comments like:

Becky Ford: Wow... another heavy storm coming again tonight! Protect yourself and be careful. Yes... you are heading into the heavy monsoon season in Arizona. Floods are very dangerous and can sweep you away.

Pete: If your hair starts to stand on end, that is a sign of electricity and you may be about to be struck by lightning. Drop to your knees and cover your head!

Holly Baskin: Avoid large farm equipment, golf carts or other large metal equipment. Not good when you're pushing Caesar...

As I read those comments, I thought, I must be the only freaking thing in this barren desert pushing a big metal object, the monsoon storm is probably licking its lips right now at the thought of having a lump of metal and a skinny stupid Brit for target practice. The wind strengthened and I gripped Caesar tighter. Lightning bolts landed all around me as if Zeus was doing some javelin training. The only shelter I knew of was a security checkpoint 8 miles ahead that I had found on Google Earth earlier that day.

As I clung on to that hope, the lightning seemed to steer off left, the wind chasing its glow.

A message from Anna: "You're in between two storms, but it looks like they're both going to miss you. Love you."

Phewwwwww.

As the storm peeled away I was left to run on alone into the darkness. I checked my watch, it was 4 a.m. and the temperature was 40°C. I'd nearly completed my marathon when I made it to the checkpoint. It was a plain concrete building with no windows and a red-and-white-striped barrier blocking the road. I got chatting to the security guard and said that if I carried on running I'd have to sleep outside in the daytime heat and I was scared. I asked if there was any way I could stay at the checkpoint for a few hours' rest. He wasn't keen. I had to take it to the next level. "Erm, could I speak to your supervisor, please?"

He called his supervisor and gave me the phone. I explained the situation.

He replied, "That building you see is a place where we might have to put illegal immigrants so it's not possible for you to stay there, but feel free to take shade anywhere around the area."

I was pretty gutted not to be able to rest in the one and only cool building, but I totally understood his reasons. I looked around for shade, but all I could see was a dirty metal container. It would have to do. I rolled my mat out inside and although I knew it would get hot when the sun came up, it would be fine for now.

That was until the security guard came back. "You can't sleep there," he said. "You have to be away from our vicinity. There's some bushes over there." He pointed out into the desert.

I was a bit riled. "There's no way those bushes will offer any shade, they're only waist height. Are you sure I can't stay here? Your supervisor seemed to say it was okay. Can you put him back on the phone?"

His tone had changed. "You can't be near our building," he said tersely. "You need to take cover somewhere in the desert."

"But there is no cover, you know that!"

"Look, I've called my superior to get permission, but he's not answering so you can't stay here."

I had to play my final hand. "Do you think if your superior knew there was a man running across America for kids' hospitals and that the only shade for miles and miles was this rusty old container then he'd give the okay for me to sleep in it?"

His tone softened. "Yes, I'd like to think he would, but that's why we're a law enforcement organisation, not a humanitarian organisation."

Although I felt utterly deflated, I knew I had to run on. I looked at the security officer one last time, he shrugged his shoulders sympathetically. As I left the checkpoint behind, my anger grew. I couldn't understand why they wouldn't let me sleep in the bloody shipping container. I know rules are there for a reason, but at some point you have to make exceptions and I felt like this was one of those moments. Fuelled by the angry situation, miles passed quickly. Anger can be a great source of energy and, in turn, therapy. At first it drives you on, but then as you get into your rhythm it becomes calming, a kind of beautiful meditation that makes negative thoughts and emotions evaporate and leave your body.

After 6 miles, the sun started to rise, and my anger was lost to the desert. An orange light began to flood the sand. It warmed me quickly and by 8 a.m. I knew I had to get out of the sun before I started to frazzle. I'd run 28 miles. A side road appeared, and a small truck stopped at the junction. I'd only seen a few lorries through the night, so I ran over and explained I needed to hitch a ride to the town of Blythe before it got too hot. Without hesitation, the Mexican man named Mario said yes, even though it was an extra 20 miles off his route.

A week ago, a social media follower, Adrian Hilton, had said he'd put me up in the Hampton Inn Blythe, which was so kind. I asked if Mario could drive me there and he kindly obliged. An hour later we arrived, I thanked Mario and slunk into the hotel lobby.

The lady at reception read Caesar's sign and said, "Wow, that's amazing what you're doing. Are you hungry? Come and have some breakfast."

I didn't need asking twice and gorged on porridge with chocolate chips sprinkled all over it. Then it was waffles and honey. Along with a blueberry yoghurt, a chocolate muffin and an apple. Hey, a runner's got to refuel! My eyes were hanging out of my head as I crashed on to my bed. I lay back thinking about how people had rallied around me, knowing I'd made it through my first monsoon and had ticked off another day in the desert. It wasn't pretty, but we were doing it.

PART 17

OUT OF THE FRYING PAN INTO THE FIRE

The next night as the temperature rose even higher, I blasted through the run. Suddenly, my head torch lit up a sign: "Arizona – The Grand Canyon State – Welcomes You". I thought it was going to read, "Out of the frying pan into the fire". As hot as it was, I'd run through California, one of the longest states in America. I felt pretty chuffed.

With the excitement of a new state and being in the Arizona desert, I ran hard and sweated harder, all the way to the cusp of dawn. I looked at my watch; 6.36 a.m., the sky melting from black to blue and now a purple haze that bleached the horizon. I knew I was close to completing another marathon. I set up my camera on Caesar so I could live-stream the sunrise. A flood of followers joined and one said, "Wow, Jamie, you look good having just run a marathon." Everyone was so supportive, but I could see myself on the iPhone screen and I looked absolutely beaten up.

The sun had started to pierce the horizon and the desert burned with reds and oranges. Seeing the sun rise above the cactuses was another victory moment. I breathed in through my nose tasting the dry and dusty air that carried a hint of herb in its scent.

"Anyone know of a place to stay?" I said into the camera.

Sandy Jimson replied, "Already on it, Jamie. Head to the firefighter service when you reach the town."

Sandy, although I'd never met her before, had been following my adventure through social media, and out of everyone commenting, I noticed she was following my every move. She knew where I was going to end up finishing a run before I did, which was amazing as it gave me one less thing to worry about.

Then, I saw something jump from behind a bush. WURGHH! What was that? A dog? It was as dark as the night I'd just run through, its body wiry, its muscles taut.

I showed it to everyone.

"That's a coyote, Jamie, be careful!"

Then I saw a comment from my mum: "J, get out of there fast, he might kill you!"

Trust my mum to go straight to the death scenario. The coyote was curious, it began to skulk toward me. I wasn't taking any chances, I stood tall, put my arms in the air and started pounding my feet and barking like a crazy person until it scarpered off, much to my mum's delight. It was like I heard her sigh of relief from the other side of the world.

As I plodded into the tiny town of Aguila, a fire truck pulled up and a fireman leaned out from the window smiling. "Hey

Jamie, one of your fans has been in touch, follow me, we've got a bed for you."

When we arrived, I discovered it was a voluntary firefighter's unit. I was greeted by two ladies who were just starting work. They showed me around, while the firefighter assembled a camp bed. He decided to try it out to make sure it was comfy and it collapsed in a heap on the floor. We both burst out laughing. Fortunately, it was able to withstand my weight.

Before bed, I decided to call Dr Fred as I had been experiencing a mild headache for the past month.

After explaining to him that I wasn't taking electrolytes, and that I was trying to get my body to adapt to the desert naturally over time, he quickly butted in. "Jamie, you're a f**king idiot! Human bodies aren't supposed to naturally adapt in that kind of heat, a month-long headache means you're seriously dehydrated, you can die from that! You need to consume electrolytes immediately."

Luckily, I was at a station that stocked electrolytes and sure enough, 30 minutes after taking some, my headache cleared.

I set my alarm for 4 p.m., and loaded up on salts and electrolytes. I was starting to feel like I was in control of the desert.

After my daytime sleep, that night the heat was a brutal 48°C. I'd set off well-rested and knew I had to cover a marathon to make it to the next town of Wickenburg. The desert air was still but unrelenting and after a brief chill-out period enjoying the air conditioning of a Mexican restaurant I clocked up a fairly quick 10 miles. But I was now 10 miles from civilisation in one direction and 16 miles from it in the other. And that's when the mountain lion lady came a-calling. At first, she was reluctant to tell me. It might have been nothing, but her maternal instincts got the better of her because she might have been sending me to my death otherwise. And then she did it, she said she had seen a mountain lion in the direction I was running.

In shock, I just let her drive off until her tail lights were out of sight. My brain was a mess, my heart smashing against my Adventureman suit. The question was, what the HELL was I going to do? I didn't have much in the way of protection except for some tired legs, to aim weak kicks at it. Should I run back? Run in the direction of the mountain lion? After a few minutes, I managed to calm myself and let logic take over. It was simple, either I ran 10 miles back to the tiny town, or I ran forwards, perhaps into the gaping jaws of a mountain lion, and hoped for the best. My final thought was, "I'm going to have to run this stretch at some point anyway," so I decided to go with the second choice.

As I turned to run in the direction where the mountain lion had been spotted, I didn't feel like a superhero – I was PETRIFIED. I grabbed my penknife and turned open the blade, its sharpened edge glistening under my head torch – not that it would have done any good, I'd probably do more harm to myself than the lion if I used it. I began to run hard, head torch scanning the road from left to right, one hand on Caesar, one on the knife. I listened intently, every noise giving me whiplash as I jerked my neck to shine a light on whatever stirred. Most noises were plastic bags, caught on cactuses, bristling in the wind. But my imagination was off the scale at this point – all the rustles were *definitely* the lion getting ready to pounce on me and Caesar.

Suddenly I had a light-bulb moment, a couple who lived in Arizona had given me their number a week ago and said to call if I had any problems. This was their territory – they'd know what to do. I jammed my AirPods in, not hopeful they'd answer at this hour, but I had to try. The phone rang...

"Hello?"

"Hey, it's Jamie. You know, the idiot that's running across America."

"Oh, hey Jamie! We're still up drinking beers. We were talking about you this evening! Everything okay?" she said in a relaxed manner.

I explained my situation.

"Oh, okay, I see. Let me get my boyfriend, he's better at this type of thing."

A minute went by and then I heard a guy's voice. "Hey Jamie, so this isn't good news I'm afraid. Just the other day, a friend of mine had his cattle eaten by two mountain lions and you know how big the cattle is out here! The mountain lion isn't going to be afraid of your size, I'm sorry to say. Do you have a gun?"

"No, I don't have a freaking gun!" I shouted.

"Well, your best bet would be to keep shining the light, act big and keep making noise where you can!" he said with all the fear of a man sat in an armchair with a cold beer.

All I could think was that's what I had done with the coyote earlier and it still came towards me – but this time it was a goddamn lion!

He carried on. "Jamie, still there? Listen, if we were close to you, we'd pick you up, but you're too far. You're in the middle of nowhere. Let's just hope the lion isn't hungry!"

"Okay, cheers for the advice. As you say, let's hope the lion isn't hungry! Good night," I said, throwing in a fake chuckle.

It was back to being alone, in the darkness, listening to the desert and hoping a roaming mountain lion wasn't hungry. Focusing on my breath to keep me calm, I made it through an entire hour, until I saw something on the side of the road. Instinctively, I ducked behind Caesar. Then I peered over and shone the light in its direction. I took a step closer, then another, until I was just a metre away. It was what I thought it was, I was eyeballing a giant tarantula.

It was the first time in the most intensive two hours of my life that I stopped thinking of the mountain lion. And what was the distraction? A flipping TARANTULA. Spiders are one of my greatest phobias. This one happened to be half the size of my foot and as hairy as my head. I knew I had to film it, but the camera didn't quite capture just how big it was. So, for perspective I placed my left foot next to it. Spiders don't really do perspective and it must have felt the vibrations from my foot because it reared up on all of its eight legs and scuttled towards me in attack mode. I jolted back on to the road and let out a huge scream. The tarantula didn't stop, it kept coming and I kept running. I grabbed hold of Caesar and pushed off. There was only one problem. I spotted another one. Another tarantula. This time in the road. I yanked Caesar to the left to swerve it and let out another scream. This was a nightmare – and it had only just begun.

They seemed to be everywhere. I flicked my head torch on to light up the road, only to see them spread all over it and all along the sandbanks. Literally hundreds of spiders everywhere. I was jumping out of my skin with every step, although they were more like leaps. I began sprinting over them, trying desperately not to run them over with Caesar, but the inevitable happened: "CRUNCH." I stopped to see if it was alright. But as I looked down the indestructible tarantula was still coming for me. I'd just accidentally spread 60 kg of weight over its hairy bottom and he still wanted a piece of me. I screamed into the hot desert night until after a couple of hundred metres, my legs whirring like Usain Bolt, the hairy beasts gradually vanished into the darkness from where they came.

Of course, once the tarantula torment was over, my brain was straight back to the mountain lion. Now I had that fear running through my veins. I just wanted it to be over. As each hour of darkness passed, I felt closer to safety and then as the first embers of daylight broke on the horizon I spotted a little town ahead. To my surprise, and relief, a cafe was open and the thought of getting some hot food inside me was magnificent.

As I walked in, I saw three men eating breakfast. One, wearing a trucker cap, said, "You look like you've had a rough night." I caught sight of myself in a mirror on the wall; my hair was frizzy, my skin dry and my Adventureman suit tinted orange from all the desert dust. My reply told the rest of the story: "It's been one of those nights!"

"I'll say! What you doing dressed like that anyway?" said another of the breakfast diners.

I quickly gave them my bedtime story, not skipping on the mountain lion part. "I swear I could hear that beast out there in the desert, I'm certain he was there," I said, recalling the nightmare.

They all burst into laughter.

"You think that's funny?!" It was tarantula time. I regaled them with the part about the spider-strewn road.

This time two of the men nearly fell off their chair in hysterics. But the other was ashen-faced.

"Wow, man," he said, "I can't believe you came across a tarantula's nest. That's really rare. I've heard that's what happens in monsoon season. You know, people travel the world to see that. Witnessing that, you were really lucky."

I frowned. "Lucky?"

"Seriously lucky," he said with a straight face.

As I cruised into the fringes of Phoenix, I couldn't stop looking at all the sandy brown-coloured houses. Like Vegas, it was another city that had somehow adapted to survive the heat. I looked at my watch, it was 19 August – my birthday! Fortunately, I had a destination, I was going to be staying with Stefan, a personal trainer from EXOS. With a couple of miles to go he came to meet me and we ran the last stretch together. We arrived at his house both dripping with sweat. Stefan's wife Mallory and their two kids, Gavin and Zoe, were at the door to meet us. Gavin was dressed as Batman.

I said to him, "Woah, you're Batman?!"

He just replied, "Nah, they're just jammies."

After being in 40+°C temperatures for the past 8 hours, the air con that blasted my face felt so refreshing. It was probably the best birthday present I could have wished for. But there was more. I was shown to my room where I found a package with a note that read, "Welcome Jamie. Here are some goodies we thought may come in handy."

I turned to them and said, "This is lovely. It's actually my birthday today!"

Mallory shouted "WHAAAAT? Why didn't you tell us?"

I opened my first present – it was a small toilet roll with a hook.

"That's so thoughtful," I said. "Every cross-country runner loves toilet roll and it's got a hook so I'll be able to hang it off a tree."

The family chuckled, but I wasn't kidding.

I'd been connected with this family via a friend back home, Mark Hughes, and they'd been following my journey on Facebook ever since. More pressies were to come, they got me shampoo, electrolytes, body glide (to help with chafing), smart socks (that keep your feet dry) and a sew-on patch of the Arizona flag. It genuinely felt like my birthday, actually, a surprise birthday. After my daytime sleep, I woke up to a huge dinner and then, as the lights got dimmed, a cake popped up from beneath the table with burning candles. This family, who had been strangers just a few hours ago, were now singing me happy birthday. It was all getting emotional.

Unlike California, I was now getting through states at speed. No sooner was I leaving Phoenix and the cactus-coated city of Tucson, Arizona, than I was in New Mexico. Running from west to east, I knew I could rip through this state – and I needed to as it was full of swamps and mosquitoes. Fortunately, running at night – and speed – I managed to get through in eight days until I crossed my next border. Sometimes after big runs, my head would hit the pillow and I'd wake up 19 hours later, and sometimes I'd sleep that long without once having to go to the toilet for a pee, which I didn't think was even possible.

I was now in one of the largest states, Texas, and soon the dusty orange desert was filled with life. With mountains in the distance, the flat sprawl of El Paso city ahead seemed like a mirage. Its tall buildings and bustling streets felt bizarre after the nothingness that had come before it. Places were coming thick and fast and I only realised how far south I was when I looked on Google Maps and saw I was getting closer and closer to the Mexican border.

As I exited the El Paso city at night, by 3 a.m. I was back to running in complete darkness. I looked up and around and couldn't see a speck of light anywhere. Away from the conveniences of the city, the Texas desert was as dry as a bone. It looked like it hadn't rained for a thousand years, yet strangely there was a scent of wet dirt. Although it felt like there was nothing ahead of me for hundreds of miles, in the desert there's always some form of life.

My head torch had caught sight of something on the ground. I crouched down to investigate – it was a giant centipede. I'd never seen anything like it. It seemed to wriggle like a snake, but had thousands of claws to hover and feel its way across the ground. Feeling like I was David Attenborough, I began filming, thinking, "This is so cool that I have the desert all to myself." My nature bubble was about to burst though.

"Hey you, what you doing out here?!"

I stopped, having no idea where the voice was coming from. Everything was black. I shined the torch all around me, but its light only carried a few metres.

"Hello, I'm running across America," I said hesitantly.

"What you doing back there shining a torch like that?" said a man's voice.

"I was filming a centipede," I said, like a big nature-loving legend.

As soon as I uttered that, I realised this was getting weird. I was stood in the darkness at 3 a.m., in the boonies, convincing a man I couldn't see that I was running across America. Then I started to think, "Hang on, what are you doing out here?" A torch beam fell upon me, blinding my vision.

"I'd be careful if I was you. I wouldn't be surprised if you get a visit from the border patrol," warned the mysterious voice.

"I think it will be okay," I replied, wondering what he was talking about.

In all honesty, I was quite scared of this voice in the darkness, having no idea why he was out here. I got the impression he didn't have as good an excuse as I did. I ran on. Five shaky minutes later, a truck's engine roared into life, sirens blared and blue lights flashed from all angles as five quad bikes raced up alongside me.

"Stay where you are!"

Holy smokes.

A man in police uniform climbed down from the truck. He wore a big moustache and a sheriff's hat that showed his senior rank. "What are you doing out here?"

Again, after explaining, my story didn't look good.

"What's in there?" The policeman said, gesturing at Caesar. "Any drugs?"

I half smiled, hoping he was joking. But his serious face said otherwise.

"They're my belongings," I said, while opening Caesar and showing him my bits and bobs.

"Give me your passport," the moustache maestro fired back.

As I handed it over he grunted, "Wait here," and went back to his truck.

While I was waiting, I grabbed my phone and went on Google Maps and it dawned on me where I was. I was 200 metres from the Mexico border and they probably thought I was a drug runner for the cartel hauling a load of illegal party supplies inside Caesar. Well, I mean, I was a runner, just of a different kind.

I was wondering how they would think I was a suspicious character, then I stared down, all I had on was a pair of shorts, a pasty-white hairy chest and a loosely tied fluorescent high-vis jacket, the one that Anna had given me, that I swore I would wear at night. "Bingo!" I thought, my Freddie Mercury look was attracting the wrong kind of attention. After a long 10 minutes, the policeman and the other patrolmen got off their quad bikes and approached me. Right, here we go.

The straight-faced policeman came close, his moustache bristling, and said, "So you really have run from the state of Washington?"

"I really have," I said, puffing out my pasty-white hairy chest proudly.

Before I knew it, we were all laughing away. I wasn't carrying any illegal contraband, other than my toilet roll with a hook, which after what I'd just been through would have proved useful when they sprang out of the pitch black.

Just before heading off, one of the patrolmen handed me some water and said, "Texas is the biggest American state. I have no idea if you're going to make it, but good luck you crazy Brit."

PART 18

GOING BIG IN TEXAS

The policeman was right, Texas was huge. They say "Everything's bigger in Texas", from the ranches, to the skies, the cowboy hats and cowboy boots. It's the second biggest state after Alaska, so the biggest in all of continental America and little old me was the tiniest of tiny dots just trying to run across it. A big state meant big runs, with big distances to cover between places for a big bed and some big-time air con. I needed to up my mileage, which meant all that marathon running had come in handy because now sometimes I would need to run up to more than 50 miles a day.

Luckily, I had my very own Texas Ranger, Sandy Jimson, a Facebook follower who was at it again, intensely and virtually involved in my run. She was now my "full-time worrier" who kept in contact with people ahead of me so she could score me a bed, food and keep me safe. I'd never met Sandy before, over the past few months we had been sending messages to each other via social media and that's how we got to know each other.

I kept telling her how grateful I was for her help, and eventually she opened up. "Jamie, it's important that you know, I suffer with anxiety and your run is giving me a purpose. It's helping me. So, thank you."

She had decided I needed someone in this role to support me. And with so many miles to run, who was I to argue? I just couldn't believe it was her thanking me!

It meant I could focus solely on running, after all, my visa was only for a year and it was quickly running out. I was at the halfway point, six months in. I'd run six of my planned 24 states. I had completed 2,800 miles (the equivalent of 110 marathons) with 120 more marathons to run. If my calculations were correct, I was 10 marathons behind schedule. And that certainly put a rocket in my engine.

Next was my biggest challenge yet – how to conquer 80 miles of nothing. A point-to-point run with no handy drinks stores, air-conditioned restaurants or comfy beds in between. Luckily, Sandy had scored me a bed with a guy named Lyn in a tiny town called Eldorado at the other end. That was a relief, knowing that I had a place to sleep and rest my wailing legs after 80 miles.

My first part of the run was through the night, it was somewhat cooler with the breeze, so I ran strongly covering 20 miles till 5 a.m. Pitching my tent along the roadside, I left my door unzipped to let a breeze into the tent. At 8 a.m., I was awoken with a start.

Peering through my tent door was a Texan farmer wearing a cowboy hat. "Morning, sir," he said in a thick southern accent. "I don't mind y'all camping here, though I waddn't recommaynd keeping yawww tent door open. It's a rattlesnake haven round here. And trust me, y'all don't wanna sleep with one of those."

With the risk of a rattlesnake alarm clock I thanked the farmer for his advice and decided to get up and get going. Packing up, my eyes glanced on something moving a few metres away, and sure enough, there was a rattlesnake, slithering through the dirt. After I packed up pronto, I attached an umbrella to Caesar to keep me shaded. I looked like Mary Poppins. As I cranked out the first few miles, something felt different, the sun reflecting down on the road was hurting my eyes. I realised it had been three long months of running in the dark every night. As my eyes gradually adjusted, I noticed there was dusty sand on either side of the road. The bushes were green and very much alive, as if rain was common around here. Knowing the shrubbery was thriving gave me hope I'd survive this stretch too.

I'd decided to set myself the mission of getting to Lyn's house in one more push, so I'd have to run 60 more miles, on top of the 20 I'd already run. After conquering the Arizona and New Mexico deserts, I felt like I could do anything. I began believing that my limitations were endless. Or at least they were with running. I was battling to keep the umbrella flying away with the stiff breeze. A local trucker pulled up ahead and kindly helped me fix it back in place.

As he did, he said, in another slow Texan accent, "Say, sirrrr, do y'all smell that? That's H2S. That's a poisonous gayaas. You don't wanna be breathing that in too much, y'all should keep on going." As he drove off, he shouted, "Run, buddy, run!"

Running all day in the heat I'd covered another 30 miles, but I was burned out. My legs had gone to jelly and as the sun turned into darkness so did my brain. I pushed harder and harder, but my body was breaking down both physically and emotionally. I needed something. Rummaging through Caesar, I grabbed a purple Powerade, which would have electrolytes and sugar in to give me a boost. I necked the entire bottle and ran on. Although it got me going, physically my mind was shot. I collapsed by the roadside. Knowing I should film some of the gruesome moments, I got out of camera and saw myself on screen – my eyes were bloodshot and bulging, I looked as if I should be lying on a hospital bed, not the side of a Texan highway.

"Come on Jamie, get up," I said to myself. I got hold of Caesar and began running, but as I did my head started to fall downwards. I had one eye open and my chin on my chest, I knew this wasn't good. I let out a "Roooarrr" and pounded my chest to create some adrenaline to keep me awake, but nothing came. All through the dark of night I battled thoughts that I wouldn't make it, but eventually the first light of morning hit the road and the sun pierced my eyes and sent an orange glow to my brain. I felt my eyes widen, like the sun was the answer my brain had been searching for all night. I said to myself, "It's a new day, you're going to make it."

At 8 a.m., I called Lyn to let him know I was in town. He drove out to see me, explained he needed to run some errands, but gave me directions to his house and said to make myself at home. As I opened Lyn's door, I kept saying "Hello", hoping I wasn't in the wrong house. Then, I collapsed on to a bed. I'd run 80 miles, with one 3-hour sleep by the roadside. I was physically broken, yet deep inside me I could feel my confidence not only growing, but glowing.

At the back of my mind, I had always wondered if I'd ever be able to do a run that was the longest or furthest in one go ever known to man or woman. In 2013, that idea sparked in my brain while I was running 5,000 miles across Canada. I actually booked myself on a record attempt to run the furthest distance ever recorded in seven days. The existing Guinness World Record was held by Sharon Gayter who in 2011 ran a total of 517 miles, in seven days, on a treadmill. Unfortunately, at the end of my Canadian run, I had chronic tendinitis in my foot and was too physically destroyed to try and attempt it.

Something felt different this time, I had been running strongly, had more life experience and seemed to know how to not get injured and stay healthy and strong. With over 100 marathons in the bank, I could sense my human limitations (like when I was in Canada) were increasing once again and any fear I had was falling by the wayside. For me, slowly beginning to push and break through boundaries one day and one step at a time seemed to be working.

At Lyn's house, I didn't tell anyone, but went ahead and re-opened my online application from 2013 and booked my next record attempt. I dated it for a few weeks after my US visa was up. That would mean my year's run would end in America with

6,000 "training" miles under my belt hopefully giving me the best possible chance to break the record. As my hand hovered over the send button, my heart raced, I pressed it and moments later I received a notification from Guinness World Records that read:

Application accepted

Dear Jamie,

Thank you for reopening your application for the greatest distance covered on a treadmill in one week. The current record stands at 832.5 kilometres (517.3 miles).

We wish you luck!

Guinness World Records team

I made some quick calculations using my iPhone calculator – it was nearly 20 marathons in seven days. My head flushed with thoughts of how I wasn't even capable of attempting it last time. And now here I was physically broken again from having just run 80 miles. To break the record, I was going to have to run what I'd just done seven times over, non-stop. My mind drifted further, I pictured the treadmill in the heart of my hometown of Gloucester surrounded by friends, family and loved ones and that seemed to ease the fear. Realistically though, at the end of this run I knew I had set myself up for a huge challenge and maybe a gigantic, big fat fail.

PART 19

WASHED AWAY

I woke in Lyn's house to a delicious breakfast of pancakes and his wife's home-made jelly jam.

While wolfing it down, I had a smile on my face and could feel that today was going to be an enjoyable run. Canadians Shawn and Peggy were here to join me. They had followed my journeys in North America ever since they saw me running alongside a highway near Toronto. They were runners too. Every year, they did an organised marathon and this year they wanted to run a marathon with me. They had written me a Facebook message saying they would fly to a nearby airport, rent a car and track me down. It would help share the pain of the run and could lead to even more donations. What a beautiful gesture. How could I refuse?

Shawn got out of the car with his warm face and bald head and greeted me with a big hug. Then Peggy with her bright blue eyes and bobbing short hair hugged me too. Even more lovely were the bright-red home-made Adventureman T-shirts they were wearing. You could see the excitement on their faces and although they were in their 40s I felt like I was with two teenagers madly in love with each other who were about to begin their next great adventure.

We began running at 9 a.m. It was 22°C and there was a cool breeze as the temperature had dropped dramatically overnight. As it began to rain, Peggy was doing her small shuffle steps alongside me, which was perfect for my pace.

"Can I give Caesar a push?" she said with a grin.

"Of course," I replied.

"Wow. I can't believe I'm pushing Caesar," she said giddily. "I've seen him on your social media videos and read about him in your book. This is so surreal, Jamie."

It felt incredible to have someone who had as much of an emotional attachment to Caesar as I did.

As we ran along a beautiful, quiet road just listening to our steps and feeling each other's warmth, I felt she truly knew me, I didn't need to say anything. After 13 miles, it was time for them to switch around so Shawn could run while Peggy drove behind us. As Shawn started to get going he had a skip in his step, you could see how much he was loving this adventure.

"I saw the video of you dodging the mountain lion. I mean, maaaaan, it's crazy out here, huh?"

"It really is. I'd take the bears in Canada any day of the week," I said with a chuckle.

The friendly company meant the marathon was completed before I knew it. Shawn and Peggy knew I was "roughing it", so they treated me to a hotel. Our fun run ended at the Econo

Lodge in Junction. As we were checking in I noticed the skies had turned really dark, much darker than normal.

Shawn invited me to their room. "Beer?"

"Absolutely, we've all earned it," I replied.

As we swigged down an icy cold brew they surprised me with a donation sheet with lots of Canadian names: "Jackson $20 donated", "Olivia $10", "Tre $30".

"Who are all these people?" I asked.

"They're from our community back in Canada. Once I told everyone what you were doing, they all wanted to help. We've raised over $1,000," replied Shawn.

"That's incredible," I said in amazement.

It was so lovely to hear that while I was running, they were rallying their community to help the cause. Knowing those lonely desert miles had been helping earn donations in another part of the world made me so happy.

We sank some more Dos Equis XX beer, ate some Cadbury chocolate and decided to get an early night as we were doing another run tomorrow. As I relaxed on my hotel bed, I could hear the rain pelting down outside, it gave me a warm, fuzzy feeling being inside all cosy and dry. That night in between dreams I kept hearing someone shouting. I sleepily opened an eye and noticed it was only just getting light, which meant it was around 7 a.m.

I tried to ignore the yelling man, but it was relentless. I couldn't believe someone had the audacity to be shouting at this time of the morning. I put my head under the pillow and kept rolling around trying to block out the noise. Eventually, I cracked and ripped the sheets off, storming to the door ready to explode at this idiot.

As I opened the door wearing nothing but a pair of pants, I saw the man hanging over the balcony and heard his screams clearly for the first time. "Grab that tree there, HOLD ON!!!"

I looked over the balcony and 20 metres below was a raging river flowing next to the hotel. A campground across the road (where I would've normally been sleeping) was completely underwater. All you could see were the roofs of around 30–40 caravans and people were everywhere holding on for dear life.

"What's going on?" I said to the man, my heart racing.

"Last night there was a flash flood, people from the caravan park are being swept away."

He continued to scream at people below, "Hold on! Help is coming!!"

It had rained so hard that it had created a fast-flowing river out of nowhere. I rushed to put some clothes on and by the time I came back out everyone was out of their rooms and screaming from the balcony. As I stared helplessly at the fast-moving water, one by one, people who weren't strong enough to hold on were just being swept away. Seeing people's heads disappear underwater had to be one of the most disturbing scenes of my life. I felt helpless, there was literally nothing we could do but stand and stare at what felt like a massacre.

I spotted Shawn and Peggy on the other side of the hotel. "Shawn, Peggy, you okay?"

Shawn looked completely pale and Peggy horrified. They didn't respond and they didn't need to. Their faces told the story. Eventually, there was just one large man clinging to the branch of a tree sticking out of the water. Everyone was yelling at him to hold on tightly. The man began trying to take his clothes off, the water must have been sucking him down and his clothes dragging him under.

It was awful to see this man fighting for his life, scrambling to take his clothes off, it looked impossible to stay afloat. I felt as if I was right there in the water with him, trying to peel my own clothes off. After many fraught minutes, he did it. He was completely naked. Suddenly we heard a helicopter fly overhead. It hovered slowly, getting closer and closer to the man as everyone was screaming at him to give him strength and energy to hold on.

The helicopter dropped a rescue sling and somehow the man was able to hook it around himself. The only way to know if it was secure was to let go of the tree, but as he did the raging torrent swept him away. We all gasped, thinking this was it. At that moment the helicopter flew upwards and the naked man was hoisted from the water – the sling was secure. As they flew away, the man just hung limply as though he had died from exhaustion.

Eventually, the helicopter landed on some higher ground right next to us. Shawn, Peggy and I watched as his feet touched the ground and he regained consciousness. Everyone began clapping and, as I turned to Peggy, I saw she had tears rolling down her cheeks. Seeing someone cheat death with the help of a rescue helicopter gave me a new-found love and appreciation for the people who truly save lives.

That day, it wasn't safe to leave the hotel, let alone run. I felt incredibly grateful and lucky that Shawn and Peggy had got me a hotel. If they hadn't, I would've camped and there's no way I would have survived the flash flood. We heard that some of the people who were swept away were found miles down the river, alive, but there were four people who were never found.

After a few contemplative days, I was back on the road running. I kept stopping at BBQ shacks, and became addicted to barbecue beef brisket. Texas was definitely a place to eat and run, or run and eat. As I headed to Austin to meet my friend Craig Joseph from Inty, who said he had a surprise waiting for me, Mother Nature was far more calm now. The dust and sand were gone, and the trees were blossoming in brilliant pinks and whites. Above, the clouds seemed to be relaxed, blending into the blue skies. Some days, I was hitting 30 or 40 miles, I was running as well as could be, but Caesar's wheels were squeaking like crazy and no amount of oil would get rid of the noise.

Incredibly on such a quiet stretch of road, I had now reached the halfway mark of my run – 115 marathons. I screamed, "I'm an animal", thinking how strong I was, but wondered who was going to break first, me or Caesar. Eventually, I made it to Austin, running along the sparkling blue Colorado River, seeing all the skyscrapers ahead shining in the golden sun. I felt grateful to be back among people. Craig had managed to get me an after-dinner talk at the III Forks Steakhouse with a tech company called Acronis. They were donating to my foundation and treating me to tickets to watch Formula 1 along with backstage passes to meet the Williams racing team. It was a great experience seeing professionals racing around the track. It was the first time I'd seen Formula 1 racing, I only wished I had that kind of speed in my legs! It was all worthwhile, after a rallying cry from Acronis vice president Ronan McCurtin we raised well over $5,000. It was crazy to think that at any moment I could receive a $5 donation from someone where that was all they could spare and the next donation could be thousands. For me, they all come with the same weight of importance, it's giving, it's human connection.

I looked around at the fancy surrounds with everyone drinking beer and reminiscing about Lewis Hamilton's victory and thought of getting to bed. Craig went to book me a hotel until I heard it was going to cost $530 for a single night.

I said, "Don't you dare pay that! I'm off." And then said to the cloakroom attendant who was looking after Caesar, "Can you give me my buggy, please?"

Craig and Ronan stared at me open-mouthed.

Craig said, "You can't just leave, you idiot. It's 11 p.m. You can't run a marathon after a load of beers!"

I grabbed Caesar and said with a smile, "It's all part of the training."

As I began running out of the 5-star hotel lobby, it was worth doing the run just to see the look on their faces.

After my booze-fuelled run, the next few days and nights rolled into each other. I was passing at speed through lots of little towns like Elgin, Giddings and Brenham as I ran north of Houston, heading through woodlands to stay out of the busy city traffic. It was mostly flat, but the sheer width and size of Texas was beginning to grind me down. One night, running along a barren stretch of road, a man pulled up alongside me. Incredibly, it was Jim! Jim was the guy who had helped me all the way back in Washington state and driven 400 miles just to give me lights for Caesar.

Jim said, "I can't believe you've made it this far." I was in total shock that he was here, so he continued, "Here, I've got something for you in the car."

I was blown away that Jim had surprised me, this time nearly 3,000 miles later. I felt like he was always watching over me, like he was my kindred spirit.

Walking over to the car I said, "What are you doing here, Jim, there's no way you drove this far just to see me?"

Jim's face changed. "I'm actually here visiting my parents who are both in hospital. I'm glad I've seen them, but it's looking like they're not going to make it."

I could feel Jim's sadness. That he'd also driven another 200 miles to see me, considering the situation, blew me away.

"I needed some positivity, maaaan, and I knew that you would bring it to me," he added.

As we got to the car, when Jim tried to open the door he realised he'd locked his keys inside. After a short period of panic, Jim called a guy, who knew a guy, who would drive out to help. Thirty minutes later, a Mexican couple showed up. Alfredo and Madelaine barely spoke English, but managed to get into the car and retrieve Jim's keys. As Jim went to pay the $50 call-out fee he explained my story to them. The couple spoke to each other in Spanish and before we knew it, Alfredo handed me the $50 and said, "Give this to the kids."

Jim and I looked at each other and we felt our hearts swell.

Then Jim said, "I rarely see this in the world we live in. I knew you'd bring some positivity to my life, that's beautiful, maaaaaan."

After spending some time hanging and chatting with Jim, the kindest of souls, he handed me a new selfie stick knowing I'd lost the one he had given me a few months back.

We hugged and as we parted I said, "As we say in England Jim, you're a gentleman and scholar."

PART 20

A TASTE OF THE SOUTH

As I neared the end of Texas, I decided they were right, "Everything is bigger in Texas" – especially the feeling I had in my heart. I'd seen some amazing things and faced some difficult challenges, but what endured was the kindness of the people. I was on the verge of completing six of the 24 states – and better still all of the states from here were tiny compared to the others.

The first of these "tiddlers" was Louisiana. Crossing the border over the bluey green of the Sabine River, physically I was getting stronger and stronger. I'd run through the summer heat of Arizona and Texas, and now the trees were becoming bare and leaves were scattered across the roads. Autumn had arrived, but I could already sense that winter was not far away too. Luckily, within a day I was given a nice warm southern welcome. Sandy had contacted a man called Alfred who was going to let me stay at his house. Better still,

Pastor Alfred – who was a tall and large man – his wife and friends wanted to take me out try a local Cajun dish at D. I.'s Cajun Restaurant. It was a large wooden shack with pictures of fishermen everywhere. A live band were playing and the sound of a fiddle was out in full force. This southern music was far different to the British kind, but I was loving it.

"Wha' would yew like, Jamie?" said Alfred in a lovely, soft Louisianan accent.

"Whatever the locals eat," I replied like a true local.

What was placed in front of me was the biggest plate of fried food I'd ever seen. Although I had no idea what it was as it was all covered in batter. Piece by piece, I gave it a whirl... oysters, chicken, shrimp, catfish, cheese... you name it, they had it and it was all fried. I got to an unusually shaped piece of golden batter.

"What's this one?" I said, holding it up.

"Frowwgs' legs!" said Alfred.

It was shaped like frogs' legs, but I wasn't convinced.

"You're pulling my leg," I said, laughing.

"Tayyste it!" said Alfred.

I threw it into my mouth and began chewing, the texture was like chewy chicken and, well, it tasted like frogs' legs. After I swallowed it, sure enough, there was an aftertaste of pond in my mouth. I wasn't a fan and it was written all over my face, but if there was ever a time I was allowed to eat a plate full of heart attack it was after running 3,500 miles. You could say I'd earned those legs.

The one thing the fried food didn't help was the constant feeling of pain. As I broke into my 135th marathon, I noticed the familiar nag of worn tendons, creaking joints and bruised muscles, but it seemed to be the norm now, like I was supposed to feel pain day in, day out. Late at night with a warmish breeze, I was running on Route 190 when I came to a bridge lit by the moonlight. It was straddling the slow and wide flowing inky black of the Mississippi River. As I scanned the bridge, there didn't seem to be a hard shoulder to run on. As cars and trucks rumbled past at speed I knew it would be too dangerous to cross. The bridge was too long without either Caesar – or more likely both of us – coming a cropper. I was gutted. My goal was to run every inch as I crossed America and this was going to be the first stretch where I couldn't. There was no other way. I ran back to a gas station and began asking anyone if I could get a lift. Every person I spoke with seemed to have an edge about them, whether it was their hood up, bloodshot eyes or just an uninterested demeanor. Something had changed from the friendly Louisiana I had experienced as I entered the state.

Eventually, around the 50th person I asked agreed to help. He was wearing a cap pulled low, was in a bright orange top and work clothes and had a thick moustache. He too had bloodshot eyes, but seemed friendly enough. We loaded Caesar on to his truck and got going.

"Thanks so much, what's your name, by the way?" I asked.

"My name's Ricky," he said. "Where you from?"

"England," I said proudly.

"Okay, okay," he said, slurring slightly. "Do you know this area? Baton Rouge?"

I shook my head.

"Pretty bad here in Baton Rouge." He pointed to the other side of the bridge. "All that there is what they call 'projects'. You know anything about projects?"

"What does that mean?" I asked.

"Projects are low income – drug dealers, crime, just bad areas."

"So, I need to run fast then, do I?" I said, trying to lighten the mood, but Ricky's face stayed serious.

Driving over the bridge I said to Ricky it would be fine to drop me on the other side and I'd take the hard shoulder and be on my way.

"That's the least of your worries," said Ricky, eyes scanning the surrounds. "We're going to get you up here a little ways where there's more lights. All this and all that back there is bad – especially for a white boy. They wouldn't care if you were a preacher they'd still rob you, and anyone that's willing to rob a priest, well, you know there's something wrong with them."

I tried to stay calm. "Do they have guns around here?"

"A lot of guns, man. A lot of guns in Baton Rouge. We're very lenient with our laws and they got shootings almost every night."

I asked him if my West Country British accent would be able to disarm the gun gangsters. Ricky smiled and drove me a mile out the other side of town, eventually pulling over.

"Now, still be careful. We're just on the outskirts of the hood."

I was really grateful for the local knowledge (at least one of us was streetwise) and him steering me away from a sticky situation.

I didn't get the impression Ricky was a hugger, so I offered a firm handshake and thanked him. He replied with, "You're welcome, bud."

With Ricky gone, I pulled out my iPhone to check Google Maps. After a few minutes I looked up and saw two men, hoods up, walking towards me. Maybe it was Ricky who had put me on edge, or the American ghetto films I had rolling around in my head. One thing was for sure, I was perhaps the only guy dressed as a superhero at 11 p.m. in Baton Rouge – probably ever – so I grabbed Caesar and began to run.

PART 21

A SOUTHERN THANKSGIVING

The next day was 22 November. It was Thanksgiving and Hallie Delaney, who had followed my progress on Instagram, had invited me to stay with the Sisson family. The timing was perfect, ABC News wanted to film me eating turkey and celebrating with over 40 people. After a bellyful of tasty turkey, which reminded me so much of Christmas Day, I told them Caesar wasn't doing so well and I wasn't sure if he was going to make it.

It turned out that the dad of the family, Vaughan, was a world-class engineer and had a shed where he would build "things". He managed to not only get rid of Caesar's squeaky wheel to save my sanity, but built new bearings inside the wheels so they would hold up to the finish line. Caesar had "rolled" over 5,000 miles across Canada and well over 3,500 miles across America, and had a lot of thanks to give for his shiny, new wheels!

I was enjoying the southern hospitality a little too much by the time I reached New Orleans, scoffing jambalaya – a sausage, chicken and prawn rice dish with more Cajun spices – down my neck at every turn. Needing more motivation than southern food, I made a visit to the magnificent Children's Hospital New Orleans. Waiting for me were news crews, the president John Nickens – who greeted me with a warm hug – and even more importantly a little eight-year-old boy named Joe who was battling a severe condition.

Joe was really inquisitive. "So, you're running 6,000 miles as a superhero?" he gasped.

"Yes, it's true," I said.

"Wow!" he replied.

I couldn't believe how much empathy Joe had, almost like he understood how difficult every mile was. I felt really connected.

After 10 beautiful minutes Joe said, "Jamie, Jamie, I've got one more question for you!"

"Ask me anything, Joe, absolutely anything!" I said, feeling proud that Joe believed I was a superhero.

"When you reach the end of this run across America..." He stumbled on his words, like he was thinking.

"Yes, Joe?" I said.

He gathered his thoughts and with a serious face said, "Are you going to run back again?"

I must have looked confused.

My superhero status was hanging on this answer. "Mmmmmm, well Joe, when I reach the end, I'll need to think about that one."

Luckily, he nodded and agreed.

Nearing the end of Louisiana, I crossed the border into Mississippi. My first night was in a hotel. I was hoping for a proper night's rest, which you can't always get in your tent, though at $35 a night, I should have known better. It was filthy and I got bitten by bedbugs. That morning I was called a liar and told bedbugs didn't even exist by the hotel owner. That negative experience seemed to flip something in my head. As I ran on, I reflected on the past few months, and how strong I'd been and what I'd been sharing on social media and everything was mostly positive – so I decided to come clean, be honest and vulnerable, writing a message and posting it online:

It's been brewing for a few days in my tummy and it's properly hit, a big wave of feeling overwhelmed and "What the heck am I doing – this is all a bit much to handle".

For a good couple of months now, my little legs have been cooking on gas and, emotionally, I've been super confident and strong, pretty much every step.

But three days ago, my tummy went tight. I couldn't work out why and the fact is, I still can't.

Usually, everything seems possible in my mind. Even the 70 marathons ahead (in midwinter!) but right now, everything seems a challenge. Even writing this post is a challenge.

I'm feeling alone and that this entire adventure is on my shoulders and it's all down to me to complete it, to hit the big fundraising target, all of it. Which I know is silly and irrational as now I'm getting more support than ever.

All I can do is try to keep the wind at my back and drive my legs forwards – I have to keep going.

During that day on my 140th marathon in the rain, I spoke to Anna, my loverrr, over FaceTime as we share every tiny bit of our lives together – the good, the bad and the ugly. Today, I just spoke about every part that was ugly. Things like...

"What if my visa doesn't come in?" (I had applied for an extension recently which would take me to April for the full year's visa.)

"My immunity is low – what if I get sick? I can't afford to get sick!"

"My tummy isn't breathing in and out properly, the pressure feels so bad I wanna throw up."

"I just wanna be home, it's been a year since I've been home."

"Everything is a challenge and I can't work out why I'm feeling this way!"

Throughout the chat, Anna just listened, asked questions and then at the end said, "You sound exhausted, J."

It was everything I needed to hear, I just needed someone to listen.

After the chat, I felt a little better and it had helped me work out why I was so overwhelmed. I messaged Anna: "Starting to feel much better my dear after chatting to you. I'm running well again."

Anna replied: "Oh good, my lover. I'm very glad. It's totally normal to feel like that when you are taking on the world – remember like the buddhas say... I can't take your pain away, but I can sit next to you while you go through it (rubbing my Buddha belly, and yours). Love you lots."

I carried the last of the anxiety with me on my final few Mississippi marathons; head down, slogging on as if an invisible state line would bring about a brighter state of mind. Miraculously, it did. As I reached the Alabama border I was greeted by a sign that read, "Sweet Home Alabama". It put a huge smile on my face as the Lynyrd Skynyrd tune popped into my head and I began singing. To make things even sweeter the sun was beginning to shine again, outside and inside me.

This put my turbo boosters on as I ran full of endorphins and hope to the Alabama USA Children's Hospital. Here I was shown into the playroom where I met a poorly child named Dylan. Dylan was having fun playing with a light-up globe, spinning it around and laughing to himself. If there's one thing I remember about being a sick kid, in pain, the power of distraction really helps.

I said, "Hey Dylan, can you find where we are on the map?"

He quickly found us and said, "We're here!"

As well as showing him my America route, I also showed him my 14,000-mile bike route from Thailand to England through 20 countries. While pointing with my finger at all the countries, it dawned on me how accessible they all are to travel – even countries like Iran and Iraq, which I cycled through.

"Look Dylan, I flew here, then started running there." He followed the trace of my fingers. "I just pedalled over this border, easy peasy."

Dylan smiled at the possibilities.

When I was a kid – ahem, a very long time ago – I had a globe sat next to my bed. My mum put it there because I used to have nocturnal epileptic fits and I was afraid of the dark. Little did my mum know, she was sowing the seeds for my future, as every night I'd whirl the globe looking at country after country, imagining what each of them was like. Looking at Dylan and his situation brought back all those memories. I knew I had to forget my worries as they paled into insignificance against the bigger picture. I just had to keep running and hoping people would be generous enough to help make lives like Dylan's better.

After running a state like Texas, Alabama felt tiny, it was only 200 or so miles wide, so if I headed in a straight-ish line I'd be in and out within four double marathons! It was a warm and friendly state. With me running so many miles and running into the evenings, petrol stations became my haven for fried chicken, although one that I stopped at felt different. After refuelling on chicken and chips, I was sat outside and noticed two or three people hanging around in groups with their hoods up. It didn't overly bother me, but I guessed I probably shouldn't hang around too long. Moments later, a truck pulled up and a man with a cap started to fuel up.

When he was done, he walked over to me, crouched down, looked me square in the eye and said, "Bet you don't feel safe around here, do you, boy? All these n*****s hanging around."

My jaw must have dropped 10 inches. I was in shock. I didn't say anything. As he went into the station, I decided to get running just to get away from him before he came back out.

Moving through the town of Bayou La Batre I began to smell the sea salt of the Gulf of Mexico as I ran on to Dauphin Island. Trees, forests and ocean were drifting by as I ran, it felt relaxing and more like my natural habitat. Excitingly, I had to catch the ferry over to Fort Morgan. It was great fun riding the small waves of the deep blue sea. The nearby houses were so colourful: blues, yellows, even pinks. I relaxed and breathed the fresh salty air, as if the boat ride was a victory parade.

Seeing the sign "Welcome to Florida: The Sunshine State" brought back so many memories. As a kid, my mum and dad didn't know the outcome of my life, whether I'd end up in a wheelchair, or worse, not survive. So, when I was nine years old, they took me and my brother Lee to Disney World. As you can imagine, that created a memory that's stayed with me to this day – it really is a world of dreams!

Now I was on my ninth of 24 states it had given me hope that I was going to make it. Better still, I knew one of my best friends from back home, Mont, was in America to see me. The idea was that when Mont turned up, he would get into the spirit of the adventure and join me for a run. True to his word, he did just that, running a whole 2 minutes to the nearest Irish pub where we slugged back a couple of pints of Guinness.

While I ran marathons, Mont had other ways of chipping in, putting me up in some nice hotels for a few days. In one hotel, we found the most wonderfully kind manager, Bill, who heard my story and decided that instead of doing Christmas presents with his kids they would instead give donations. It was strange to think it was approaching Christmas, the weather was still around 15°C and usually at this point in the UK we're wrapped in coats, scarves and gloves. After a few days Mont left me to it. It was a good mini-boost seeing such a familiar face and it spurred me on as I headed towards Panama City.

If the tarantulas swamping the desert road was nature's way of doing surreal, here man had taken over. First, I trotted past the giant "upside-down" building plonked by the side of the road and then the Ripley's Believe It or Not! building, which was a huge boat sticking out of the ground. Florida had a way of making everything look wacky and Disney-like.

Reaching Panama City, a social media follower, Joe, joined me for a run. Joe had a sweep of grey hair and a huge silver moustache that glinted in the Florida sunshine. He was 70 years old and ran in order to "Stay on this side of the ranch", which wasn't a phrase I'd heard before, but I liked it. A lot. We were both enjoying the moist sea air in our lungs and the shade of huge apartment blocks looming over the long stretch of white sand, when we stumbled across an enormous boat that had been tipped over in the water. It looked as though a rogue wave had just simply flipped it upside down, yet strangely the sea was a wash of gentle white ripples.

"What happened there, Joe?" I asked, genuinely inquisitive.

"A few months ago Hurricane Michael powered through here. A lot of people died and over a million homes were wiped out. As we keep running and you head to Mexico Beach, it's going to look like an atomic bomb went off," he said.

During our run, sure enough, we saw that trees had been placed impossibly on top of buildings, branches and sticks covered the roads so you couldn't see the tarmac any more. It's something that I've never experienced in Britain and maybe never will; my heart felt sad for all the damage and devastation. Joe had kept my spirits high and casually completed a marathon with me – as 70-year-olds do. As we parted with a hug I ran on into the dark evening pushing on to Mexico Beach. When I got there, it turned out Joe hadn't been kidding, it really did look like it'd been flattened by an atomic bomb. I shone my torch where houses had once stood, seeing foundations, clusters of bricks and wooden planks that had been thrown around. Occasionally, there would be one house that had stood strong, but its lonesome upright position only added to the sense of devastation around it. It was so eerie seeing all these homes now scattered across the ground. Sadly, it seemed it hadn't stopped desperate opportunists taking their chances as I saw one sign that said, "Looters will be shot on sight."

As I ran into the broken heart of the town, a couple who were driving past spotted my red cape and tired face.

"Where you heading?" said a man with exhausted eyes.

After I explained he warmly said, "Come and stay with us."

I was in such a state of disbelief I had to ask the question, "Do you still have a home?"

"We do, just."

Though most of the homes in their neighbourhood had been destroyed, a mile up the road there was a single house still standing – their home. Once inside, I noticed the whole house was slanted, they showed me a crack in the walls where the hurricane had done its best to try to blow it down.

They cracked open a box of wine and it seemed only right I join them. We "cheersed" but I could sense their hearts were as broken as their home.

Sitting down listening to country music, I said, "It's bonkers you live in territory where this can happen any day of the year. Why do you stay here?"

The man, George, said, "Twenty years ago, we decided Mexico Beach was the spot we'd call home. We have the beach, the sun and an amazing community. We just never imagined in our lifetime that something like this would happen."

PART 22

CHRISTMAS ON THE RUN

The next day I ran along the coast and saw more places the hurricane had torn through. I'd now completed my 150th marathon. A big milestone. But with nothing around me and not feeling too much like celebrating, I took a break by the side of the road and checked my Fitbit watch. I'd now hit over eight million steps in eight months. For a little entertainment and some help with motivation, I pulled out my iPhone to calculate the average person's steps over eight months – the answer was 720,000 steps. I was now stepping more than ten times what the normal person would. It felt weird to see those stats, because I am a normal bloke, but if it came down to the most miles covered every day for eight months, I had a hunch I would have been number one in the world. Oh yeah!

It gave me a burst of confidence – that was until I did some calculations to see how many steps I'd have to take to break the seven-day treadmill record and it was over one million steps. I felt my stomach tighten. I let out a big sigh and thought, "You better get training." And immediately leapt up and got running. As much as the stats gave me a pep in my step, with it now being Christmas Eve, I'd be lying if I said I wasn't missing home. That night, I camped in a bush in the boonies and woke up alone on Christmas Day. I'm actually a home boy at heart and Christmas is my favourite time of year – and this wasn't exactly what I had had in mind. I decided to do what I knew best and that was to run. I connected to Facebook Live for some human connection, but like all technological communication it didn't quite have the same effect as talking in person. After 13 miles, I sat myself on a deserted roadside, no cars in sight, and squeezed peanut butter gel through my big scruffy beard into my mouth. "Not quite turkey and all the trimmings," I thought.

As I reached mile 16, I began to think about where I was going to stay that night, when I got a call from Mike Cornford. Mike does all the tech for big events and years ago he saw me speak on stage at a conference – he had been an amazing supporter ever since.

"Hello, Mike!" I said with my AirPods in so I could keep running. "What you doing calling on Christmas Day?"

"Merry Christmas, Jamie! Where are you staying tonight, you mad bugger?"

"Well, it's looking like I'm heading into boonie land so I reckon it'll be a night in my tent."

"There's no way you're staying in a tent on Christmas Day. I've checked your tracker and I can see a motel ten miles ahead."

"Really?"

"Yes, really. I'm booking you in for the night."

"You don't have to do that, Mike," I said, feeling uncomfortable about the big gesture.

"I know I don't, Jamie, but I want to, so stop being daft. It's done. I'll text you the details. Me and my wife Suzi have been collecting money since the start of your run too and we'll be donating that to your charity. You're doing so well, keep going. Merry Christmas, Jamie!"

"I don't know what to say. Thank you, Mike."

"Don't thank me yet. It's called Cindy's Motel. Who knows what I've just booked you into!" he said, laughing.

After the call, my heart soared and my run became strong. Within minutes my world had been turned around. I was on a runner's high, skipping on air. I thought, "I might be missing out on Christmas dinner, but at least I'll have a bed for the night". As I floated into the tiny town of Mayo there wasn't a soul in sight. I pushed through the door of Cindy's at 8 p.m. and was greeted by the owner, Roger.

"Hey man, you made it – I've been waiting for you! Your English friend Mike told me you were coming!"

I was blown away by the warm welcome, I couldn't stop smiling.

"Have you eaten?" Roger said.

"No, not yet. I've got some peanut bars with me so I was going to eat them," I said, trying to look enthusiastic.

"Well, how would you like a Christmas dinner?" Roger said.

I felt my jaw drop.

"One of our local ladies did an extra dinner for you when we knew you were coming. Do you like turkey? Oh, and I've got one beer left in my fridge if you fancy that too?"

Roger had no idea he was spouting absolute gold dust from his mouth. He took me to my room. Blissfully, the heaters were already on. The Florida winter definitely felt like it was on its way. As he flicked on the TV for me, one of my favourite films ever was on – *Forrest Gump*. You just couldn't write a better script. I pulled my PJs over my sore legs and watched Tom Hanks run instead while eating a microwaved Christmas dinner and sinking a cold beer, all cosy and warm. This Christmas, Mike and Roger were the best presents I could have asked for.

There were more presents to come. Anna was coming to town. I hadn't seen her in over three months and this time it had felt like a really long time. To make it easier for her, I needed to run 37 miles to Lake City to meet at the most convenient spot. And after all the turkey and seasonal goodwill, my body seemed to be in a positively strong state. I knocked out the "love miles" double quick.

I made it to Lake City around midnight, with Anna arriving shortly after. She'd booked us into a nice hotel, but we were too late for food. Those love miles had made me so hungry I was considering gnawing my arm off, so we headed for a date night at 1 a.m. In a sleepy town at sleepy time, there weren't many options, in fact the only place open was a McDonald's so we smashed 20 chicken nuggets each – well I gobbled some of Anna's too. Then she pulled out some Christmas pudding that her Mum had made.

I scoffed that down in a flash too and in between mouthfuls of sweetly spiced sponge mouthed, "Bloody hell, Anna, I've missed you."

It felt like my Christmas had really started with Anna back by my side. The next day, she donned her Wonder Woman outfit and we ran east knocking out a few marathons and camping en route, until we made it to Jacksonville. Here, a British man named Simon let us have his home for New Year's Eve, where Anna and I had a quiet night. By morning, having reflected on the year gone by, I had this overwhelming feeling to share a love letter to America on social media:

Dear America,

My mission is to ensure that no sick child is ever without the treatment they need, but can't access or afford, both in the US and around the world. You are one of the biggest English-speaking countries, so after Canada, it only seemed right to run here to continue towards that mission. What I'm saying is, I want us to continue together.

Now, 2018 wasn't exactly an easy year for us. We've toughed it out through 160 marathons. I've been very up and I've been very down, but I wouldn't change any of it for the world.

I'll never forget that hot and steamy three-month fling we had in the 120°F (50°C) desert. Or that time you sent me some surprise gifts – yeah, thanks for the mountain lion, tarantulas and scorpions. You really have kept me on my toes!

To be fair, my naivety means my planning is a bit lax at the best of times, running through Arizona at the hottest time of year, but hey, it's just easier if I blame you.

Over these eight months, I've noticed that people seem to give themselves a tough time about you, and the rest of the world gives you a bit of a tough time too. I'm British, we have a similar thing going on back home too.

Sure. You eat more fried food than I've ever seen, and you have a few oddballs here and there — but what country doesn't have those?! I'm pretty odd myself. I mean, I run around in just the one sweaty superhero costume. That's a big question mark against me right there.

From what I've seen running across you though, is that you are one of the most kind-hearted and generous countries on the planet. Please, give yourself a break. I've run more than 4,000 miles across you, and met hundreds, if not thousands of people. Not everybody gets to see a country like I am, but if you did, you'd see there's more that unites you than divides you.

You don't need to be great again. You're already pretty bloody great. Thank you for that.

You've looked after my skinny behind more times than I care to remember and you're pretty good at giving — we've raised $150,000 so far after all! This is all money going towards your state children's hospitals, with money raised outside of the US going to fund grants my charity can give to families around the world who can't afford or get easy access to medical treatment.

So, dear America, as we head into the next 70 marathons up the east coast together, and into the depths of the winter, I'd like to put in a small request for you to keep your temperature tantrums to a minimum. Please.

I don't mind the odd snowstorm here and there, but I'd really appreciate you not giving me a frostbitten nose. I got one of those while running Canada on my last adventure and I don't fancy it again. You know what they say, once frostbitten, twice shy.

I still have no idea if you're going to allow me to finish off this 230-marathon thing we've started together. But ever since being a sick kid myself, spending the first nine years of my life in and out of hospitals, I've learned to keep going, even when times are tough. I'm willing to keep pushing my body, mind and spirit beyond anything I've ever put it through before and keep chasing down that dream I told you about – to help as many sick kids as I possibly can.

I guess what I'm trying to say, America, is I'm pretty proud of how far we've come and I just hope you know... I'm committed. Let's go from "it's complicated" to "in a relationship".

Yours sincerely, and with high, huge hopes for 2019,

Adventureman

That morning, Anna was mighty peeved to find out she didn't have a letter of her own and so departed back home to England. Just kidding, as always, it was mighty tough to leave her. We'd just had a taste of "normal" life again as a couple. We even went to the cinema and watched *Aquaman* – which I loved, by the way, I'm a big superhero-story fan! I didn't want our date nights to end. With Anna not coming out again until the end, it felt pretty definitive that these last three months really were going to be the "last leg".

PART 23

GEORGIA ON MY MIND

Heading north on the east coast, the running conditions were perfect, if slightly cloudy. That was until they got cloudier and cloudier and cloudier until they merged into one big dark behemoth of a cloud. Seems like down south, after the calm comes the storm. I checked my weather app and, yep, a huge storm was heading my way. As I stood looking at it coming straight for me, a car pulled up and a man got out and walked over.

He put his hand on the left side of his chest and said, "Man, I saw you on TV last night. You really touched my heart." And then he handed me a $5 note. It felt like he'd donated $500.

With the storm coming, I knew I was going to get a soaking, so I took off my top and cape and tucked them into Caesar to keep them dry. I was wearing nothing but shorts and must have looked like a madman facing up to the end of the world. And sure enough, as my legs opened up, so did the skies. The rain hammered down all over the road and all over me.

After two hours, just when I thought it couldn't rain any more, it came down even harder until the road began to flood. My feet felt like flippers swimming through a monsoon. Soggily slugging through, all I could think of was the man who had donated $5. I had a big grin on my face. Every once in a while, I'd see a car drive past and people's faces peering over the steering wheel, looking at this grinning fool getting battered by the rain, thinking, "What the hell is that nutjob doing out there in the damned rain?"

As the rain stopped, I made it to the border crossing sign, "Welcome. We're glad Georgia's on your mind", which caught me off guard. Truth was, it totally wasn't, with my goldfish brain I always forget when I'm crossing into another state. Still, it was a welcome sight. As dusk fell, I plodded into a little town called Kingsland. Starving hungry, I bowled straight into Steffens Restaurant, an old-school diner that had a 1950s vibe to it. Walking in, having changed into my dry Adventureman suit, cape and all, I felt pretty awkward. More awkward than normal. I felt the energy change and people stare. I sat up at the bar, ordered fries and a pork chop and scoffed the lot, especially the fat from the pork. Oof, Georgia was on my mind now, but not in a particularly good way.

Come the morning, it was still the nearest place to eat, so I went back for breakfast.

This time, as soon as I ordered a lady named Emma came up to me and said, "I just read your sign outside on your stroller, it's amazing what you're doing. My 21-year-old daughter,

Madison, is outside and really wants to meet you, she's spent years of her life in hospital too."

It turned out her daughter had too much fluid up near her neck and brain. It was a similar condition to mine, though I had too much fluid on my lower spine. We walked outside and I gave her a big hug. It turns out she'd just graduated as a nurse because she wanted to help sick kids too. My heart grew proud. As I walked back into the restaurant, more people came over, all wanting to donate. It was beautiful. The night before in the same diner I had felt like Awkwardman, now I was back to being Adventureman. It's strange how your perception of a place can be so easily swayed by the people you meet. Georgia had totally redeemed itself.

As I ran on, I noticed there was a banknote between Caesar's solar panel and sign. I stopped and pulled it out, it was $5. Someone from the restaurant must have stuffed it in while I was eating. Just as I was marvelling at this casual act of generosity, a car pulled in.

The window wound down and the person inside said, "Here, it's not much, but put this to your cause," and handed over another $5.

There was so much giving, I couldn't quite take it all in, so I said, "Thank you," and waved the other $5 at him adding, "I just found this on my buggy as well."

The gentleman replied, "You're doing a good thing, sir. Keep going."

Running out of Kingsland town the roads were quiet and I noticed the trees were taller and beginning to look bare, the grass either side of the road a blend of greens, rouges and browns – it felt like autumn was tipping into winter. A few miles in, a notification popped up on my phone. I get a fair few and I'm ashamed to say I do miss some of them, but this one I couldn't help but notice.

It read: "When you're sitting in a local diner and you see some weirdo eating alone wearing a superhero outfit, you notice the website, look him up and realise he's a pretty amazing individual and not that weird at all... wish I would have known who you were before you walked out the door, my family would have loved to have bought your dinner."

It made me smile and think, "So it really is true, people really do think I'm a weirdo."

The marathon that day, number 163, after the morning I'd just had was one of my easiest yet. On my 164th marathon, I was flying and had convinced myself that I could run the world in a day! My legs had a bounce like never before, my grin was wider than all the states and hitting mile 20 felt effortless. It was only slightly tempered when I began running over swamps just as the sun started to set. Inland from the Georgia coast, the Altamaha River turns into a series of slow-winding streams and inlets. I know this scene well, and I know what it brings – mosquitoes. They love my British blood and began swarming in, landing on my shoulders, neck and everything else that doesn't bounce when I'm running. I was doing everything I could to shoo them away, flapping my cape and slapping my neck like a madman, but I knew they were having a feast.

As I ran and swatted, I began looking at Google Maps and spotted a little town called Darien and, even better, a restaurant called Waterfront Wine & Gourmet. I love a nice glass of wine, so that was clearly the best spot to get away from the mosquitoes. As I arrived at the front, the bartender spotted me and said, "Where have you come from?"

"I've run from the state of Washington, just well... a bit of a weird route!" I replied, casually.

He stopped in his tracks, "WHAAATTT?! You're kidding me??!! Come on in. Let me get you a drink!"

He took me out back, sat me with the locals around the bar and poured me a glass of red from Horse Creek Winery, a local Georgian wine. I'd love to tell you how I savoured it and how it had tasting notes of cherry and sandalwood, but I poured it down my throat faster than you can say "Cheers!" I felt like I'd earnt it after all the miles and mosquito munching. With another glass in hand, I shared the story about me pooping my pants over the mountain lion in Arizona and, honestly, everyone in the bar howled the house down with laughter.

One of the locals, an ex-FBI agent called Rich, leaned over and said, "Where you staying tonight?"

Slightly tipsily I replied: "I'm not really sure."

He said, "Well, you can stay at mine if you like?"

I gratefully accepted. After the wine starter, he took me for dinner at B&J's Steaks and Seafood.

He joked, "It's a small town so not too many choices for dinner, but you'll enjoy it."

The menu was a southern delight, I chowed down on freshly caught shrimp with a side of alligator. I'd never tasted alligator before, or had it as a casual side dish, and to my surprise it just tasted like chicken. And I loooooove chicken.

The next morning as I was getting set to leave, Rich handed me a bracelet that read "WIN".

He explained, "I created this slogan bracelet to remind myself and others that whenever a tough situation occurs, and as an agent you come across some pretty hair-raising stuff, all that matters is you remember, 'What's Important Now'."

That day, I ran on strongly and smashed way beyond 26 miles – hitting marathon 165. At the end, I saw a text pop into my phone, it was from Rich.

It read, "Thank you for allowing me to be a small part of your journey. We grow as people from every person we meet. Safe travels my friend."

I replied, "Dear Rich, you're so right about how we grow as people from every person we meet. I just ran 41 miles, so you fuelled me in more ways than one. Thank you."

With the thought "What's important now?" bouncing around my head, I felt more motivated than ever. As I approached the border, the sun was bright and brilliant, and I was on a flat, straight road surrounded by shimmering lakes. As I took my last few paces in Georgia, a shiny black car pulled in and a middle-aged lady beckoned me over. She was waving some envelopes from her window.

As I got closer she said, "I saw you on Fox News last night. Here, take these."

Instinctively, I said, "Thank you," but had no idea what was inside.

On the front of each one "Merry Christmas" was written. I thought, "A little late for Christmas", but inside each envelope was a $10 note. As generous leaving gifts go, Georgia knew how to ensure it would be staying on my mind.

PART 24

SOUTH CAROLINA

THE SWAMPS OF SOUTH CAROLINA

I was now 12 states down when I ran towards the next one with its welcoming sign – "South Carolina: smiling faces, beautiful places". I was heading north now, and I seemed to be ticking off the states quickly – almost too quickly. I was now up to 167 marathons. And for the first time a flicker of thoughts darted through my head about the finish line. You get a lot of time to think things over when you're running, thoughts come and go and people's faces pop in and out. My mind flashed back to Anna. While she was with me, and being a far superior planner, she noticed that my finishing point – West Quoddy Head Lighthouse in Maine, which was the most easterly point of the US – was in the middle of absolutely nowhere with no Wi-Fi. Which, quite frankly, would have been the worst spot for family and friends to join the last part of the adventure. With no cell towers in sight, I wouldn't be able to live-stream, which would have been terrible for fundraising.

I remember Anna saying, "J, there's a town named after your home town – Gloucester! It's a small fishing town in Massachusetts. Why don't you finish there? How cool would that be?! The Gloucester boy runs all the way to Gloucester."

I'd dismissed the idea almost instantly because it would have meant running 5,500 miles through 22 states instead of 6,000 miles through 24 states. I was genuinely worried that shortening the run would upset my social media supporters and the kind people who had donated, as if I'd cheated them somehow. It had got me in quite a tizz. But as always with running, sometimes things become crystal clear. As I headed north on a quiet, old road that ran parallel to Route 95, my mind begin to sync with my surrounds. I noticed the tall, bare trees, the distant sound of cars and a gentle wind that swirled between us all. It cleared my mind. Anna's idea made total sense – especially finishing in Gloucester – it really would be a home from home. Also, knowing I'd be attempting the treadmill world record at the end, which the followers didn't know anything about yet, meant I'd have to run 20 marathons in seven days, so that would easily cover the missing 500 miles and I would have run well over 6,000 miles.

I began to get excited, picturing just what this American version of Gloucester would look like. Did it have a beautiful patchwork of farmers' fields, a cathedral, my favourite pub? Well, if I wanted to find out I best carry on running. As well as the finish, I needed to focus on my next hospital visit, the Medical University of South Carolina Shawn Jenkins Children's Hospital. I had over 100 miles to cover if I was going to be on time to meet the kids. With the tight time schedule, I decided to take a shortcut through a forest. After a few miles, the roads became dirt tracks and everything suddenly looked exactly the same. I was navigating with Google Maps, but the app wasn't playing ball, right now I was supposedly hovering over water. I looked behind me, wondering if I should go back to the road. I didn't know how, so I continued on. Suddenly, the smell of sewage hurt my nose, I had landed in Swampsville.

There was a mountain of dirt and trees covering the track with a swamp on the other side. I had no choice but to lug Caesar over it. I was sweating from the sheer panic of the place I'd found myself in. As I dragged Caesar up the dirt and slid down the other side, my feet slipped into the brown, stale water. It looked like it had been there for 500 years and smelt that way too. Smelly feet are my kryptonite. I pulled my soggy shoes from the water and looked at the gunk that was now covering them. Disgusting. I had to find a way out of this bog of stench, and after taking many twists and turns following the snaking swamp I finally made it back to the main road. As I did, I crouched down and placed my hand on the road in thanks. I'd spent almost a full day lost in the swamps and forest. I'd literally had a stinker.

That mistake sent a rocket up my backside. I did two back-to-back days of over 40 miles and made it to North Charleston and the hospital just in time. As I made my way around the play area, seeing dozens of smiley faces made it all worthwhile, although I was slightly embarrassed by the pong from my smelly feet. Luckily, the kids found the yucky smells absolutely hilarious. With their laughter ringing in my ears, I took my stinky feet and ran through Georgetown, Myrtle Beach, where I sensed more and more people were hearing what I was doing. Cars drove by honking their horns, people were handing me home-made food and I had runners joining me.

On one run, a lady stopped by in her car and said, "You're that duuuuude! I just saw you on CNN all the way up in New York."

I thought that weird, but nice. I hadn't even done an interview and my story was being shared.

I was getting notifications on my phone as well – "Just saw you on the news," with a link to an article from ABC News with the headline: "Is it a bird? Is it a plane? No, it's Adventureman!"

It was all coming together, donations were rising too – we were now at over $150,000. All my worries about not raising any money were dissipating. All the effort I was putting in when I wasn't running – the interviews, video editing, posting on social media or replying to people – was really working. Even though I was always on the go in one way or another, I could sense the momentum building, even if I couldn't find the time to take a poop.

THE GUNS OF NORTH CAROLINA

With 13 out of 22 states complete and 175 marathons (4,585 miles) down, I had just made it to my next state. HELLO North Carolina! Unlike the other states' welcome signs, North

Carolina's was a little more curious: "North Carolina – The Nation's Most Military-Friendly State". That morning, after waking up at the house of a firefighter who had very kindly taken me in for the night, I phoned my dad.

As soon as he answered, I said, "Dad, I've only got 35 marathons left to go! I've learned how to fix my body from what Sylvia's shown me through trigger pointing and I'm getting so much support. I really do think I'M GOING TO MAKE IT!"

Now, my dad is the most positive and optimistic man on the planet, his enthusiasm is infectious, but after I'd shared my excitement he paused before speaking.

"J, that's amazing and I'm so glad you're feeling confident that you can finish this thing. It was never a doubt in my mind. Can I just say something though?"

"Of course, Dad!"

"Don't get complacent. NEVER get complacent."

I love my dad because he fuels me to believe in myself. He's always been there for me and always seems to know what the right words are at exactly the right time. He knows how to keep my feet on the ground too. I'm so grateful. Of course, he was right as usual. This wasn't over. I still had nearly a thousand miles to run – and although I was feeling strong, I knew I couldn't take my body for granted. It was exactly the grounding I needed.

Knowing what my dad said, I continued to do longer periods of trigger pointing, sometimes using a golf ball, pushing into my tight, tired legs, just like Sylvia had. Self-management of my body became even more important, if I stopped at a restaurant or went into a supermarket, I'd buy anything that was green – spinach, broccoli – and eat it raw. I wanted to stay healthy and not get sick.

Passing through the seaside town of Wilmington and continuing along Route 17, although my body felt good, running in the pouring rain meant I was struggling for motivation. Mentally, every step felt like a marathon. Dad was right, things can change quickly. I kept stopping to gulp some honey, hoping its natural sugars would boost my legs and my negative mind, but nothing seemed to be working. To make matters worse, I didn't know where I was staying and I was mentally preparing myself for a night in the tent hoping it could withstand the pouring Carolina rain.

The rain had soaked right through my costume and I was starting to feel cold. As I trudged towards the end of the marathon, I spotted a gas station and popped inside to see if there was anywhere to stay.

I asked the checkout lady, "Hey there, I don't suppose you know anywhere warm and dry I could put my tent up, do you?"

The lady looked confused at this drowned rat of a man, until the guy behind me – cap, long hair and a big, bushy moustache – blurted out in a an incredibly thick Carolina accent, "Y'all can stayyy at mine!"

"Really?! That would be lovely!"

He gave me some quick southern-style directions. "Take a lay-eft at the ay-end of this rowd and it's the how-us at the ay-end."

As I got close to his house, I used Google Maps to navigate because I never trust my directions. Staring at my iPhone screen while running, I thought the road was called "Machine Gun Road". I thought there's no way it could be called that! I stopped, used my two fingers to zoom in and sure enough I was staying on "MACHINE GUN ROAD" in the Nation's Most Military-Friendly State. Oh man.

I tried to remember what my saviour looked like, had he actually been a gun-toting nutjob? Too late, I was on his doorstep knocking on his door.

Tim answered in his awesome southern accent. "Well, come on eee-in," he said warmly. "Y'all have timed it purr-fectly, the Super Bawl is about to start."

His accent was so strong I was struggling to catch what he was saying. Sitting down, I wondered if Tim was going to gun me down in a hail of bullets. Instead, he went into the kitchen and knocked up beefburgers, mac and cheese and baked beans. He was going to take me down with a banquet fit for a king. Afterwards, Tim sat on his couch and began chain-smoking cigarettes and gulping down beer after beer. As I looked at him relaxing in a haze of cigarette smoke, I thought never judge a book by its... in this case, road name. Yup, I had a soft spot for Tim.

PART 25

RUNNING BACK TO MY CHILDHOOD

The marathons kept coming, as did the state borders, I was now feeling more focused than ever. I was running strongly late into the evenings, I'd often listen to music in the darkness, soothing myself with songs I'd listened to as a kid, especially Motown and especially Marvin Gaye's "I Heard it Through the Grapevine".

One night, I ran on until almost 2 a.m., huffing and puffing to the border. I shone my head torch towards the sign wondering what this one might say for the state of Virginia. Virginia, home of golden tobacco? Virginia home of the knackered marathon runner? No, instead it read, "Welcome to Virgina: Virginia is for lovers". Suddenly I saw flashing blue lights in the distance. Argh! Had the police seen my flashing torch and mistaken me for a nocturnal lover – what we refer to in the UK as doggers – on the prowl for some late night lovin'…?

The sirens went on, they were hurtling towards me and they weren't going to slow down anytime soon. There was a screech of brakes, the burning of rubber and the car skidded to a halt next to me. I stopped, wide-eyed, as a policeman flew out of the car.

"Everything okay?"

"Yes, officer, all good, just doing a little run."

"We had a call ten minutes ago saying there was an old lady pushing a baby down the road. Is that you?"

I'd just run over 50 miles, nearly a double marathon.

"Yeah, that's me, officer. Though there's no baby here!"

"Oh, you're that guy, the runner?!" The officer's stance softened. "The whole town is talking about you. You're doing so well. Here, take this snack for the road, kid – and stay safe!"

As I ran on into the Virginia night I thought, "It really is all love here."

I was going to feel some more love for my next marathon too. I was being joined by two British navy boys who were training in the States – Julian who had strawberry-blonde hair and Ben who was tall and stocky. As a gift, and a taste of home, they'd brought me some chocolate Bourbon biscuits, something I hadn't seen, nor scoffed, in a year. It was a strong and steady biscuit-fuelled run. We took backcountry roads, zigzagging through fields of cotton. The skies stretched on for miles and the Virginia plains were as flat as a pancake, while there was a hint of a breeze in the air making it perfect for running. We strode rhythmically alongside one another, like troopers, as the quiet country roads stretched on ahead, with the only sounds to be heard our feet striking the ground in perfect synchronicity and our gentle circular breathing. We knocked out 20 miles with relative ease.

As we counted down the miles to the marathon distance, Ben said, "You haven't even broken sweat, Jamie!"

I replied, "There's no such thing as an easy marathon," knowing how quickly things can change.

But at the moment I did feel like I was getting stronger and that's exactly what I needed if I was going to break the treadmill record in just six weeks' time. The world record was already on my mind even though I hadn't finished this challenge yet – so I decided to combine the two.

After the navy boys left, I tried to complete the longest run of my life, three marathons in one go, over 75 miles, without a wink of sleep. I wanted to remind myself what sleep deprivation felt like and to get used to the miles. It didn't end well. As I got to the end, I genuinely felt broken. Skipping a night's sleep, I immediately felt the repercussions. My brain wanted to shut down and I could barely open my eyes. The physical pain was excruciating, it burned through my legs and all the way up into my back and my shoulders. If I was to break the treadmill record, I'd need to do this for seven days straight on just a few hours' sleep. My confidence dropped and I wondered whether I had bitten off more than I could chew.

I was approaching Richmond's tree-lined streets when I worked out I had just over 20 marathons to go, so plenty of time to rebuild my confidence and supercharge my fitness.

As I ran through the city's outskirts a woman driving past stopped, wound down her window and yelled, "Hey you! What the hell are you doing out here?!"

After sharing my story, the lady, Connie, said, "Where's your entourage?"

"It's just me!" I replied.

"OH MY GOD," she shouted, "I've never met anyone who's done anything like this. You're staying with me. I want you to meet my son too, he has spina bifida."

Hugging 13-year-old Daequan, I could feel the shunt, a small tube surgically placed in the brain that helps drain fluid and protects it from too much pressure, running from his head to his belly.

Connie said, "He was born with a hole in his spine. He also has hydrocephalus, which means too much fluid was travelling to his brain – he could have died. He's lucky to be alive. The medical bills are just so high and it's only down to the donations and funding he's still with us today."

By morning, Connie said, "Meeting you like this has brought hope and inspiration back into my life. And, annoyingly, I'm going to be worrying about you now. You know, I'm convinced you're my brother from another mother."

As I ran from Connie's home still laughing, I waved goodbye and as I neared the end of her driveway I turned and said, "Thank you for everything. And just so you know, you're my sister from another mister!"

As I left Richmond and passed through Fredericksburg, I neared the end of Virginia. The sky had turned a winter milky grey and had begun to come alive in front of my eyes. It was the middle of February and it was snowing. As I ran, the sporadic drops of cool snow propelled me to the end. Inevitably, although my 190th marathon was over, I heard a ping on my phone and thought, "The work never stops". Although the WhatsApp message I received was a goodie. It was from a friend, Michael Gugger, whom I had done some filming with.

"Jamie! I'm linking you here with my best friend Steve Soleimani. He works at Google NYC and wants to organise a talk there!"

Minutes later Steve joined the WhatsApp chat and said he'd managed to get me a talk at one the biggest companies on the planet. A date was planned, 6 March, I just had to get there in time. It was 300 miles away. It meant that I'd have to run every day from now until then. I was going to have to push myself to my limits to make it, but I couldn't miss out on the opportunity to make more connections and hopefully more donations.

Pushing on to Washington DC, I was accompanied by Martin and his daughter, Lauren. Martin was dad to Sylvia, who'd been helping me with my trigger pointing. They were on bikes and had decided they would be my tour guides for the day. For the first time on the trip, I felt like a full-blown tourist. The only difference was that I had to run to see everything. As soon as we hit the heart of the city, I felt the magnitude and history – all the buildings were white, mighty and heroic. We stopped for a break at the Lincoln Memorial where the reflecting pool runs all the way out in front, then trotted on to the Vietnam Veterans Memorial, a wall with thousands of names of all the people who died. Finally, we made it to the White House. All my childhood memories of American films came flooding back, especially the movie *Independence Day* where the spaceship blows up all the monuments – even the White House I was now stood in front of. It was surreal and spectacular all at once – as if I was running through my own movie set – bar the exploding buildings.

Maryland was only a short run from the American administrative capital. It was a strange entrance, I was so used to seeing the border signs welcoming me with their catchy little sayings, but I wasn't even aware I'd crossed the border until I hit the fringes of Baltimore – the biggest city in the state. It seemed a little sketchy in some places – it had a similar feel to Baton Rouge. But within a block of the grittier parts of the city, I saw a clean, white and expensive-looking building – the tremendous hospital at Johns Hopkins Children's Center. Inside, I was welcomed in and went live on air to their kids' TV channel, which was broadcast direct into all the kids' rooms. Kids were able to call in with questions.

"Are you really a Superhero?"

It felt really nice to reply, "I was a sick kid too, now that's my superpower."

There seemed to be superheroes everywhere. A friend from back home, David Redvers from Tweenhills, had a connection with the Clancy family who had arranged a surprise for me, one that meant I didn't have to worry about navigating my way north to Philadelphia. An army of runners were going to tag team in and out offering big smiles, snacks and more importantly local knowledge about the best route to Philly. Again, I felt an extra wave of energy and excitement as I saw so many smiling faces, received so many words of encouragement and knew donations were flying in. It gave me the push I needed and I ran through Delaware in a single day. Without realising it I was over the border and into Pennsylvania, reaching a city I'd always dreamed of visiting, Philadelphia.

My obsession with Philadelphia comes from being one of the biggest *Rocky* fans ever. This was Sylvester Stallone's home city in the movies and its backdrop featured in many key scenes in the film. As I neared the city centre, I felt like I'd been in the ring with Rocky though. My feet and ankles had started to deteriorate. There was a nagging discomfort and I could feel my body beginning to slowly fall apart. To make matters worse, I could barely feel my feet. The temperature had dropped to −8°C and my feet were crazy cold from the snow and ice that had covered all the paths and roads.

It was a real slog, my cheeks were numb and burning with the cold wind that battered into them. But again, good people kept popping up – finding me on my tracker and handing me dry socks and hot drinks – one man even invited me for a Guinness, which I have to admit really helped for a few miles. I found my way to the Gaehring family's house, who were connected to another family who had taken me in days before. The sense of community and warmth was incredible, I was being passed along like a relay baton. Cara, the mum, had a roaring fire ready for me and on my bedside table had placed some chocolate.

After I freshened up, I met Matt, Cara's husband, and their 11-year-old daughter Amelia.

As we sat getting warm round the fire, Cara said, "So in the past few years we found out Matt has vascular Ehlers-Danlos syndrome. It's a rare condition where he bruises easily and his organs can shut down. It's pretty life-threatening. Unfortunately, it's been passed down to Amelia, so we have to be careful with her."

I looked around at this warm-hearted family and their unflinching attitude to the hand they'd been dealt.

Cara continued, "With you having had a rare condition too, we think it's amazing Amelia gets to meet you."

I looked at Amelia and smiled. She was really quiet, but a smile never left her face.

Cara told me the difficult decision they'd had to make. "We were worried if we had any more kids the condition would be passed on, so we've started the process of fostering."

"Really?!" I said in awe. "My mum and dad fostered too when I was younger. We had over ten kids pass through our home. You're in for a ride, you'll really enjoy it and I can already tell you'll be amazing foster parents."

I felt our bond strengthen on an even deeper level. Cara just smiled, you could see how much she wanted to have more kids.

That night Matt gave me directions to the Philadelphia Museum of Art where the famous *Rocky* steps were. I was so excited. In the morning we did a quick visit to Fox News. The news stations were covering me every day and donations were flooding in. I left Cara, Matt and Amelia with a warm glow as I headed back into the cold. Within minutes, my face was frozen to my cheekbones, but I kept thinking of all the training scenes from the *Rocky* films; the mad montages set to "Eye of the Tiger", where he's dragging sledges and running in knee-deep snow. (If you want to put the song on and do some one-handed press-ups or hit some rocks with a sledgehammer just like he did, then please do.) As I bumbled along the frozen streets of Philadelphia trying to get warm, I reached the foot of the famous *Rocky* steps for the first time. I looked at the top to see the Philadelphia Museum of Art monument – just like in the movie.

As I prepared to sprint up them, just like Rocky had, I spotted Cara, Matt and Amelia waving a British flag. What a brilliant surprise, they'd turned up to see me.

I went over to them, giddy with excitement. "I gotta do this!"

Cara said, "We'll look after Caesar. You do it, Jamie!"

I looked at Amelia, still quiet as a mouse as she smiled from ear to ear. I felt a surge of adrenaline as my first foot hit the steps. I began sprinting as hard as I could, panting, thinking about all the challenges this adventure had thrown at me and remembered one of my favourite lines from the film.

"It ain't about how hard you hit. It's about how hard you can get hit and keep moving forward."

I began imagining the *Rocky* theme tune where the saxophone is going, "Da da da da da". My lungs were burning, working hard, breathing in the icy cold air, the city grey, but my mood was electric. As I reached the top, I began shadow-boxing, punching the air.

There were a fair few people around, I didn't care, I shouted, "I've reached Philadelphia," and then, just like in the movie, "Yo, Adriannnnnn, I DID IT!"

Reaching these steps was fulfilling a lifelong dream and brought memories of my childhood rushing back as I thought about watching all the *Rocky* films as a kid. I totally believed Rocky was real back then and I looked up to him as a role model – he was always the underdog. With my illness, I was in and out of hospital as a kid and having dyslexia meant I had to go back to school years after my classmates had left. I had always felt like a bit of an underdog, as though I would never really amount to much. But, what I've always had is heart and I know I'll always keep moving forwards, no matter what, and that's my gift to the world.

As I made my way back down the steps, I had my photo taken at the Rocky statue and a tour guide nearby was playing the *Rocky* theme tune through a "duck" whistle. As an adventurer, I'm not one for playing tourist, but right then I was the happiest one in the world.

PART 26

NEW YORK – CITY OF DREAMS

As I was nearing New York City, I knew I had a group of runners from the UK joining me. For years, I'd been involved with a business named Unite Students, giving talks, as well as supporting some of their staff on a cycling adventure from John o'Groats to Land's End which raised £250,000 for Sport Relief.

This time though, I got a message from Ali Hastings, who works at Unite Students as the social impact manager, saying, "How about we support you on your adventure?!"

They donated £10,000 and wanted to send over four keen runners who had to apply within the company (they have thousands of employees) to join me for support. The idea was for each of them to run a marathon – for most of them, it was their first one. I was super happy to be part of four runners' dreams as they were helping my dreams come true too.

The runners touched down while I was still 57 miles away from Google HQ. The next day I was due to give the talk. I knew I wanted to run a few miles on my own and leave exactly 52.4 miles, a double marathon to run with the others. So logistically the only way I was able to make it work was to run a marathon for the first part of the day with two of them and let the other two join in for the second marathon. Double whammy. Waking up, it was the coldest day so far, −11°C.

When Sophie, the logistical queen and van driver arrived, I greeted the runners with a big hug because it was so cold and then said, "Who's first?!"

Tamsin and Alistair raised their chilly hands. As soon as we began we found out Tamsin had never run a marathon before, so I said, "Great! Me and Al are looking forward to destroying you for your first ever twenty-six-miler."

Our British sense of humour was off and running before we were. We got going and were in a rhythm before we knew it. It was superb having them by my side, we were full of chit-chat as our breath spilt clouds of condensation into the air. But as always, post-20 miles, we fell silent, each of us battling our own inner demons as we fought for the finish line.

When we were almost at the marathon distance, Tamsin said, "Wait! According to my watch we might not do a marathon. Wait here." Then Tamsin ran back a couple of hundred metres and joined us again, "Okay, let's go."

Back running alongside each other, Tamsin said, "I've been overweight most of my life and my dad always said I'd never run a marathon, I had to make sure."

"Really?!" I replied. "Well, you've now got the Strava distance to prove it. Your dad can eat his words."

We increased our pace for those last few steps crossing an imaginary finish line together. We all had a celebratory lunch as Tamsin and Alistair sat tired, but smiling. Then, as I cosied up next to a heater it dawned on me that my day was only just getting started – I had to do it all again. The other runners were waiting for me. This time it was Saffa and Tom.

As they jumped out of the van, I said, "We have virgin marathoners joining us – wahoooo!"

Saffa and Tom laughed and seemed happy to be out of the van and shaking off the nerves as they got ready for their first marathon.

As we ran, I was intrigued to know what their motivations were.

Saffa began opening up. "We had to apply to the company. I wrote a bit about why I wanted to come on this adventure and what my motivation was. We've had a lot of tragedies in our family. We actually came to the UK from Sudan when I was seven for the purpose of getting better medical treatment for my sisters. One of my sisters, Sahar, who is now twenty-six, contracted malaria when she was one and was lucky to survive. She had complications and ended up getting cerebral malaria, which led to cerebral palsy and scoliosis. We also think she may have autism. She's in a care home and is wheelchair bound now."

My heart sank hearing what Saffa was saying.

She continued, "When I was sixteen, one of my other sisters, Hanadi, ended up getting glioblastoma, an aggressive form of cancer in the brain and spinal cord. She actually spent lots of time in Gloucester Children's Hospital, which I know is the hospital that you stayed in as a kid."

I couldn't believe it, her sister went to the same hospital as me.

"So, for like a year, Hanadi went from being really healthy and running around at school to being really, really sick and in hospital. After many operations, it wasn't enough and she passed away."

My heart broke.

"So, my main motivation for running is for my sister Sahar who can't run and my other sister who's no longer here. You have to really appreciate your body and what we can do. We should run, especially for those who can't."

We didn't say anything, we just knew it was true. As we ran on in silence the sun was setting and the temperature plummeting. As golden light slipped to purple, blue, then black, there was a haunting beauty to it. By mile 22, with our head torches piercing the darkness, we were running together as a team and I was giving updates on how far we'd run, mile by mile, counting them down.

Tom said, "Surely we're still not on mile 22, Jamie?!"

I double-checked my iPhone, which was being drained rapidly by the cold weather, but it was true.

"Sorry, Tom, we're still on mile 22."

"I think I need to stop to take a drink," he said.

As I pulled Tom's drink bottle out from Caesar, I said, "Uh, sorry, Tom, the water's frozen."

The temperature was now at −13°C, and our fingers, toes and faces were freezing up. I thought the only solution was to keep moving. We all agreed and got running again, picking up the pace.

I turned to Tom and Saffa with a frozen smile and said, "I can't believe you're having to do your first marathon in this!"

They looked over with a mixture of misery and sadistic pleasure, managing to crack a smile through quivering lips. I knew when they were sitting somewhere warm many years later this would be one of the most memorable experiences of their life, to be a part of that felt magical. Those last few miles were pretty brutal and by the end I think the pain had been numbed by the cold, but eventually we made it – even though our eyelids had nearly frozen shut.

As we reached the hotel the rest of the group ran out to clap us in.

We hugged, steam coming off us, as Sophie announced, "We have pizza and beer inside if you fancy some?!"

As we were drinking and stuffing our faces, I felt overwhelmed with emotion seeing everyone achieve their marathons and grateful they had flown thousands of miles to help me through this tough, cold leg. The timing of their support couldn't have been better, I was now only 6 miles away for tomorrow's talk at Google.

I got to bed late at 4 a.m. having stayed up to finish editing a vlog for social media. I had set a 6 a.m. alarm, ready for the Google talk, although on only 2 hours' asleep I wondered how I was going to be able to speak. Luckily, I was only a short ride away. I caught a taxi to Google HQ, seeing New York City for the first time. The city was just waking from its winter slumber; big city, bright lights, but only those who were awake could see it. I was lucky enough to be one of them.

As I stood outside the Google doors, it was a good moment. I'd been racing for weeks to get here and had made it just in the nick of time. I'd pushed my body past its limits and in the last two days and nights I'd only had 5 hours' sleep, so I was seriously worried that the biggest talk of my life would flop. I met Steve and he took me for breakfast, where I gulped down as much hot coffee as my throat could take. The cafeteria had every cuisine you could ever imagine, needless to say I gave tinned fish and butter a wide berth.

It looked like an amazing, crazy place to work. As we walked to the rehearsal, I saw people travelling down the corridors on scooters. We passed a Lego room, sleeping pods, bars, more restaurants. There were ladders and poles that led to weird and wacky rooms. It was one big playroom for adults. You never had to leave the building. An hour before the talk, I was doing all the techie stuff and getting miked up.

Slightly panicked, I just kept telling myself, "You're going to do this, pull yourself together, you're Adventureman!"

Five minutes before the talk, I looked at the audience and there were five freaking people. FIVE?!!! I started to get really embarrassed, would I be speaking to five people!? No, suddenly, with one minute to spare, hundreds of people flooded in. Pheeewww.

A surge of endorphins kicked in, along with a voice in my head telling me I could do it.

I was about to take the stage where Lady Gaga, Sadhguru and Ryan Reynolds had spoken. I looked around, the curtains were red, blue, green and yellow – the Google colours. I peered down at my Adventureman suit, and apart from the blue, they were exactly the same colours. If there was a made-up Google superhero, I was it.

When I hit the stage, I came alive. At one point, I shared a story about my previous adventure going wrong and how I thought Google Maps was broken – which got a roar of laughter, and by the end tears were shed. Afterwards, I signed Adventureman books and hugged everyone. I honestly don't know how I pulled it off in my exhausted state.

Steve came up to me, a big smile on his face and said, "Jamie, that's one of the best talks we've seen here at Google."

As one last treat, Steve took me and the Unite Students to the top of the Google building where we looked out over New York City. There were skyscrapers as far as the eye could see, the sun glinting off their mirrored windows. We were so high, I wondered if I'd be able to see where I was finishing in Massachusetts.

After the Unite Students left and the Google experience was over, I was handed over to Sandy Jimson's relatives, the Pape family who lived in Navesink, New Jersey. In between runs, they took me to the 9/11 memorial.

Mum of the family Terri said, "Look there. It's a huge statue of an eagle and in its claws is an iron beam from one of the buildings that collapsed. There are 2,977 names engraved on it for the people who lost their lives that day."

For me, it brought back memories, so many memories, of the scenes I watched on TV at home. It didn't quite feel real back then, but being here, looking at the eagle and seeing all the names, I could physically feel the pain and trauma and the sadness it must have brought, and still does to this day.

Leaving the Pape family the day after, I caught a ferry back into the city, travelling past Staten Island and then sailing past the iconic Statue of Liberty. A Scottish runner called Aileen met me from the ferry and as we ran along the canal path she pointed out the Empire State Building. All I could think was that was where King Kong had swung from in the film. I was back to being a tourist again and was loving it.

Tonight, I was staying with the Ullrich-Wardell family, who took me to a famous Broadway show, *Ain't Too Proud: The Life and Times of the Temptations*. There were plenty of men in flares thrusting their hips and singing one of my favourite heart-warming songs of all time – "My Girl". Afterwards, we stopped in Times Square, the adverts and lights flashing all around us was exactly like I'd seen on TV – I even spotted the *Back to the Future* car on show. I was experiencing so many childhood memories, and was enjoying not running and acting somewhat "normal". I never thought I'd say that. I was relaxed, I had less than ten marathons to go, I knew I was going to finish this US run, though in the back of my mind I still had one of the toughest world records to break.

PART 27

BREAKING DAD

As I ran out of New York and into Connecticut, I travelled through Stamford and Bridgeport, and made it to Hamden. Anna had arranged for me to stay with her 70-year-old great-aunt, Ann Altman. As I arrived at her big wooden-slatted home that had a lovely tinge of green, the hospitality was already in full swing. A towel had been neatly laid on my bed and Ann had been cooking up a storm.

"I hope you're hungry," she said, "I've made a lot of pasta."

Shattered, I popped my PJs on and joined Ann in the kitchen at the back of the house where she spoke eloquently about her time studying at Cambridge and Yale. The sun was setting outside and as I went to spoon a big mouthful of meatballs into my mouth, we heard an enormous "BANG BANG BANG". Both our hearts burst from our chests. It sounded like a hammer hitting the kitchen window.

"What was that?" I said, terrified.

Ann spat out her food. "I have no idea. I don't have visitors at this time," she said with a startled look.

The noise was so loud, I began thinking the worst. It must be intruders. I puffed my chest out and went into defence mode. I stormed to the window cupping my hands to the glass and staring into the gloom. There was someone there, banging on the window with a fist. I saw a man with a grey beard down to his chest, he had no top on and his chest was covered in hair too. All he wore was sandals, a pair of shorts, a red cap back to front and a red superhero cape around his neck. He had his arms above his head. I kept staring in disbelief. Trying to comprehend what I was looking at.

Ann shouted, "What is it? Who is it?"

I looked back at her, confused as hell and said, "It's my dad."

"I guess we better let him in then," Ann said.

As we walked to the front of the house, I began to process that my dad must have flown out to surprise me. Ann threw open the door, took one look at my dad wearing a cape and practically nothing else and said, "What the f***?"

Not quite the well-spoken, Yale-educated lady I'd just been chatting with, but I couldn't blame her – Dad looked ridiculous.

With a big smile and clearly emotional he said, "Can you believe I found you...?"

He had barely got the words out, but I was already hugging him. I couldn't believe it. It had been over a year since I'd seen my dad. We hugged tightly for the longest amount of time I'd ever hugged my dad. I felt his warmth and pride.

Luckily, Ann, who had no idea my dad was surprising us, had made a stack of pasta so Dad joined us for dinner. Sat around the kitchen table, he was like a kid on holiday relaying the story of how he'd got to us.

"At the airport I told the taxi driver I needed to find you. I showed 'em the tracker on the web and said to 'em, 'err, that dot you see is my son. The taxi driver was keen to join the adventure, but as we got really close my phone was just about to die and I thought I wouldn't be able to find you and then, right at the last minute, it brought me here. I wasn't sure it was the right house, but thought I'd check the back window and bingo, there you were!"

The next morning Dad had another surprise for me. He was wearing a red cap, a yellow T-shirt and very short red shorts.

"What do ya reckon, J? I'm going to run with you till the end."

"As Forrest Gump?" I replied, staring at his long beard and mad outfit.

We both began laughing hysterically.

As we got ready to hit the road, Dad was trying to put his enormous suitcase on Caesar. I said, "Dad, couldn't you have brought something a little smaller?"

"Ah, it'll be alright son!" he said with a grin.

Caesar was now pregnant.

As we went to head off, I said to Ann, "Do you think he looks like Forrest Gump?"

"Foreign scum, more like!"

We left Ann with a wave, giggling like two kids. We were less than a mile in when I suddenly realised there was only six marathons to go, but that was still a heck of a way. I looked at Dad and said, "Dad, have you been training for this?"

"Training?!" he said with a look of outrage. "I'm a McDonald! We don't need to train."

As the miles began to disappear Dad turned to me and said, "It's weird. It's been so long since I've seen you but now I'm here, it feels like only yesterday."

Boy, I'd missed him.

After 15 miles we stopped in a pizza restaurant for a drink in a place called Middlefield. And when I say drink, I mean a beer.

As we gulped down a cold one, Dad said to the waitress, "Can you like and share my son's page?"

The waitress looked confused. Dad was trying to be supportive, but he doesn't have a clue about social media. As he tried to explain something he didn't know anything about, the commotion seemed to make everyone curious and they began asking what we were up to.

Before I knew it, Dad had made friends with everyone and Tony, the owner, came over with a large margherita pizza and said, "That's on the house!"

We left stuffed on pizza and kindness and it propelled us to mile 22 where I noticed Dad had begun running a little funny.

"You alright, Dad?"

"My hips. Knees. Feet. They're all a little sore," he said, laughing.

As we reached the marathon distance, ending at a cheap motel, I looked at Dad's face and saw the laughs had disappeared, he was now grimacing.

"But, Dad, we made it," I said, smiling.

He gave me half a smile before we got him back to his normal self by finishing the night in a diner, eating cream and pancakes. Lads on tour!

————————

As I awoke to the gentle sound of birdsong, no, wait, the rhinoceros-style snoring of my dad, it was clear he was sleeping very well after the marathon. That was until he woke up and realised he was going to have to do it all over again. He moaned and groaned just pulling the quilt off. As we checked out, I noticed he was limping heavily.

"Dad, it's a forty-four-mile day, shall I look for the nearest bike shop?"

"Do I have a choice?"

I'd broken Dad after one day. I couldn't stop giggling.

We found a bike shop just down the road and got a second-hand bike for $200 and off we went.

As Dad climbed on, all I could hear was him muttering, "This is so embarrassing!"

Our destination was Boston and we were looking for nice, peaceful trails to get us there. We hit a gorgeous dirt track called the Air Line State Park Trail where Dad and I could share some quality time together in the wilderness. We listened to my footsteps crunch and his wheels gruffle through the dirt. When we spotted a beaver dam, Dad got all David Attenborough on me, pretending he knew loads about beavers. It felt incredible to be with him, just us two in nature. It was something we'd never do back home. That's what adventure can bring.

At the halfway point, we found a bar in the middle of nowhere and they had crackers (and lots of butter) and home-made soup, which was delicious. On the way out, a lady put The Temptations song, "My Girl", on an old jukebox, so Dad and I got up and had a sing and dance with her. It was a perfect pit stop. We headed back to the trail and, as night fell, began hitting monster hills one after the other, with a bright moon shimmering in front of us. On the uphills, Dad kept getting off his bike to help push Caesar with me. I told him that very early on in the adventure, when I was badly injured after just a few days and feeling anxious, I had thought of Grandad on his deathbed and used the memory of his breathing to calm my own.

"Your grandad was a Glaswegian doorstep baby, you know. He had to be adopted," said Dad.

I truly felt like my grandad's roots travelled through my dad to me. I think that's where a big part of my fighting spirit comes from.

"We don't know where our roots come from exactly. That's why your grandad said, 'Us McDonalds, we're a rare breed!'"

He said it in such an animalistic manner it was as if the McDonald grit was right there at that very moment.

Hitting mile 40 on an 8 per cent incline, my feet were slapping on the ground as I was having to pull Caesar and my dad's suitcase back as hard as I could so they didn't run away. I started to feel nauseous from all the miles and my body became limp.

Dad must have sensed I was hurting. "You know, J, it's just bloody amazing what you're putting yourself through. I'm just so proud."

With Dad's words driving me on, I kept digging in and at 1 a.m. we made it. The way we'd worked it out, that was the last day of running where I'd have to hit more than a marathon in one day.

Dad said with a tired smile, "Unbelievable effort, J. Seriously unbelievable."

I'd reached marathon 206, and maybe it was too many miles from the day before, but my knee ligaments were in agony, so much so I could barely run. Panic set in, was I really only a few marathons from the end and suddenly my knee was buggered? I picked up the phone to Sylvia and she told me where the trigger points were to ease the tension. As I pressed against my knee, for the first time it didn't work.

Dad, obviously, had been earwigging on the conversation and said, "Don't worry, son. I'm an ex-bricklayer and I've got hands of steel."

So, by the side of the road on a grass verge, Dad cracked his knuckles and went to town on my knee, pushing his thumb in – hard.

"You've gone white in the face, J. Is that a good sign?" said Dad.

Turns out it was. Within 5 minutes I was back running, and although moving a little better, it still felt sore.

Dad got off his bike and said, "Here, give me Caesar. I'm pushing him now."

It felt amazing to have Dad with me, I could now concentrate on the running, knowing he would lead the way. I knew he was in pain too and I kept asking if I could take Caesar back, but Dad refused every time.

We ground it out, mile after mile, and I felt like we were sharing the pain.

As we finished the marathon, Dad said, "When I saw you in agony this morning, I just thought, right, it's time for Dad to step up. I don't care about the pain. You've gone through 5,000-odd miles of pain! The time and effort I've put in today is worth everything – and I mean that. I just didn't realise what you do day, in day out. You don't just run; watching you do all the social media, the blogging, the video editing, the stretching, the interviews – from what I've seen it just goes on and on. And you still gotta run the miles. So, this was a tough day, but I know it's all worth it. It's more money raised for the sick kids, that's what it's all about."

And then there were only three marathons to go.

PART 28

DON'T STOP BELIEVING

The next day in Rhode Island a Facebook follower, Justin Czar, picked up Dad, Caesar and me in his truck. He took us straight to do a local radio interview where Dad joined in. Of course, he spoke more than I did. Afterwards, we headed to Justin's house and met his son, Landon, and his Portuguese wife Norma. While eating Portuguese tapas with fish stacked high on the table, Justin held out his phone to show me a $1,000 donation he'd made.

He said, "I run a fencing company, it does alright. That said, this is one of the most inspiring things that I've ever seen in my lifetime."

Dad, with juicy tapas fingers, got up, said nothing and went straight over and gave him the biggest hug.

We couldn't stay for too long as we were being picked up by the McStravick family. About four years ago at the end of the Canadian run, I received a message with a picture of a cute kid holding a big glass bottle with lots of money in it. It read:

Dear Jamie,

My name is Chip McStravick. I am eight years old. Last month at my birthday party, instead of presents, I asked my friends to donate money to adventureman.org. I am glad to say that my friends and I raised $400 which we've donated to the IWK Health Center Foundation in the Maritimes.

My family and I enjoyed following you on your journey across Canada. My dad even recorded a video of me copying you putting your hand in the water in Newfoundland.

I hope you're doing well and I hope your legs are feeling better.

Your friend,

Chip McStravick

I'd been receiving countless messages from Chip's mum, Melissa, making sure I stopped by as my run went right past their house. It was totally meant to be. When we arrived, I met her husband, Peter, and their four kids: Chip who was now 12, Avery 15, Read 11 and Sullivan 8. They were quick to share the video they had made for me, showing footage from the start of my run across Canada – let's just say I was a little excited in that video. It was wonderful to have my first ever tribute video. That day we all went to their school, Pine Hill Elementary, where I gave a talk to over 400 schoolchildren. It was really special, especially with the McStravick family and my dad there watching.

The hype was starting to build as the run was coming to an end. My friends from back home had arrived too, Rich Leigh and Victoria Clark aka "Lady-V" (I call her this because she's the poshest lady I know – even posher than Posh Spice). She'd been helping me arrange all the hospital visits through WhatsApp. It felt amazing she was here in the thick of the adventure, in real life. We carried that energy into marathon 208. Dad and I were smashing it. He ditched the bike and was now back running, fist pumping with every mile and shouting, "The McDonald machine is back!"

I politely reminded him of his own mantra, never get complacent. "The machine can break at any moment, Dad!"

With 10 miles to go, Lady-V decided to use my dad's bike to join us, she looked a right sight on this beat-up bicycle wearing her sophisticated jacket and high-heeled boots. As we were chugging along, Dad put a finger on his nostril and blew hard to let out all the snot.

Lady-V wasn't impressed. "Oh, Donald, that was disgusting. I had to swerve a big dollop of your snot!"

Luckily, more pleasant and less slimy things lay ahead. As the sun started to set, we had a surprise visit from the McStravick family who came out to run the final few miles. I gave each kid a turn pushing Caesar and could see from their laughter how excited they were. After a mile, Sully the youngest was beginning to struggle so we paused until Melissa pulled up in the car, blasting out "Don't Stop Believin'" by Journey – which, as we all burst into song, got us moving again.

As we hit mile 25, our heads bobbing along to the music, I said to Chip, "I hear your mum is pretty upset with me. Apparently you told her you were going to run across Canada too?"

He smiled and said, "It's true. I'm going to do it in a faster time!"

I looked at Dad and said, "What do you reckon, Dad? Do you think he can do it?!"

Dad responded with the line he's ingrained into my psyche: "The challenge is on! But as you know, there's walking and there's talking!"

I handed Caesar to Chip and said, "If you're going to run across Canada, you better get used to pushing Caesar uphill!"

Chip was just about tall enough to see over Caesar's handlebars, he had to push hard and breathe even harder, but couldn't stop smiling – he was more than up to the challenge. We finished the marathon with a flourish, buzzing off each other's energy and giving high fives all round.

Two marathons to go.

It was so hard to leave the McStravicks – it was like saying goodbye to old friends even though we'd only been there for two nights.

As we hugged on the porch Melissa said with a very serious face, "Your lessons of combining adventure with philanthropy to make the world a better place to live are your biggest legacy. They've had such an impact on our kids, more than you'll ever know. But you do realise that if Chip runs across Canada that will be your fault and I will find you, and kill you."

We travelled to the exact spot we finished our last run. Over the next couple of marathons I was going to be joined by a different runner for each. At the start of my run, Gavriella, Jeff and SuperTed, who had booked me to speak at their

Microsoft conference, held a fundraising auction. They raised nearly $20,000 for the charity with a prize for two people to join me and each run a marathon – and here they were. First up was Yannick Debaupte. Yannick was an Ironman, so running a marathon wasn't too tough for him.

He was really excited to be here and said in a thick French accent, "Jamieeee, can you believe you've made it here to the other side of the US, eh?!"

"Time has just flown, hasn't it?" I replied.

"Yes, but I flew here. You ran here. Big difference, eh?!"

Yannick's wife, Patricia, was our support vehicle and kept us fed with French classic canelés de Bordeaux, crispy pastries filled with custard and buttery goodness. It was the fuel we needed, and Dad needed too, to get us to my final state, Massachusetts. My final state. I couldn't believe it.

As we blasted out the miles, passing through blissfully quiet country roads near Wrentham, more people joined in. We had a surprise visit from an Englishman named Steve who had driven across the entire state of Massachusetts just to run 2 miles with us.

Steve's only request was: "Jamie, please can I run with Caesar?"

Steve seemed to be obsessed with Caesar.

Yannick said, "See, Jamie, no one is coming to see you, they are all here for Caesar!"

As everyone showered Caesar with the praise he deserved, the miles flew by and camaraderie was high. That's when we saw a sign saying "Entering Boston" and a few moments later hit the marathon mark of 26.2 miles.

After a night in a nice hotel, the following day we were joined by Paul Simpson, who would be running the final marathon with me, he had a big smile and a big bald head like my dad's. Before we ran out of Boston that morning, Paul came with me and my dad to Boston Children's Hospital.

I would have expected him to want to skip that part of the day as a kids' hospital isn't always the easiest place to be, but Paul said that his daughter, Merrill, was diagnosed with spina bifida and had spent most of her life in hospitals. It was nice to share the visit with Paul and to know I would be spending the rest of the day running alongside someone who really understood the mission. The hospital was the perfect motivation for the final marathon. After completing that we'd be only 6 miles shy of the finish line. We set off giddy with excitement, especially Paul and my dad who were like two peas in a pod, both singing their bald heads off as they ran. We all agreed that if anyone asked who they were, we'd say Paul was my dad, and my dad, with his long beard, was my grandad.

Dad's bike got some use too. A friend of mine, Chris Nyland, had flown out from England. Chris wears nerdy glasses and is a trustee of the charity, and helps with our website and getting donations. Halfway through, we stopped in a pub and our meal was paid for by some people who had seen me on the news. Again, Dad was the first over with the hugs.

As we ran off with big bellies and big smiles, Dad said, "I'm lapping up all the glory at the end, and rightly so, it was me that made you!"

We ploughed on, striding confidently, knowing that every step forwards was a step closer to the finish line. Then we saw the first "Gloucester, Massachusetts" sign. The excitement cranked up another notch as we began chanting my home town rugby club's song, "GLAWSTERRR, GLAWSTERRRR." Car horns began honking – it felt like everyone knew my run was coming to an end.

Passing through Beverly, in the distance, I could hear bells ringing and teenagers cheering. It was getting louder and louder until we saw more than 500 students from Landmark School on the roadside, cheering and going bonkers.

At first, I didn't think it was for me, until the teacher said, "All these students have been waiting over two hours for you to arrive so they could say hi. We've been following you all the way. It's so inspirational. We salute you!"

We pushed on buoyed by all the support and on the final mile Paul pulled out his harmonica and played a tune as we danced the final mile. As we crossed the line with a jig, it felt simply incredible, I'd done it, I'd completed my final marathon. That evening, Anna flew in from the UK, just in time for the final run. She'd been suffering the past week with tonsillitis and I was worried she might not be able to join us, but like a warrior, she was here. It wouldn't have felt right her not being there at the end of this adventure. With just 6 miles to go, I had an urge to drink beer, but instead, that evening was a quiet one, reflecting on the journey. I felt emotion bubble to the surface at the magnitude of what I'd achieved, though I didn't let it flow, I hadn't quite completed my run across America, just yet.

Six miles to go.

I woke to see the sun bursting with brightness, supported by clear blue skies. I could feel the butterflies floating in my belly, nervous, yet excited to finish this coast-to-coast, 5,500-mile adventure across America. I knew the number of people running today would be high because of Good Morning Gloucester, a high-reaching blog and podcast, which had been promoting it every single day for weeks on end – I just didn't know how many people would show up. For the final 6-mile finish, we decided to stagger the miles so people could join in and run with me. We'd worked out a system depending on people's ability and how far they could run, so anyone could join in.

Our first spot was Sweeney Park in Manchester-by-the-Sea, with the goal to make it to Gloucester, to the Fisherman's Memorial statue on South Stacy Boulevard, then making it to Pavilion Beach which overlooked Gloucester's Outer Harbour, where I would finally dip my hand into the North Atlantic Ocean. We made sure my live-stream was on, so people could tune in from anywhere in the world. Alongside me were about 20 people: friends, family, Anna in her Wonder Woman outfit, my dad and complete strangers all dressed as superheroes. The only people who weren't dressed up were the sheriffs who were escorting us – I thought that was pretty damn cool having a group of sheriffs cheering us along.

After a 10-second countdown, we were off in a hail of flashbulbs from all the news camera crews, including Billy Baker from *The Boston Globe* who was running backwards to get the right picture, pure talent. As we ran, I felt like I was floating on air, I could barely feel the ground. It was as if I'd had five shots of coffee, but without the caffeine shakes. It was dreamy, I felt like I could run forever, stay in this moment forever. Although I had the world record in the next week or so, I let go and let myself enjoy these final strides. Every few minutes I was knocked from my dreamlike state by the sheriffs putting on their sirens. "Whoop whoop – it's the sound of the police!"

After the first mile, I needed a wee and made a quick dash into the woods, I looked at the sheriffs, but with the feel-good mood they turned a blind eye to my toilet break out in nature. There was a party atmosphere, with everyone chattering and smiling, it gave me a moment to reflect on all the people who had helped and supported me along the way. A little shiver went down my spine, a smile broke out on my face and I had an overwhelming feeling of the kindness in humanity.

By mile 4, the sheriffs had begun blasting out the *Rocky* song, "Eye of the Tiger". People began coming out of their homes, waving at us, some joining in and running. Goosebumps broke out across my back and a surge of tears bubbled to the surface, but I wasn't ready to let go just yet, there were still a couple of miles to go. The road was quiet, the tarmac smooth and the trees stood strong and tall, the bright sun shining through their bare branches. I looked ahead, down the road and caught the salty scent of the ocean. I began imagining the sea and what it would look like when I got there. Then it was back to the moment, as I saw two little kids on the side of the road holding a sign that read "Adventureman is Awesome". A bit of late drama – we had to halt the run – for high fives!

As we all ran on, I saw a sign that read "Entering Gloucester est 1623" and heard a cheer. After that, I kept hearing, "Hello Adventure-dad!", I looked around confused, thinking that's not my name, until I saw my dad with a big grin on his face. People must have seen him on my social videos and given him a nickname. I think he was chuffed with his new name because every few steps he kept shouting, "Who's the daddy?"

Another sign, "Gloucester loves Adventureman" – we definitely had to get a picture with that one. As the energy built, I had the feeling I was running into my Gloucester, my real home town. With 1.7 miles to go, the mayor, Sefatia Romeo Theken, was there to greet me with a warm hug.

"Welcome to Gloucester," she said.

This Gloucester really did feel like a home from home. I was joined by another 50 runners, so many of them kids dressed as Batman or Superman. As I looked back, there was a sea of superheroes all bobbing along behind me, one lady even had a bright pink wig!

As I looked down beside me, I saw that I now had a tiny human running alongside me.

"Hey, how old are you?" I said.

"Six! My name is Dash," he replied with a cute lisp.

I looked to my left to see a Gloucester local had run up alongside me.

"Jamie, just you wait till you get to the Boulevard, it's insane!"

As we neared the park, I saw all the townspeople lining the side of the road, cheering and clapping. This was amazing. The energy from everyone was so positive. I felt like we were on the final stage of the Tour de France. I checked my livestream and spotted a comment from someone that said, "I'm getting emotional." I was too. My throat was closing up, I was getting overwhelmed.

Another runner shouted, "Are you going to be sad when this is all over?"

I couldn't help myself, it all poured out of me. "I've gotta say, I've craved getting to the end the whole time, especially in the tough moments. But because I've done a few of these now, I realise how special they are. Every day is so unique. You can never recreate any day, they all feel like once-in-a-lifetime moments, like right now. So yes, it is sad, but I wouldn't change it for the world."

I was worried as a Brit in America there would be no one here for the last stretch, but I shouldn't have been. The American people had been fantastic all the way through and they weren't going to fall at the final hurdle. As we reached the last checkpoint meaning there was only 0.7 miles to go, hundreds of people were waiting.

I let out a big, "Come on, let's finish this off!!!" and fist pumped the air, which got everyone cheering.

My mood lifted higher than ever and tears bubbled to the surface. Listening to everyone's steps was like being part of a stampede. I was being carried along by the electric energy from all these different styles of runners.

With just 200 metres to go, a little kid with a superhero mask asked, "Are you tired?!"

I replied, beaming from ear to ear, "Not at all. I'm floating on air."

Then I saw all the people ahead, there must have been more than a thousand lining the streets. The *Rocky* theme boomed out from different sides of the road, chants of "Glawster, Glawster" floated up into the blue sky and tears flowed down my face. I didn't know where to look, there were so many smiling faces, until I saw a huge banner placed across the road, it read, "Welcome to Gloucester, Adventureman!"

Everyone was screaming, "You gotta run through it!"

So I put my hands in the air, closed my eyes and burst through the banner, ripping it in two. The crowd erupted and a 2-litre bottle of beer was placed into my hands.

I threw it down my neck, with people shouting, "Drink that growler!" as it went all across my face. Beer had never tasted sweeter.

The miles were done, all 5,500 of them, but with my journey being "coast to coast", I had to get to the beach. So, just like Forrest Gump, I just kept running. We passed Gloucester's iconic Fisherman's Memorial statue, where a man stood holding the wheel of a ship, looking out to sea, which was where I was heading. The sandy beach was on my right, just a few metres away and I felt a cool breeze whipping in from the ocean. I closed my eyes for a second and thought again of all the people who had helped me. As I opened my eyes, the ocean unfolded before me. Seeing the water shimmering in the sun, I saw more people clapping and cheering. I ran past, smiling, high-fiving, feeling every ounce of their goodwill and began running across the cool sand and into the sea, my steps splashing as I got deeper and deeper until I took a deep breath and dived into the freezing cold Atlantic Ocean. I held my breath and stayed underwater, feeling every drop of the ocean on every inch of my skin, as if it were washing away all my frustrations and worries from the past year. I'd never known if I was going to make it and as my head appeared above the water smiling, I let out a huge breath of relief. I looked at the beach with all my family, friends and the people of Gloucester smiling back at me and thought, "We did it."

PART 29

FROM ONE SIDE OF THE WORLD TO A WORLD RECORD ATTEMPT

DAY 1: FIRST STEPS

Within an hour, the world record attempt would begin. But some people were already up and running, dashing back and forth around the marquee making sure all the final bits were in place. The treadmill was being lined to make sure it was on a fair surface, security cameras being fitted as Guinness rules stated it had to be filmed 24/7 and a huge banner tied up on the front that read, "Adventureman's World Record Attempt – The greatest distance covered on a treadmill in seven days. Jamie McDonald supporting Superhero Foundation." Gulp. No pressure then.

The night before it had felt like the Last Supper. I was having dinner with Anna when I went to hand her the mustard only to get the response: "J, what are you doing? I asked you to hand me the broccoli."

"Oh, sorry," I replied.

"J, you okay? You don't seem yourself?"

That question hit a nerve, I realised I'd been stuck in my own head all day long, like a space cadet.

I grabbed Anna's arm and blurted out, "I don't know if I'm going to make this. It's just dawned on me I'm about to attempt something that's way beyond what I'm capable of. This is going to hurt more than anything I've ever done before." Tears were rolling down my face. "There's a really good chance I'm not going to make it," I said, my head slumping down...

Anna, as always, recognised it was just little old me and not quite the superhero people thought I was and said, "It makes total sense why you're feeing this way."

It was what I needed to hear. I let out an enormous sigh and said, "What the hell was that? Where did that come from?! I think that's been brewing for a while. Back to Planet Earth."

It had been exactly one month since I had finished my run across America. Since then, I'd been taking it easy, running a few miles a day, but mostly just resting. I was eating healthily; I went dairy free, sugar free, gluten free – trying to make my body as pure as possible. It felt good to cleanse myself of the American pancake dinners. I had a strict diet where I was only eating nuts, vegetables and lean meats, especially salmon. And I was drinking like a fish – but only water and strictly no coffee. No coffee means things are definitely getting serious. I spent most days trying to strike the balance between resting and recovering, but not taking too much time off running as I didn't want to get soft and lose my physical strength or my warrior mentality that I'd built up over the past year.

It was 1 p.m. when I stepped on to the treadmill for the first time. I looked around the marquee, here I'd be spending the next seven days running pretty much non-stop. The nerves were still there, my hands shaking.

I reached forwards to start the treadmill, but as I did Victoria shouted, "Stop! Before you begin we need to get a picture of the monitor so it shows 0 miles for the Guinness World Record rules."

Considering the fun times I'd had on the black stuff, these Guinness folk were fussy fellows, but rightly so, if you're going to break a record you have to do it properly.

Victoria (or Lady-V) was the person who organised all the hospital visits across the US. She's a total power planner, everything I'm not, and now she was taking care of the volunteers and helping organise this attempt too. Incredibly, we'd also managed to fly in Sylvia, my trigger-point therapist, from California. She was the only person on the planet who knew how to fix my body when it broke down. I was so happy that I had everyone in place to try and break this record.

I knew this was it. I put my shaking finger over the "Go" button on the treadmill, paused for a second, pulled back and thought, "Am I really ready?" I knew that once I hit the button this was it, my life and feet would be glued to the treadmill and wouldn't leave until I'd run more than 517 miles, in seven days, the distance of 20 marathons!

I looked at everybody; friends, family, volunteers, the mayor, the news crews, and said, "What the bloody hell have I got myself into?"

Everyone laughed, but I meant it, I was quaking in my running shoes.

The countdown began, "Ten, nine, eight, seven, six..." my dad's voice getting louder with each number, "... five, four, three, two, one".

I hit "Go" and the treadmill creaked into life. I looked for the "speed up" button, but with lots of people watching, I started to panic.

It felt like they were thinking, "Come on, hurry up!" so I quipped, "Sorry, it's a bit of a slow burner."

Everyone laughed again and my stage fright disappeared, I found the button and broke into a little run. What felt like a gazillion cameras went off, flashing in front of my face. Somehow, I didn't fall off, instead speeding up and breaking into a strong run. It felt incredible to be moving at last.

I looked up at the crowd, put my arms above my head in a power pose and said, "Let's 'ave it!"

Getting into my stride, I glanced at the polar heart-rate monitor connected to the treadmill. I looked at the reading – 150 bpm. My adrenaline was higher than the sky. Over the past few days, I realised I'd been like a caged animal and, finally, I was released.

I took some deep breaths to calm myself, then turned to everyone and said, "Right, so this is it for seven days then."

All that running across America had been worth it. I easily got into my stride and was already about to reach my first marathon when I had a special visit from one of the Superhero Foundation families we had supported.

Superhero Foundation is the charity I founded five years ago. In the UK, I volunteer my time supporting families who need treatments the NHS can't fund, which means sending kids around the world for pioneering operations, including America. It was Charlotte Thornhill and her little boy, Archie. A few years before, Charlotte got in touch to tell me about Archie, how he had cerebral palsy and had to spend most of his time in a wheelchair. There was however an operation in America that could keep him pain-free and give him the best chance to move his legs again. The problem was it cost £80,000. We supported Charlotte and Archie through their journey including a fundraiser where Charlotte danced non-stop for 36 hours in the exact spot I was running right now. Charlotte had moves like Mick Jagger, Jamiroquai and Prince combined as she smashed the target and got Archie his life-changing operation.

"Hey, Archie!" I said cheerily.

Archie didn't say anything as he's very shy, he just gave me a giant smile from under his Harry Potter-style glasses.

Charlotte said, "He's been asking all day if he can join you on the treadmill and run a mile next to Adventureman?"

Archie looked up with a hopeful grin.

"A mile? Wow. Of course. Hop on, Archie!" I said.

Archie stepped on to the spare treadmill to my left and started it up. To my amazement, he began running, to the point I could barely see any sign of his cerebral palsy.

"Easy, Archie!" said Charlotte as the crowd noticed the little man's achievement. "If he hits a mile, that will be the greatest distance he's ever covered!" she added.

The crowd cheered and someone shouted, "Come on, Archie, you can do it!"

Archie was about the same height as the treadmill, so you could just about see his little head bobbing away above the support bars as he ran. But he wasn't done yet. He stuck his finger on the "speed up" button, looked across at me and gave me a big winning smile. My heart melted. I felt like I was watching a world record being broken right in front of my eyes. As he smashed the mile, everyone cheered and Archie looked really proud. I think he might have given my world record a go if Charlotte hadn't peeled him off the treadmill.

As they left Charlotte said, "Thank you, this has made his day!"

Little did she know, it had made mine too.

That wasn't the only surprise, shortly after two more superheroes from my charity arrived. The Bottger family and Alex Paterson, aka Captain Armless. In 2014, the Bottgers became the first family I helped on their fundraising mission. We supported their dad, James, to climb up and down our local hill 75 times until he reached the equivalent of Mount Everest (yup, we broke him, but he achieved it). This helped get their daughter, Charlotte, a life-changing operation in the US. Charlotte, who had always been wheelchair-bound was now walking on the treadmill next to me. What an incredible sight.

Then there was Captain Armless. He was the most recent person we had supported and was now casually hanging out by the treadmill. In 1980, Captain had a motorbike accident. He hit a tree so hard he had an arm amputated and 40 years of ongoing phantom limb pain. Captain approached me before my US run about a new treatment for a bionic arm that was going to cost over £40,000. We supported his fundraising knowing he was a guinea pig for the treatment, but it was a huge success. So much so, his treatment is now being rolled out to other amputees and Captain works for our charity to help others in similar situations.

As I looked down at my legs pounding the treadmill, seeing the first people I had helped, the Bottgers, and the most recent, Captain Armless, it really brought home what this was all about. They were the bookends of the charity, old and new, and were now in the same room laughing together. My heart swelled with pride. It was the start I needed to knock out some easy miles and run with a sense of enjoyment, because soon I knew I'd forget what enjoyment felt like.

It was gone midnight when I broke the 50-mile marker. I felt tired but wanted to make sure I went to bed completely exhausted – so I pushed on until 4 a.m. It was then I gave Sylvia the nod I was ready for sleep. Lying down, Sylvia put my noise-cancelling headphones over my ears, playing white noise to make sure every last ounce of sound was blocked out. We were slap-bang in the middle of the Gloucester Docks, a public place for Guinness rules, so it would only take one drunken buffoon to stumble in, disturb my sleep and the record would be over.

Sylvia was doing some light trigger pointing on my aching muscles. It was amazing having her to nurture me to sleep and help manage my body, it meant I could concentrate on the running and now – the sleeping. We planned – if the plan was to come off – that I'd have three hours of sleep every night. I knew how important it was to calm my energy down, but my heart was racing. The idea of rest just didn't feel fitting, even though I knew how important it was. I tried breathing. I tried counting sheep. I tried counting sheep backwards. I think I counted a thousand sheep, but was feeling more and more awake. My frustration grew, the sheep scattered and I knew the game was up.

I ripped off my headphones and shouted at Sylvia, "I can't do it! I just can't! Let me get back on that treadmill."

Tears rolled down my face at the thought of having to run another 24 hours until my next sleep cycle. Getting back on the treadmill I let out a guttural, "RAHHHHHHH!" Then another. And another. I flushed out the frustration as quick as I could and then with all my emotions screamed out, turned up the speed and began running again.

DAY 2: HUNDRED-MILE HIGH

Around lunchtime on the second day, Rich came around to help with social media.

"We're gearing up to completing nearly four marathons, that's a hundred miles, Jamie. I reckon we should do a video of you to share on social. You okay to do that?" he said.

"Yes, I can do the video. It's actually laughable at how painful this is," I replied, smiling through a grimace.

The camera started rolling and the countdown began, three, two, one... "One hundred miles!" I shouted.

There was a small cheer. Rich turned the camera to me, but all I could think to say was, "I can't believe I've made it this far. I've never, ever covered this kind of distance before, I don't know how I'm going to do this five times over. I'm just going to have to dig so, so deep. Like I am now. Just digging."

That was what I said to stay positive, though really, I felt like I was digging for something else – my grave.

After 28 hours of running non-stop and fairly hard, I was 115 miles in, and more importantly 15 miles and 4 hours ahead of the record. It was a huge lead and a tactic I felt was right. My theory was that after a few days of running I'd be completely broken anyway so it would be better to be broken ahead of the record than be neck and neck throughout. Though, by going hard early, it was clear me being "broken" was coming around earlier than I'd expected. Maybe my grave-digging fears were about to come true.

That evening, Ben Limbrick, who has a bright mop of blonde army-style hair, arrived to see how I was doing. I'd spoken to Ben a week before the record, he's a professionally trained medic, so I had asked if he would be on call in case I needed any medical attention. He was super keen to help and having been in the army understood about pushing your body to the limit.

"How you doing, Jamie? I must say, you look like s**t!" said Ben.

"Cheers, Ben. Be a little more honest, why don't you?"

I was trying to have some banter, but I wasn't feeling good.

"Yeah, I'm okay in the circumstances. My ankles have swollen up like balloons and I didn't sleep a wink last night. I just want to make it through this evening so I can get my head down for sleep later."

"That's good! I'm going to do some checks if that's alright," said Ben with a doctor's tone.

As I ran, Ben gave me a device to put in my ear so he could check my temperature. It bleeped, he looked at the reading and it said 36.2°C.

"Are you cold?"

Sweating from head to toe topless in just a pair of shorts, I replied, "Do I look cold?"

"It's strange your temperature is so low. Here, let's check your oxygen saturation levels." Ben put another device on the end of my finger. Another bleep. He checked the results and he read out, "Eighty to eighty-three..." with a look of concern on his face.

"Is that good or bad, Ben?" I said.

"I'm going to be honest with you, Jamie. That's not good. It looks like your circulatory system isn't carrying blood around your body like it should."

"Well, what's the answer? What do I need to do?" I asked, seeking hope.

"I need to get you off that treadmill, Jamie"

"What, Ben?! Don't be bloody silly. Let my body just work itself out," I said pleadingly.

"Your body doesn't just work itself out, Jamie. How much water have you drunk since the start?"

"I'm not sure. I keep taking sips every once in a while," I said, thinking Ben had it all wrong.

"Let me know when you next need a wee. I want to see what it's like," Ben said.

Thirty minutes went by. "Okay, Ben, I'm ready."

We went to the portaloo and as I started to pee Ben peered over my shoulder and said, "Jamie, that's your problem right there. Your piss is like treacle and it freakin' stinks!"

"Great," I thought. "Now my number ones stink too."

As I got back on the treadmill, Ben said, "Listen, I should take you off the treadmill, but I can see you don't want to stop. For now, we're going to get you hydrated so it's not up to you whether you want to drink, the support team will tell you when you drink. Deal?"

He pulled out some electrolyte sachets and tipped them into a glass of water and continued, "I'm going to do more routine checks and if things don't change in the next twelve hours, I'm going to have to pull you off. If I don't, you're going to die."

"Relax, Ben. I've been training all year for this. I don't think I'll die," I said with a smirk, trying to loosen up the energy.

Ben spotted my carefree look and replied, "You're absolutely right, Jamie. I'm probably overreacting. What will actually happen is your organs will fail and you'll spend the rest of your days using a dialysis machine and your mum will have to feed you through a straw. So, actually, not as bad as you think, really."

It wasn't all death, pee and me resisting medical help. That day there was a string of welcome cameos. First, a surprise visit from the loveable adventurer, Ed Pratt. In 2018, Ed became the first person to unicycle the world, pedalling 21,000 miles in total. I know. One wheel. Ridiculous. He, of course, turned up with his unicycle and jumped on to the treadmill next to me to see if he could pedal and stay on. He successfully achieved at least 3 minutes and only 17 near-serious accidents, but it kept me entertained as the miles went by.

Later on, an old running partner, Wayne Mayor, turned up. Years ago, we used to run together. I remember looking at him, remembering our 3–4 mile runs and thinking "never in a million years would I have imagined I'd be attempting something like this". It was a bizarre reminder that I still felt like an "everyday runner" yet I was attempting a record that professional athletes wouldn't even dream of doing. It was a weird realisation.

As the night drew in, I started to sink into a new realm of discomfort. My ankles burned and my pace slowed, then dropped off a cliff completely. A wave of doubt crept in, a dark emotional shadow that was beginning to suffocate me. Freddie Burns, a professional rugby player who had played for England, popped in. Seeing him gave everyone a thrill and should have excited me too, but I couldn't snap out of my dark mindset. I was embarrassed by my pace, I couldn't get above 2.8 miles per hour. My ankles felt so sensitive and icky, like they might break at any moment.

Although I was feeling terrible, visitors still came; this time it was Craig from Inty. "Alright, Jamie! I've got a surprise for you."

He whipped out an enormous cheque for the Superhero Foundation – £5,000. I forced a smile, but something inside of me was so dark. I felt like a fake, I didn't want people to see the pain I was already in.

"Hey, can we FaceTime my girlfriend Kimberley in the US? She wants to see you," Craig said excitedly.

I thought, "How can I refuse a man one call after he's donated five grand?"

"Sure," I said.

Craig held up the phone and, within a few words, I said, "Sorry, I can't. Looking at the screen is giving me motion sickness, I'm going to throw up."

It was really hard not to be my bubbly self, but I knew I couldn't let anything affect the mission. As it got late into the night, people were jabbering away and there was a real party atmosphere in the air. But after last night's sleep fail, I knew I had to calm the energy and get myself ready for bed.

"Craig, and everyone else. I need total quiet. I'm sorry, I've got to go to bed soon," I announced.

The fun police had arrived. Special Grumpy Officer Jamie McDonald, shutting this party down.

I hobbled over to my bed to lie down. I was desperately seeking sleep, but trying to wind down was almost impossible. My head was in a spin, I couldn't sleep the night before and if that happened again, the record was over.

After 15 restless minutes I yanked my noise-cancelling headphones off and said, "Sylvia, trying to sleep is the real challenge, I just can't do it."

Sylvia was calm as she dispensed sleeping advice. "Just let your mind go to places it wants to, let it wander."

I put my headphones back on, took a breath and followed her advice. Immediately, I saw a dog's face, tongue wagging, behind it, clouds, white and fluffy, behind that a storm with lightning bolts. Then, I was flying through it. Every few seconds the visuals changed, until my eyes opened.

I said to Sylvia, "Did I do it? Did I sleep?"

Sylvia smiled. "You did, Jamie. It's 4.30 a.m. That's three full hours you've slept for."

I breathed a sigh of relief. I'd completed my greatest challenge so far and weirdly it was what I, or anyone else, would have considered a terrible night's sleep.

DAY 3: GETTING LEGLESS

Still in a daze from my brief snooze, Sylvia started her routine – lifting and stretching my legs to get blood back into them.

"Okay, Jamie. You're ready," she said with purpose, like it was "game time".

But when I went to move my legs, they wouldn't budge.

I laid them out straight, I tried them again, still nothing.

"Sylvia, I can't move my legs..."

The moment I said it, I flashed back to my childhood. I remembered saying the same thing to my mum when I was five years old. During that night I'd woken in pain and couldn't move my legs. It felt as if a ton of bricks were on me. As I screamed the house down, my mum and dad ran in to comfort me. As I lay crying, so did my mum, I could feel my dad was petrified too. Now, as a 33-year-old man, I felt the same wave of fear rush over me again. It was completely out of the blue as it was a memory I never thought about and now, of all times, it was seeping its way back into my subconscious.

"Sylvia, seriously, I can't move my legs," I said again, panicking.

Sylvia replied in her soothing Californian tone, "That's okay, Jamie. Let's just move one leg at a time."

I tilted my body forwards, we both grabbed under my left leg and edged it closer so it was hanging off the bed. We did the same with my right.

I was terrified. "It's over, Sylvia. This isn't right."

"It's okay. We're going to get your legs off the bed and on to the floor," Sylvia said calmly, while gently moving my legs so my feet touched the floor. "You're all good, Jamie. You're doing well. Now, put a little weight on them," she said.

As soon as I lifted my body and put the tiniest bit of weight on my legs, they burned with pain.

"Arghhhhhh!"

"Well done on your first attempt," Sylvia said consolingly. "Now what I'd like you to do is go again, but this time do a long 'ommm' noise when you feel the pain."

"What?"

"Have you ever done a yoga class where you've had to do deep 'ommms'? Try after me. Here we go, let's stand."

Sylvia got under my left arm to take my weight and we both let out a deep "Ommmmmmmmmm".

I was still in excruciating pain, but it seemed to take the edge off. I looked down at my legs. "Sylvia, I'm standing! I'm standing!" I cried.

"That's great, Jamie. Now let's work our way over to the treadmill and keep up with the oms," Sylvia said positively.

With each tiny step, I was doing my best to om away the pain, but it would sometimes slip into an "Ommmm – argh – mmmm". I sounded like a man trying to give directions with a mouthful of toffees. But I kept persisting and before I knew it, I was pushing "Go" on the treadmill. The bleeping noise kicked in and I was off running again.

Despite the scary incident, I felt a change in the energy of the tent. As the sun came up, more and more people were arriving. We had an NHS nurse from the children's ward and a policeman in uniform arrive to run by my side. It wasn't just a warm feeling I was getting from all this support though, it had started to feel like the warmest day temperature-wise too. When you're running your guts out it's amazing how quickly hot weather can make everything feel twice as hard, I knew this from the desert. The tent seemed to soak up the heat of the sun like a greenhouse. We had two fans pointing at me on full blast, but I knew it wasn't going to be enough. I shared my worry with my dad, he responded without hesitation. "We need a swimming pool with ice!"

My dad is only one of 200 people in the world to have completed the ice-mile challenge. That's swimming a whole mile in freezing water, so I wasn't at all surprised about his suggestion. Within an hour, a kiddies' paddling pool was being filled next to my portaloo. Luckily, there were restaurants and pubs nearby, so finding ice wasn't a problem. It wasn't long before I reached boiling point. I managed to get off the treadmill and into my "bedroom" – a makeshift area of privacy – where my dad stripped me naked. I didn't have any swimming shorts, so I struggled into a pair of boxer shorts.

Hobbling over to the ice pool, I said, "I'm dreading this, Dad."

Although, in truth, I think my testicles were dreading it even more.

"I know, but afterwards you won't. I promise," said Dad.

Seeing the paddling pool, I spotted a load of rubber ducks. "What are they doing in there!?" I said, confused.

"Well, you don't want to swim alone, do you?" said Dad with a big grin on his face.

Lowering myself in, I felt the burning sensation all over my skin, I gasped for air.

"That's it, J, that will sort you out. Get your head in there too!"

I dunked my head in and heard the ice jiggling around my ears. Every worry in the world disappeared. All I could think was that my head was turning into an ice pop and it felt good – really good. After 15 seconds, I took my head out and unlike my usually sleep-deprived brain, it felt crystal clear as if I'd downed a litre of coffee.

"That felt incredible, Dad. I feel like a new man. Let's go!"

As Dad helped me out, he said, "I knew it would."

I was hooked. Only a few hours later, I was craving an icy dip again. This time though, there were fewer people around, so I called over a stranger who'd come to watch.

"Here, what's your name? Could you help me into the pool?" I asked.

"Uh, yeah, my name is John. Of course..."

As we got in my "bedroom" I said, "I'm sorry to ask, but you're going to have to strip me naked."

John's eyes widened. "Oh, right." He seemed to take a few seconds to process what I was asking. "Um, of course, of course."

After my ice dip, I was back in the bedroom and knew that I was unable to bend my body in any way from stiffness to get myself clothed, so I lay on the bed, shivering naked, and said jokingly, "You know what they say about cold water and the effects it has on you, don't you, John?"

That broke the ice, so to speak, and John quickly helped me get dressed and back on the treadmill.

As I got back into my stride, I turned to him and said, "So that's a pretty big surprise, having to undress a naked stranger, huh?"

John said, "Well actually, Jamie, you don't know me, but it's kind of weird because I feel I know you really well. I've followed all your adventures, I love your strength and courage, I've watched all your videos, and read your book at least five times."

Wow, this guy was a superfan, he was chatting like he really respected me, like I was big and strong. Well, I'm certain that dream was crushed after he saw a naked, skinny boy from

Gloucester. I was a lot smaller than he made me out to be... in every sense.

OFF-TRACK

Most girlfriends' parents are the norm, they'll live a fairly standard lifestyle and, as a normal boyfriend, you can usually connect and go about showing you're a good suitor for their daughter. Anna's parents are Olympians. Rowers to be exact. They both competed in the Moscow 1980 Olympics. Ian won a bronze medal and Sue came 7th. There are more than 7 billion people on the planet, so when people make it into the top ten in a sporting field, they're legit. Sue was also a rowing coach and had helped youngsters win gold medals at the Olympics, so it was safe to say that trying to run more than 500 miles on a treadmill wasn't completely bonkers in their world and they understood what was needed to break records. And, as a complete surprise, here they were. They had driven a few hours from London to Gloucester for the afternoon, just to say hi.

"Hi, Jamie, you're looking well," Sue said, smiling, a glint in her big blue eyes.

I wasn't so chirpy, but it was the mother-in-law so I smiled back and gave Sue the warmest energy I could. After a bit of chit-chat, I noticed Anna pull them aside with Ben, the medic. Their faces looked serious.

Sue returned to the treadmill and said positively, "Right then, how's your speed?"

I nodded. "Okay I think."

Sue launched into action. "What are you eating, Jamie?!"

I pointed to the table. "I've got peanut butter, avocados, tinned sardines, rice cakes, food that's full of fat and easy on my stomach – no dairy or gluten. That's about as much thought as I've given it really."

Sue replied not so cheerfully, "Are you joking, Jamie? Have you not got a nutritionist helping you? I've been speaking with Ben and you need more calories. I can assure you the calories you have on the table and what you're going to burn for these seven days will not be enough. I mean, rice cakes? There are no calories at all in rice cakes!"

Sue departed hastily and an hour later was back with an armful of bags from Holland & Barrett. Suddenly the table was full of milkshakes.

"Are they milkshakes, Sue?" I said, confused, thinking that wasn't a typical athlete's diet.

"Yes, Jamie, they're dairy free too, so they should be easier on your gut and they're full of calories, just what you need!" Sue said proudly. She continued to offer her expertise. "What distance are you on compared to the previous record holder?"

"I'm not sure, Sue, someone will need to work that out. Right now, all I know is if I stay above three-point-four miles per hour for twenty-one hours a day, I'll break the record."

Sue's face changed once again. "So all the volunteers are logging your distances and times, but no one is calculating the comparison to the other record?"

"I created a system to know my mileage and left it with Sylvia to do the daily calculations for the other record. She updates us every night."

"Where's Sylvia now?"

"In bed resting as she's supporting me on the night shifts."

As I said it, I felt slightly ashamed at the basic system I'd created.

Sue calmly replied, "Leave that with me, I'm good at maths. I'll get a system going so we know where you're at, every single hour of the day."

I took some time to reflect on how I had set everything up. It was the first time I had someone question my set-up, and to be honest, the state I was in both physically and emotionally, I accepted I had missed some important pieces of the puzzle. My mind was a whirlwind of thoughts. I was fretting about the tent, the social media, Sylvia, the Guinness rules; the cameras, the volunteers, but the one thing I didn't think about was me performing as an athlete to break one of the most gruelling records on the planet. I thought, well done, Jamie, you've thought about every single aspect of the record, except for the most important ingredient of all – you've gone and let your future mother- and father-in-law know that Dory from *Finding Nemo* has more brains than you.

An hour later, Sue came back over. "Jamie, Ian and I are going to stay the night in Gloucester. You look like you could do with some extra support."

I felt a huge wave of relief and was incredibly grateful I had two Olympians fighting my corner. With each passing hour, new ideas we're being introduced to monitor my performance and it felt like the mission was becoming slicker by the minute. Sue created charts next to my food, a "How often does he pee" chart, a "How much water has he drunk" chart, a "How often has he eaten" chart, even a "How often does he poo" chart. In fact, Sue had more charts than Radio 1.

She was right about having "ideas up our sleeves" too. As I was slogging away on the treadmill, another person from the public wanted to join me. Callum hopped on to the spare treadmill on my left, I noticed he was wearing a tight vest, his biceps were big. I immediately thought, "He's one of those fast-type runners." As soon as he turned the treadmill on, he went to a top-notch speed and the ground beneath us started to shake. My anxiety kicked in. I didn't know where to look. I was confused, I couldn't say it was making me feel anxious, especially as he was only trying to be supportive, so I just looked down and focused on what I was doing.

Sue seemed to pick up on my energy. "Jamie, everything alright?"

I felt comfortable with Sue. "Not really, I feel really anxious," I replied.

It was like Sue had a second sense and could feel what I could.

She walked over to Callum and said, "Is there any chance you could run at the same pace as Jamie?"

Callum got it straight away, turning his speed down to match mine and within a minute I felt my anxiety drop. Feeling good, I tweaked my speed up a few decimals.

Sue shouted over to Callum, "Four-point-four is the speed, Callum."

He adjusted it and we began running in perfect harmony. Now Callum was truly supporting.

I turned to Sue and said, "I'm feeling much better now, thank you."

She gave me a warm smile and said, "We're on it now, Jamie. We won't miss a trick."

With Sue and Ian working on my speed to stay ahead of the record, I continued with my ice-pool dips to keep cool. Now it was Ian's turn to step up and offer his athletic expertise. Ian is well built and has a bald head, so when he says something, you listen.

"Jamie, the support team are saying the dips are working for you, but there's a big challenge, you're losing five minutes every hour and we can't have that. These marginal gains, or losses, will be the difference in breaking the record and not."

"It's been a lifesaver today, Ian. I don't think I could have made it without that pool," I said somewhat desperately.

"Okay, leave it with us and we'll see what we can come up with," he said confidently.

While Sue, Ian and Anna were having an emergency meeting to work out how to keep me cool, Ben was doing his routine health check. As he looked at my temperature he said, "Jamie, something's not right. Your temperature is up and down like a yo-yo. Are you cold now?"

"Nah, I'm just right," I replied, not wanting Ben to worry.

"Your temperature is right down, you should be shivering, Jamie. Are you sure you don't feel cold?"

"Seriously, Ben, I'm good, I just have to keep running."

Ben left the tent looking confused.

Meanwhile, Anna and her parents came back over. "J, we've come up with an Olympic solution to keep you on the treadmill for as long as possible," Anna said, with Sue and Ian beaming excitedly behind her.

"As long as possible? That sounds really great," I said sarcastically.

"In rowing, when it comes to competing in the hot countries it's really common the rowers wear an ice jacket to keep them cool," Anna said.

"An ice jacket? I've not heard of one of those."

"Well, you basically put a vest in the fridge or freezer and wear it. That means no more trips to the pool. I'm off to get you a jacket now," said Anna cheerfully.

"That's one of the most thoughtful presents you've ever brought me," I said, and we shared a smile.

A little later, Anna returned with the ice jacket. I'm not sure how fashionable it looked, but it felt amazing against my skin. It was the first time I felt I wasn't going to start sweating as I moved. But as I shouted, "Pee break," within seconds I knew something was seriously wrong. My upper body started to shake, then my legs trembled.

My mum took one look at me and said, "What's wrong?"

"I'm not sure, Mum, I think I need to lie down," I said with a shaky voice.

I took a step off the treadmill and my legs gave away and I went into some weird hyperthermic convulsion.

I heard my mum scream and felt my eyes roll back in my head. "Helpmepleassse..." I tried to speak, but couldn't, and dropped to the floor.

Two volunteers grabbed underneath my arms and dragged me over to my bed. My mum wrapped me with all the blankets she could find as I curled into the foetal position and began violently shaking and moaning and groaning.

My mum was rubbing my body. "Why the hell are you doing this to yourself, J? This isn't right. You shouldn't be like this. We're calling Ben…" she said, scared.

Even though I felt she was right, and feared this could be the end, I needed to put her mind at rest. Still shaking, I said, "D-d-d-don't worry, Mmmmmum, it's going to be alrightttt."

As Mum rubbed me down, something happened that's never happened before – my mind hurtled back to my six-year-old self when she would rub me down after I'd had an epileptic fit. It was her way of bringing me "back to life". The memory was so vivid, it was as if I was there. As I continued to shake in agony, thinking there was was no way I was coming back from this, it felt bittersweet somehow, having Mum nurture and reconnect me to my childhood felt cathartic and brought tranquillity to my soul.

Anna and Sue came into my "bedroom" and joined my mum in rubbing me down.

After 30 minutes, my shaking slowed and I returned to a vaguely normal temperature. As scared as I was, I knew I had to keep going, so I crawled back to the treadmill. I could sense the people who'd come to watch were concerned too, I could hear some worried whispers – which wasn't surprising as they'd heard all my groans.

As I gingerly stepped back on, I heard a clap, then another clap from the other side of the tent, then, "Come on, Adventureman, you got this!"

Within seconds the tent erupted with cheers. I turned on the treadmill and held my fist in the air to show my appreciation. As I began running, I felt a slight spring in my step, but I was still worried about what had just happened.

Eventually, Ben arrived and was by my side. "I heard what happened, Jamie, how you doing?"

"Ben, that freaked me out and I'm worried my body is shutting down."

I was worried he'd pull me off the treadmill, but I knew I had to be honest.

"I'm actually not surprised it happened, Jamie. I've been thinking about this all day; your body temperature has been all over the place. I don't think you're able to regulate your body temperature and I think it's down to dehydration. So, I've brought a solution with me!" Ben said positively.

Here I was worrying that Ben was going to pull me off the treadmill (I think I was secretly hoping he would), but it seemed our roles had been reversed. I was the one worrying and Ben was the more hopeful one.

"What's the solution then, Ben?" I said, pleading for some positives.

"I've got you some Dioralyte," he said with a grin.

"What the heck is that?"

"We used these in the army when someone was severely dehydrated. They're full of salts and electrolytes that will help get your blood flowing and regulate your temperature. Not only that..." He pulled a sachet from his pocket like a magician. "...they're blackcurrant flavour!"

Moments later I was gulping down a litre of lukewarm water full of Ben's blackcurrant Dioralyte.

"Give that five minutes and you're going to feel like a new man!" said Ben with a grin.

Sure enough, 5 minutes later I was back running strongly – clearly high on Army Ribena. I was... high-bena! But even though I was back running, I couldn't seem to shake the emotion of what had just happened. As the evening wore on, nothing could raise my spirits. The grey clouds grew darker, as if Lord Voldemort himself was running through my veins.

"J, in two and a half days you're about to hit eight marathons. It's the two-hundred-mile marker!" my dad said proudly.

I mumbled back at him, "I've just got to make it through the night."

I was 54 hours in and running on only 3 hours' sleep. With every step I was clinging on. As I kept trudging in silence, every step one of excruciating pain, I realised attempting another 300 miles on top of the 200 miles I had already covered was impossible. It felt like a switch flicked in my brain – for the first time in my life, I was going to give up and throw in the towel.

It was so late I knew now wouldn't be a good time to quit, so I made a pact with myself that I'd give up first thing in the morning. For the next few hours that thought went around and around in my head – it felt like a dirty little secret. As I finally slumped from the treadmill after more than 56 hours of non-stop moving, I clambered on to my bed in so much physical pain. It was as if I'd been hit by a car, five times over. I was emotionally numb, but I was at peace with giving up.

DAY 4: END OF THE DREADMILL ROAD?

After 3 hours' sleep, I took off my headphones and "checked in" to see what condition my brain was in. I asked myself, "Are you still giving up?" Nothing had changed. Today was the day I was going to quit, I just needed to find the right time to do so. Sylvia got me out of bed and helped me into my trainers as I howled in pain. My ankles had swollen to the size of an elephant's. Everyone in the tent looked horrified as I hobbled towards what we were all now calling the "dreadmill".

I thought, "Maybe I should just give up now. Why am I putting myself through this if it's all for nothing?"

Dad and John Myatt chipped in words of encouragement. "Come on, J, you're doing well. You got this."

That year, John represented Great Britain in the Ice Swimming World Championships held in Russia, becoming a gold medallist for the fastest time swimming a kilometre in 0°C water. I took another step, buoyed by their positivity, and started the treadmill. Two hundred miles in, I notched the speed up to 2.3 miles per hour. My legs and toes felt as if they had gone a hundred rounds with Mike Tyson while simultaneously being set on fire.

I kept pushing it out, my hands over my face in disbelief that you could feel this much pain. "Raahhhhh" I grumbled.

As I notched up the speed again, I felt my legs in burning pain again, so I said it. "Dad, I can't do this. I'm getting off. The record is over."

It was something I never, ever thought I'd say to my dad. He barely flinched, except for his forehead, which squeezed together as if to say, "I'm confused."

Then he said calmly, "No you're not. You're staying on that treadmill."

"Dad, listen, I totally underestimated what it would be like to run on a treadmill. It's completely different to road running with Caesar. Look at the state of my swollen ankles. The pain is beyond anything I imagined. It's day three and I can't even run. If I can't run, it's over."

I felt Dad was taking me a little more seriously now, but he didn't give in. "J, listen to me. As a support team, we've been learning as we go and we haven't been as good as we could be. Sue and Ian will be here today again, from now on we're going to have food on tap and make sure you're eating enough. We'll have water to make sure you're hydrated. We're going to be on it. Just ride this wave out and keep going. You're still ahead of the record, so it doesn't matter if you take it slowly."

"Dad, you're not listening. Food and water isn't going to change this. Look at me?! I can barely walk, let alone run."

Dad's resilience didn't waver. "Right then, we're going to get some ibuprofen too."

"Dad, what's wrong with you?!" I shouted. "That's not going to sort me out either. You're not listening to me!"

He grabbed a handful of sheets of A4 paper.

"J, I was going to leave these letters until tough times, well, it looks like it's time. These are the letters from all the kids who have written to you."

Dad started to read out the letters one by one. By the fifth, I started to break down, tears rolling down my cheeks.

Dear Jamie,

We came to see you in our superhero costumes yesterday. We were amazed how well you were doing and to run three marathons a day is a lot of work. I just want to give you three top tips… always believe in yourself, do what you want to do and no matter what, keep on running.

Good luck breaking the world record!

Love, Abbey

Dad then put down the letters and spoke again. "So, do you want to listen to my suggestions, or do you want to give up?"

The tent fell silent, all you could hear was the sound of the rubber rolling around the treadmill.

I looked at Sylvia, she caught my eye and said, "You got this, Jamie."

I took a deep breath, looked at my dad and thought, "You got me, you b******!"

"That's it then, Dad. It doesn't look like I've got a choice, but this ain't going to change anything. You know that, don't you? There's no way I can physically get through this," I said, defeated.

"Fancy a coffee?" said Dad.

"Go on then. I suppose it doesn't really matter any more."

Before and during the challenge, I'd decided not to drink coffee as I didn't want the quick caffeine hit only to suffer brain fatigue a few hours later. But because I was getting off soon, I didn't care.

John passed me a coffee and said, "Get that down your neck."

I tilted my head back and poured it in as if I was draining my last swig of beer before they closed the bar. This swig burned my throat, but at least it took the burning away from my legs.

A couple more volunteers filed in for their shift. The atmosphere in the tent wasn't good. I sensed everyone could feel my doom, that somehow they knew everything was coming to an end. I recognised one of the volunteers, it was James Forrest, an ex-Gloucester rugby player. I couldn't believe he was here volunteering. As flecks of dawn light began to ignite the tent, my mind was a muddle. I was mentally stressing out, thinking what I would tell people. What would I say to the newspapers? The volunteers who signed up for shifts we'd now have to cancel? I felt like I'd let myself and everyone else down. How could I be so stupid to think that running on the road was the same as a treadmill? Typical me, no planning, not much preparation – I felt like my personality, which is brilliant for thinking big picture and achieving adventures, had just come back to bite me in the ass.

As I continued to catastrophise, James nudged up close and asked the golden question. "How you doing, Jamie?"

It was normally a question I despised, because of the inevitability of the answer. This time it felt different. Like it was said with real empathy. I'd always respected James on the field so I felt I could have a man-to-man chat with him.

"I've cocked it up, James." I told him how I'd got it all wrong and now there was no chance of breaking the record.

James listened. He had this calming energy and once I'd got all my worries out he said, "That all makes sense," quickly adding, "you know your dad's gone to get ibuprofen – that's good stuff, you know. Back in my rugby days, I had a dodgy knee for years so on the big game days when I needed my knee most I'd use ibuprofen to get through. It's incredible stuff!"

"Really?! I've never taken it before," I responded, sucked in by every word he said.

"Seriously, Jamie, once you have them, you'll notice the difference."

I felt like a door in my mind had just nudged opened. Dad got back from his ibuprofen trip and shouted so the whole tent could hear; "Well, you're still going. That's good!"

James quickly passed the ibuprofen and said, "It says on the box, these will take twenty to thirty minutes to take effect."

I gobbled two tablets and washed them down with the rest of the now cold coffee. I kept my legs moving on the treadmill and every 30 seconds would see if they were ready to start running – they weren't. Five minutes went by and I had an urge to increase the speed. As the treadmill sped up I broke into a little gallop, I increased the speed a little more and before I knew it I was back running just shy of the record pace.

I looked over at my dad in complete disbelief. And to be honest, my dad had the same look.

I lifted both hands up in the air and said to everyone, "I'm doing it. I'm actually doing it!"

I felt a huge rush of blood course through my body, through my back, all the way up to my head and heart. It felt like a ray of light had just pierced my dark cloud – it was a glimmer of hope.

As I tried to get back into my rhythm, Sue walked in and asked, "Jamie, what have you eaten this morning?"

"I'm feeling pretty sick, Sue, I'm sure I've eaten enough," I said, hoping she would back off.

"What about some banana, peanut butter and honey?" she said in a tone that said, "You don't have much of a choice here, sonny."

I slowed the treadmill down and scoffed a mouthful, it was topped with my favourite honey, manuka. As the sugar hit my tongue, I felt my cheeks widen into a smile. I looked up and saw Sue, Anna, Ian, Victoria and Dad all smiling back.

Anna shouted out, "The first smile in days. And it was all down to the Adventurenana!"

After the scrumptious snack, I noticed I needed to watch out when Ian was about – in a good way – as he and Sue were always plotting to make the process as good as it could be.

"Jamie, I've got a new idea that I think is going to make a hell of a difference," he said confidently.

"What's that then, Ian?"

Ian was the master at building anticipation, he waited a few seconds then said, "Are you ready for this?"

I loved the excitement, it stimulated my brain, anything that gave me hope would be welcomed with open arms.

"Right then, Jamie, when you get off to have a pee, you get off the treadmill, walk over to the portaloo and do your business. But then you have to come all the way back to the treadmill and get going again. Do you know how long that takes?"

My pee-timer was off. "Not really, a few minutes?"

Ian replied, "It takes around four minutes. If you're going to the toilet, say ten times a day, for the next four days that's one hundred and sixty minutes wasted! That's over two and a half hours of time you could bank – and would mean a ten-mile lead over the current record holder."

I'd never seen a man so excited about going to the toilet, but Ian had a point.

"Marginal gains, Jamie, marginal gains," he said, smiling.

"That's all good and well, Ian. But what are you suggesting? We put the toilet right next to the treadmill? It stinks, I don't think I, or anyone else, wants it that close."

"No, Jamie, you're going to pee on the treadmill," he said, quite satisfied.

"You what, how?! Look over there, Ian, we're being live-streamed on YouTube twenty-four-seven. There are people walking in and out. Surely not?" I said, mortified.

"Don't worry about that. Me and Sue have a plan. You just keep running and let us know when you need a pee," he said, as if it wasn't really up for discussion.

Sure enough, an hour later, I was ready to go.

"Ian, I'm ready. How's this working?"

"Well, I'm going to hold this bottle while you pee and Sue is going to hold your superhero cape in front of you so the public can't see," Ian said.

This was the height of Olympian strategy. But at this point I was open to anything that might give me an edge. Operation Quick-Pee got under way. I turned off the treadmill and it slowed to a halt. I was happy I didn't have to get off, that small step was always carnage on my legs. Though trying to stand still was a nightmare. Even stopping briefly after 30 minutes on a treadmill, you feel the motion beneath your feet. Try being on a treadmill for a few days, it feels like the world beneath you is going to turn upside down.

Ian and Sue could see I was struggling to stand, but they knew to make it a fast turnaround too. They braced themselves, standing either side on the treadmill. Sue whipped up my cape and Ian grabbed a bottle and placed it in the required position. I noticed the bottle was transparent, they were really taking the pee now, so I said, "Did you have to choose a see-through bottle?"

Sue responded, "It's so we can check the colour to make sure you're hydrated."

This was the ultimate act of kindness you'd want from your future in-laws, it was the balancing act to end all balancing acts. I held one hand on the treadmill and the other on you-know-what. Ian gripped the bottle, while I aimed the best I could. I started to set the wee free – it was working – but the motion was weirding me out. The top part of my body kept wanting to move forwards, while my feet wanted to be swept behind me. As I was in full flow, I gripped the treadmill but noticed I kept moving forwards and that's when it happened. My body lurched forwards, my you-know-what hit Ian's hand and my dehydrated pee sprayed all over it. If the YouTube camera had been on slow motion it would've seen me mouthing, "No no no – noooooooooooooooooooo!"

I looked at Ian's fingers dressed with my urine and brought my eyes up to meet his. We said nothing. Our eyes winced for us. I turned to Sue. She realised something was seriously wrong. She peered over the cape and our eyes locked. They say the eyes are the windows to the soul, but right now they would have just screamed with mortification. It felt as if I was a million miles away in a parallel universe looking at this unfortunate wee-reality I now found myself in.

About five years ago when Anna introduced me to her dad for the first time I remember thinking, "What a lovely bloke", but I also remember thinking he had a demeanor that said, "Don't you ever mess my daughter around." Now I'd made a mess all over his hand.

Strangely, soon after, Ian left to go back to work in London. But the stream of visitors continued. Olympic and Commonwealth champion Lorraine Shaw popped in to say hi and the Gloucester rugby players Charlie Sharples, Tom Savage, and Ben Vellacott arrived having had a whip around for donations from the players. Even the Gloucester chefs brought protein and fat balls, perfect to eat on the treadmill.

It was really nice to feel the momentum and support building. But as the energy in the tent built, mine faded. When people walked into the tent they would say, "How you doing, Jamie?" or worse, "How're your ankles?"

I was trying to take their questions as a positive, and sometimes embracing pain can actually be an advantage. By focusing on it, it can give you the fuel to keep going, but sometimes it works equally well to block it out. Right now, I was trying to do the latter so to be reminded of it every 5 minutes was a struggle. As usual, Sue's sixth sense tuned in.

An old guy – a member of the public – walked in and said, "I've been watching you on the news every day, Jamie. You're doing so well, but I heard you're having ankle problems. Oh, I see them, they really don't look too good, how do they feel?"

Sue, quick as a flash, shouted across the room, "Jamie, how's your left arm?"

I thought, "What the hell are you on about, Sue?" but didn't want to be rude, so I lifted my arm, looked at it and said with a massive grin, "Actually, it feels amazing, Sue. My left arm feels fantastic!"

I realised it had been days since I said anything had felt fantastic about my body. Sue's genius tactic was working and was quickly embraced by the support team.

If anyone walked in and asked how I was, the next question from a protector would fly across the tent. "Jamie, how's your left arm?"

The team effort was really helping.

Later in the afternoon, hobbling to the toilet I heard someone shout, "You look like Grampa Joe, look everyone, it's Grampa Joe!" It was Ben playing the joker.

I thought I'd play along. "Shut it you, little rascal!" I said, shaking my fist like a grumpy old man.

But joking aside, I really was walking like a 100-year-old.

As I went to sit on the toilet I felt a huge wave of pain surge through my thigh and let out a big scream. "Arghhhhh!"

Ben was at the door within seconds. "Everything okay, Jamie?"

"Argh, I think so, I just can't bend my right leg. I need to go to the toilet, you know, a number two, and I can't."

With difficulty I got back to my bed so Sylvia could take a look. After lots of mobility movements, my leg was as straight as a board, but wouldn't bend.

"That's as good as we're going to get it," Sylvia said.

Over the past year she'd manipulated my body to extraordinary and stretchy lengths, so if she said that was it, I believed her. I slunk back to the toilet wondering how exactly this was going to work. The only way was to keep my right leg straight with my foot on the floor and my left leg bent with that foot on the toilet seat. Legs askew, my buttocks hoisted in the air at a jaunty angle – it was probably the most unorthodox number two I'd had in my life.

I kept repeating to myself, "Breathe, Jamie, just be comfortable with being really uncomfortable."

That evening, Anna created a drawing of a mountain in front of me. Then she wrote "3.5 days" at the top.

She turned to me. "See that, J, you're at the top of the mountain. You know what that means? It's all downhill from here!"

She was right, I was now halfway through and knew that every step I took was one closer to the record. Rich grabbed his camera to film a video for social media.

A crowd gathered and he told me, "Jamie, you're two hundred and sixty five miles in. That's ten marathons. And since the start of the record, we've raised twenty thousand pounds! You're halfway!"

I was more than 3 hours and 10 miles ahead of the record. I genuinely couldn't comprehend that both my legs were still moving and the whopping amount we'd raised so far. I felt an enormous sense of gratitude, then gave my usual fist pump to get the crowd going, which always got me going too. The cheers and claps sent a rush through my body and I turned the treadmill up a little faster. I felt like this was the best way to show my gratitude to everyone.

I whispered under my breath, "Thank you."

DAY 5: RAGE AND ROMANCE

The previous night I had pounded out some more miles and made it to bed at 3 a.m., thankfully dropping off fairly quickly.

"Time to get up, Jamie," I heard Sylvia's voice speaking softly to me.

As I came to, I sensed something wasn't right.

"It doesn't feel like I've slept, Sylvia," I said.

"You have. You've had two hours' sleep," she replied.

I didn't say anything. As Sylvia went through the usual routine warming up my legs, I was trying to process why I'd only had two, and not my normal three, hours of sleep, which is what we'd planned. I couldn't comprehend it, I lay there in silence trying to rack my brain.

"How you doing, Jamie?" Sylvia said, as part of our morning ritual.

"Good," I said, but it came with a slight tone of annoyance. "Why did you only give me two hours of sleep?" I added.

"While you were sleeping, the previous record overtook you – so right now, you're just behind. We agreed yesterday that if that happened, an extra hour of running, instead of sleeping, would help keep things on track. Do you remember that chat?" Sylvia asked.

Over the past few days, my memory had become increasingly blurred. I didn't remember. I felt a wave of anger surge through my system, but didn't want to upset Sylvia.

I started to rant in my mind. "How could she think that I could make it through the day on two hours of sleep?! There's just no way. My routine is RUINED! The record is over!"

Sylvia tried to make small talk, but I cut her short at every moment. I sensed she knew something was up, but I couldn't bring myself to tell her how upset I was. Stumbling on to the treadmill felt like a good distraction, an attempt to create pain elsewhere so I didn't need to confront my emotional pain. But as the treadmill began moving I felt my anger bubbling to the surface again.

My brother Lee was standing and staring at me. I felt hot and needed to be cooled down, but I lost it and screamed, "GET THE FANS ON, WILL YOU? MAKE YOURSELF USEFUL!"

Lee took it like a champ and did what I said. I felt like he was a safe haven to let out my frustrations, but it didn't get rid of the bubbling volcano.

"Anna, get me some food," I said in a harsh tone.

In the next breath, I shouted over to a volunteer, "We need music now!"

I couldn't work out why I was being so rude to everyone. It felt like my head was going to pop off my shoulders in frustration. I just wanted to get it all out. An hour came and went with me ranting at anything and everything until it dawned on me, I needed to tell Sylvia how I felt. She was one of my greatest rocks and I was worried if I told her how angry I was it would upset her and she wouldn't support me for the rest of the attempt, but I had to.

"Sylvia, come here, please. I don't want to upset you, but I have to get this off my chest," I said as if I was a kettle coming close to the boil.

"Go for it, Jamie, it's important you share your feelings," Sylvia said.

As soon as I got permission, the whole kettle top blew off like Mount Krakatoa.

"I AM SO UPSET WITH YOU. HOW COULD YOU POSSIBLY THINK TWO HOURS IS ENOUGH SLEEP!? I'M SO ANGRYYYYY!"

There were a few seconds of silence, then Sylvia took a deep breath. "I hear you, Jamie. You've got a right to those feelings. I hear you," she replied in a mothering tone.

She stood there in silence, not fazed by my outburst. I didn't know what else to say, so I ran, she stood, and we listened to the treadmill go around and around.

"Okay, I think I just needed to get that out. I feel better now."

I felt my kettle cooling and my energy calm.

"I'm glad, Jamie," Sylvia said calmly.

Sylvia turned, had a quick chat with Anna and left the tent. Suddenly, I had this huge wave of guilt. I began freaking out. "Anna, Anna. I've upset Sylvia. Please get her back, I need to say sorry," I said frantically.

"J, you're all good. I overheard what happened. I've spoken to her, she's totally fine."

"No, she's not, she's not! Get her back," I said.

Anna responded calmly, "It's all good, J, honestly. I'll call her and bring her back. Though, seriously, she's good. It looks like you're having bouts of paranoia."

"Paranoia?!" I said, clearly paranoid.

Anna continued, "Yes, just relax. I know this is important to you, we'll get Sylvia back."

Sure enough, 5 minutes later, Sylvia came back and as soon as she walked over I spluttered, "I'm sorry, I can't do this without you, Sylvia! I'm so, so sorry."

"It's all good, Jamie. Nothing to worry about. I'm here. Just keep doing your thing."

I let out a deep sigh of relief. I couldn't work out why I was behaving like this. Every emotion felt extremely intense. On reflection, I knew this was my fault, that I had forgotten my and Sylvia's conversation about only taking a 2-hour sleep instead of 3 hours. I could no longer trust my own decision-making – my head was screwed. I knew I had to snap out of it and somehow refocus. I was behind the record, but I did now have an extra hour to get ahead. As daunting as the next 20 hours looked on 2 hours' sleep, I accepted it and was ready to get after it.

As the day progressed I started to clear my head and get my hunger for miles back. I decided if I got through today, I could do anything. My feet pounded the rubber and I owned every step as if it was my last. As the afternoon slipped into evening, I hit mile 328. I'd run over 12 marathons. It was at this very moment Anna walked in, barefoot, wearing a slinky blue and pink dress, which matched her pink hair and bright blue eyes. My eyes widened. Anna never wore a dress unless it was for a special occasion. She's an adventurous girl with a style that's a little more tomboy, so whenever she wears a dress it catches my attention. She looked beautiful.

"Hello J-Boy!" she said, glancing her eyes at me. "It's been a while since we've had a proper date, so I thought I'd surprise you. Do you mind if I join you?"

She stepped on to the treadmill and began running barefoot beside me.

"I thought we could have a date night and I could do a bit of training for Barefoot Britain. What do you reckon?!" Anna said, fluttering her eyelashes.

"Let's squeeze in the romance where we can," I replied with a smile.

Anna asked her mum to play the role of DJ. One of my favourite tunes kicked in.

It was like someone had pulled a love lever. As "My Girl" by The Temptations spilled from the speaker the energy in the room changed. Then Anna, the crowds and I all broke into song, our arms swaying in the air. As we sang, I couldn't help but steal glances at Anna. I became overwhelmed by the wonder of our five-year relationship and realised how deeply in love I was. Watching her support me in a way only she could peeled back a whole new layer of love I didn't even know existed. Singing away, my heart was content, my mind rested and my feet, well, they weren't even touching the ground. She made me feel, like she always does, that I could achieve anything. My girl.

As I climbed into bed, happy, my mind drifted back to the record. As I lay down, I said, "Sylvia, when I wake up, can you tell me how far I am ahead of the record?"

Sylvia replied, "Shall we wait for Sue to do the numbers tomorrow?"

"No. I can't wait for Sue. Just work it out using the system I gave you at the start of the record. I really need to know as soon as I can," I said, just wanting to hear I was ahead.

"Okay. I'll do that for you, Jamie. Now get some rest, sleep well."

Three hours later I was awake again. All I wanted to hear was the distance.

"Morning, Jamie, you're now seven miles ahead of the record!" said Sylvia.

My mind was blown. It was everything I wanted to hear. Yesterday, I ran well and this was the validation I needed. I felt good, buzzing on adrenaline and the belief I was definitely going to break the record. A few hours later, Sue walked in. I couldn't contain my excitement. "Sue, this morning for the first time in the last few days I'm well ahead of the record. At least seven miles ahead!" I said chirpily.

"Right, okay," said Sue in a manner that didn't match my positive vibe.

I knew immediately something was wrong. Originally, I set Sylvia up with a system to calculate where I was compared to the current record, but with Sylvia doing so much work on so little sleep the team had decided on day two that Sue, as an ex-maths teacher, should be the person in charge of numbers.

"Listen, Jamie. I need to be realistic with you. That's not what my calculations were yesterday evening. I'll double-check, but I'm almost certain you're not ahead," Sue said as calmly as possible.

It was everything I didn't want to hear. I felt like a baby who'd just had his candy snatched away. As Sue went off to recalculate, I decided I couldn't wait for her to work it out, so I called the volunteers over. "Hey, do you think you can do some calculations to see where I'm at?"

The volunteers jumped at the chance to help. After 30 minutes, they came back smiling and said, "We reckon you're nine miles ahead!"

"Really?" I responded. I was confused they had a different number to Sylvia's, but if it was even better, that was great. The numbers hokey-cokey wasn't over yet – and here's what it was all about – Sue was back. "Okay, Jamie. I've done the calculations – you're behind the record by two miles."

My face dropped. I refused to accept it. "Sue, that's not possible, Sylvia said I'm ahead. I got the volunteers to check and they said I'm ahead too."

"Jamie, I've spent hours and hours on this. I'm not sure how they're doing the calculations, but it's not correct. They need to take into account the breaks you've had and the breaks you're going to have, including sleep breaks. When you sleep tonight that's going to knock you back behind the record. You have to trust me on this."

It was all too much, but I knew Sue was right. Maths was never my strong point at school – I was kicked out of class far too often. I knew I'd left Sylvia with a system that wasn't perfectly calculated. And for a record, it needed to be perfect. It was my fault. And it was hard to accept. Really hard. I turned back into the Incredible Sulk.

"Sue, this place is filthy. Look at the carpet. It needs hoovering. Can we get someone to hoover?!" I said, panicking the carpet was ruining the record.

"Yes, we'll get that sorted," Sue said, flustered.

"Sue, Sue, can we get some music on?" I was clawing at anything I could to take away my anxiety.

Sue turned on the music. "How's that, Jamie? Motown good?"

"Yes, that will do. Thank you," I said manically.

Two minutes of Al Green didn't do it for me. "Sue, Sue, the music's no good. Can you change it?" I said.

"What, Jamie? What do you want? What music do you want?" Sue said, frustrated.

"Just anything, Sue, anything. Actually, let's just turn it off," I said, not really knowing what I wanted.

As the music went off, I realised I was trying to stay in control, but knowing I was behind the record I felt anxious and truly out of control. Out. Of. Control. I had no idea how to handle it.

As I wrestled with my mind I noticed my physical condition was looking a little unusual. My belly was protruding as if I was pregnant. For days I'd been struggling to go for a number two. To try and help, all my meals were being blitzed. Spag bol, blitzed. Sausage and egg sandwich, blitzed. I was pouring meals down my neck, retching on every single one of them. As my pace slowed, it felt like my digestive system had stopped working altogether. It was at this moment I got a surprise visit from BBC presenter and adventurer, Mark Beaumont. Mark holds the world record for the fastest ever cycle around the world, over 18,000 miles in 78 days, 14 hours and 40 minutes, so he knew the strains placed on the body when attempting big endurance events.

"How you doing, Jamie?" Mark asked.

"Kind of okay, but I'm desperate to go to the toilet. I haven't been properly in days," I said, feeling he would sympathise and understand. "Mark, actually, I think I need to go now. Could you help me off the treadmill and walk me over?"

"Of course!" said Mark.

As I stepped off, Mark supported my arms and pretty much carried me to the toilet. Anything that wasn't the treadmill's movement was excruciating pain, so having Mark take my weight was most welcome. Going into the toilet and shutting the door behind me, my mind flashed back to the incident where Ian and I had become more closely acquainted then I ever thought possible. As I adopted my awkward "standing-up" position, it worked. I opened the door to see Mark's face. "Any joy?" he asked, rather sweetly.

"We have lift off, Mark!" I could feel my cheeks beam and so did Mark's. After all the toilet malarkey, Mark, being the top man he is, used his social media presence to help rustle up some donations and build awareness for the record. As we walked arm in arm back to the treadmill, I felt we had really shared a massive victory together – the battle of the bowels.

DAY 6: HASTA LA VISTA, JAMIE

Around noon, Sue had to leave for a commitment in London, her final words, "I'm going now, Jamie, but whatever you do, don't get off that bloomin' treadmill!"

I was gutted Sue was leaving, she was one of my strongest support pillars. She was worried about where I was distance-wise, so she left Anna to take over and keep cracking the whip.

"Speed up, Jamie. That's it," I kept hearing from Anna, though it felt more like a soldier's voice.

The next minute: "Drink this, Jamie," she said, keeping up her sergeant-major role.

She was doing everything: helping me with pee breaks, notes, nutrition, but it was more than a one-person job.

My mind was on the mileage, was I behind, was I ahead? I kept asking Anna for updates, but all I got back was, "In a minute."

I knew she was juggling everything, but my anxiety was so high I couldn't help myself. What was even weirder was Anna's tone, it was completely different from what I'd known in our relationship. In one sense, I was happy Anna was supporting me, but in another, all I wanted was her nurturing me as my lover.

An hour went by, I could feel the tension rising.

Anna gave me another order. "Drink this, Jamie."

My control went flying off the treadmill. "I can't take another, 'Drink this, Jamie', where's Anna? I just want you to be my girlfriend, I want Anna back."

Anna's face changed, scrunched up and she exploded back: "Well, that's all I want too, to JUST be your girlfriend."

I could feel her emotional barriers go up. Another 10 seconds went by and she burst into tears and ran off. Weirdly, I understood the extreme situation I'd placed Anna in and how difficult it was, but I was so engrossed in the mission I was more fixated about "putting it right" between us so I could keep running, rather than being concerned for her. It felt totally out of character, to feel so emotionally unattached. It was safe to say I wasn't going to be winning the boyfriend-of-the-year award.

"Sylvia, can you grab Anna?" I said. "We had an argument and I need to put it right."

I felt numb that I couldn't just leap off the treadmill and chase after Anna and a bizarre thought popped into my head: "Is this what it's like to be the Terminator!?" You understand the situation, you know what have to do to complete the mission, but you don't "feel anything". Was I turning into the Terminator? I hoped so, at least physically. An hour later Anna came back in.

I said, "I need your clothes, your boots and your motorcycle."

I didn't, obviously, she would've terminated me. Instead, I felt my old self returning.

"I'm so sorry for shouting at you. This is a really messed-up situation I've put you in. You're doing amazing and I honestly couldn't do it without you."

Her demeanour softened. "That's okay, no need to say sorry. It's all good."

I smiled.

"You're not doing this record ever again though, just so you know," she added with a smile of her own.

I nodded back, a hundred million per cent in agreement.

After dragging myself back to normality it wasn't long before the pits of despair opened up once more. This time it felt even deeper, like an emotional edge of no return. As my eyes darted around, I spotted Lady-V setting up with her band The Honey Riders. She had helped organise so much of my trips and this record, now she was going to sing too. Her timing couldn't have been any better.

As the sun began to set, its light shimmered like a dream off the nearby restaurant windows. It bathed everyone in a warm glow as they were drawn to the tent by the sound of the band playing. "Lady Marmalade" was the song, and as amazing as it was, my eyes were closing as I struggled to stay awake. Worse still, I could feel my body breaking down, almost like when a conveyor belt snaps and everything suddenly grinds to a halt. I felt like I was fighting to stay alive.

As Lady-V closed out the song, an alchemy hit me: the music, the soft light – and I felt a huge wave of adrenaline shoot from my toes all the way to my brain. I shook my head as if to say, "What the hell was that?" Another 10 seconds passed, another surreal wave of energy surged to my brain once more. Suddenly, it was stimulated like never before. The waves of euphoria kept coming and instinctively I reached for the treadmill button, ready to run even faster. I pushed it up, up past the normal speed of 3.8 miles per hour, but it wasn't enough. I turned it up again, and again – 4.4 miles per hour now. I began running with a spring as strong as a gazelle.

Anna looked over to me. "Wow, J, you're looking good."

"I know, something strange is happening, but I'm just going with it," I said, surprised at how well I was running and how alert I felt.

With every step my stride seemed to grow longer and more relaxed. For the first time, my hips were opening up and my mobility felt as smooth as the very first mile I ran.

As I rode the gentle waves, every once in a while, I'd have a "check-in", talking to my body, as if to say, "Are you really doing this?"

I kept notching up the speed, but no matter how fast I went I kept effortlessly surfing the waves of euphoria.

"Anna, I've never felt anything like it in my life. How many miles am I on now? I said in disbelief.

"That's 375 miles – over 14 marathons in total."

I was now in territory that very few people would have ever reached.

"I don't know what's happening, and I never thought in a million years I'd say this, but I feel invincible."

It was like the bottom part of my body was on autopilot and was performing better than I wanted it to. I was in tune with every stride, yet felt no pain. All I had to do, was slightly push each shoulder forwards, alternating, and my entire body would do the rest of the work with no thinking at all. I sensed the energy in the tent shift positively, no one spoke, they just left me to it. They knew and I knew, I was in the zone. Then suddenly as I was looking out on the band, the tinted windows became a purple colour. I forced my eyes to blink, I thought I was hallucinating. The purple dissolved into green, then red and yellow too. It felt entirely natural and my body and mind sank even deeper into tranquillity. I called over to Sylvia and said, "I'm not sure what's happening right now, I'm seeing colours, but I feel amazing. I want to run even faster, but I'm worried I'm going to burn out. Should I slow down, or just go with it?"

Sylvia smiled and in her laid-back Californian accent said, "Go with it, Jamie. Ride the wave."

As I cranked up the speed, Lady-V played the next song, "Play that Funky Music". I couldn't just hear the music, I could feel it. I mean, really feel it. As the chorus kicked in, beautiful colours danced all around me and infused themselves in my soul. As the words to the song kicked in, my running certainly was laying down a boogie as the funky music played. But as for playing it til I die, well, there was no way I was going to die. I genuinely felt like the strongest runner on the planet and at the same time I was as zen as Bob Marley. The miles passed. The crowds dispersed, but one person returned – it was Ian, my future father-in-law.

"Christ, Jamie, you're looking strong," Ian said brightly.

"I know, Ian, I feel incredible. What are you doing here?"

"I spoke to Sue over the phone, she felt pretty upset about having to leave you so while she's not here, I'm going to take her place. She was on the train back to London, while I was on the train to you in Gloucester – we're doing a tag team. We're going to see this through to the end, cause that's where you're going, Jamie. All the way to the end. Now look at that speed, that is perfect. Let's go."

As the sun slowly set and darkness came to greet me, my Zen state started to fade. I became increasingly tired, though every 6 seconds I kept getting huge adrenaline shocks to my brain and colours flooding my vision. They grew more intense, vibrant and fluorescent, I could no longer tell what the dying embers of the day were and what my body was projecting on me. I felt my heart jumping, I was getting palpitations, the situation was becoming overwhelming.

"Ian, Ian, I'm freaking out. This is too much. Why am I seeing all these fluorescent colours?"

"That's a good question, Jamie. If I'm being honest, I'm not sure. You're starting to reach realms where no man has ever gone. And I suppose it was always likely some wacky things would happen. There's no manuscript for what it takes to break this record. We're making it up. We're scripting it as we go. The most important question I have for you is, are you running?" Ian said rather magnificently as he calmly studied my legs.

I followed his eyes and saw my feet going back and forth.

I looked up. "Yes, I'm running."

With no concern, Ian replied, "Well then, that's all that matters."

I felt reassured that Ian, an ex-Olympian, wasn't worried.

Minutes later, Anna shouted out, "J, I've got some good news for you."

I looked over. "You've run the equivalent of Gloucester to Glasgow in five days. You've just reached four hundred miles. Waheyyyyyy!"

Watching Anna's lips say "Waheyyy" was surreal. I understood 400 miles was a long distance to run, yet I didn't feel like I was experiencing the moment at all. I was in another dimension – outer space.

The fluorescent lights were more intense than ever, like I was on the dancefloor of a nightclub. I began to lose perception of where I was on the treadmill, I kept hearing Ian's voice, "You're too far back, Jamie. Get closer up."

"Ian, am I doing okay?" I blurted.

"You're doing great, Jamie. You're on speed," he said.

Hearing Ian's voice was the only thing that felt real, everything else didn't make sense. I kept my eyes down, looking at my fluorescent feet, making sure I wasn't going to fall off the treadmill, then all the lights blurred into one and everything went black.

DAY 7: TOO HOT TO TROT

"Jamie, Jamie, it's time."

I heard a soft whispered voice. I opened my eyes. I didn't know where I was.

Through a haze, Sylvia was peering over me, she spoke again. "Are you okay, Jamie?"

"Where am I, Sylvia?" I said, muddled.

"It's Sunday. You're doing your treadmill record, Jamie."

She said it like everything was normal.

"I'm just going to do the usual routine, take your compression socks off and do some stretching."

I started to regain my senses. "Sylvia, what happened last night? I don't remember going to bed. The last thing I remember was being in some kind of trance and seeing all these mad fluorescent lights everywhere."

"Ah, yes, last night you were struggling to speak, you weren't coherent. You kept going though, you were running well. You're doing brilliantly, you've only got one hundred miles left to break the record!"

As she took off my compression socks, she looked surprised.

"Wow, Jamie. The swelling in your ankles has almost disappeared."

"Seriously? They no longer look like elephant's ankles?" I said, thinking "no flipping way".

"They're looking great. Whatever happened yesterday, it helped. Your body must have been releasing some kind of natural anti-inflammatory. I think you're adapting, Jamie."

"That's amazing, Sylvia. Let's get me back on that treadmill."

That morning, time was flying by and the donations were rolling in. We had raised over £37,000. Not bad for a few days' work. As we hit 1 p.m. and mile 448 – or 17 marathons in six days – that meant I now had only 24 hours left to reach 517 miles, and 69 miles to match the record (just under three marathons). I was behind by 6 miles (nearly 2 hours), but I knew I had all day and night to get ahead again. My maths was getting better, but not much better, all my trust was with Ian to make sure the speed I was doing was going to be enough. It was clear I wasn't going to "smash" the record, but I had a fighting chance to maybe, just maybe, "break it". That was the new mission.

It was now late afternoon, the day before the final day. Sue was back from London and my brain was beginning to shut down altogether. Listening to the patter of my feet on the treadmill was like counting sheep in my mind. Every noise, and everything around me, was saying "go to sleep". In just over six days, I'd covered 470 miles on only a few hours' sleep, I'd effectively missed four whole nights of restful sleep. My eyelids had weights on them.

Five years ago, I remembered the time I had to go under anaesthesia and thought it would be fun to fight the drug as it sent me to sleep. Right now, it felt exactly the same. I was fighting with all my might, but knew I wasn't going to make it. I could see from the corner of my eye people were showing up, waving and asking to come into the tent and say hello. I could barely wave, I couldn't speak, I felt drool sliding down my chin. As I clung on to consciousness, I heard one of the volunteers say, "It's pretty hot in here, isn't it?"

A lightbulb moment went off. That was it. Although my brain didn't exactly light up.

"That's what I need," I said to myself.

I remembered from my Canadian adventure that when I was running in temperatures of −40°C in a sleep-deprived state, my brain instinctively didn't want to fall asleep in ice-cold temperatures. I wasn't sure of the science, but I knew, like the ice baths I had at the beginning, it would work.

"Ian, Ian. It's too hot. It's killing my brain. Can you make this place as cold as it can be?"

"I'm on it," Ian said.

I saw him and Sue jump into action. Operation Chill-Out was under way. The tent doors were lifted open and I had two fans blasting me at full speed. I felt my body temperature dropping and my brain begin to wake up – it was working. I turned up the treadmill, I wanted to get to a perfect speed where I was cold enough to stay awake, but not too cold that I went into shaking convulsions like I did on Day 4. But after 20 minutes running at a strong speed to stay warm, I began to burn out.

I needed to slow down, but I was worried that if I did my body temperature would drop too low. "Sue, can we make it warm again?" I said, struggling to string a full sentence together.

The fans were turned off and the doors closed. It began to warm up again and with every degree it increased, my brain began to shut down all over again. "Sue, as you can tell, I'm struggling to speak. But we need to keep changing the heat every five to ten minutes. Can I just shout 'Canada' when I want it cold and 'Lanzarote' when I want it warm?"

"Sure, Jamie. We can do that."

Lanzarote held its own significance. It's where me, Anna, her parents and their family go on holiday every year. And it's WARM there. With this new method, cold doing its job of keeping me awake, a surge of hope rushed through my system, I felt I had a real shot at making it.

As the "Canadas" and "Lanzarotes" rolled by, it edged into evening and Ian offered words of encouragement. "Jamie, you've got one night to get as far ahead as you possibly can. We're going to get you to a distance so when you wake on the final day, you'll be ahead of the record. How does that sound?"

I sort of mumbled and slopped some drool back in response, I didn't really know what I was capable of.

"Right then, if that's the plan, we're going to have to increase the speed and start going for it for the rest of the night," Ian said determinedly.

I was past logical thinking. If Ian had told me to jump off a bridge to break the record, I would have. I ramped up the speed to 4.4 miles per hour. Now, that doesn't sound fast, but when you're over 480 miles in, it felt like I was trying to outrun Usain Bolt.

As we ground on, I started to become dizzy. "Ian, I think we need to slow down. I'm not going to make it at this speed. I'm not doing well."

Ian replied, "Jamie, you're doing great. We're on track to be ahead of the record when you wake up. Keep going."

I trusted Ian, I kept pushing as hard as I could. It felt like my hips we're wrenching and ripping apart with every stride. The lights around me, including the red digits on the treadmill, started to blur again and I became unsteady on my feet.

"You're doing well, Jamie."

"I'm not, Ian. I'm seriously not. I can't keep this pace up. I can't do it. I need to go to bed."

"Keep looking at the speed, Jamie."

I knew Ian was trying to distract me, but I was running at breaking point.

I thought hitting breaking point the night before the end was crazy, so I said again a little more sternly, "Ian. Listen to me. I'm not going to make it. I'm done. Can I go to bed, please? I know I'll wake up behind the record, but I'll have all morning to go hard at it."

"Keep looking ahead, Jamie. You're doing well," said Ian for the 501st time.

"IAN! You're not listening to me. WHY DON'T YOU JUST F*** OFFFFF!" I screamed.

The marquee fell silent.

I listened to the sound of the treadmill, acting like nothing had happened. Then 20 seconds went by and my brain caught up. "Did I just tell my future father-in-law to F off?"

"Sorry, Ian," I said. "Please, listen. I know we've gone back and forth and you've kept me going, distracting me, but I'm not going to make it through tonight. I know it's way earlier than normal and I know I'm going to wake up behind, but I'm on the brink of falling off and if that happens, it's over. Please, let me go to bed."

It was weird, as much as I knew it was the right thing to do, I wasn't at the stage of fully trusting myself.

But Ian was listening. "Okay, I tell you what. How about you go for another hour at four miles per hour and then you can come off?"

The expression on my face did my negotiating.

"Thirty minutes then?" said Ian, smiling.

"Deal."

Although I was relieved to be going to bed soon, I knew I'd be waking up behind the record. I just had to believe I had more in the tank to surpass it tomorrow.

FINAL DAY: WE CAN BE HEROES

As I opened my eyes I felt panicky like I'd slept through my alarm.

I shouted manically, "Sylvia, is it time?"

I heard Sylvia's relaxed voice. "Yes, Jamie, it's time."

Sylvia began the routine one last time: compression socks off, muscles gently stretched and her usual calming questions. "How did you sleep?"

I had to be honest.

"Compared to all the other three-hour sleeps – not great."

"Do you remember you kept trying to get out of bed?"

I gave her a puzzled look.

"You kept waking up and insisting it was time to get back on the treadmill. You kept mumbling and shouting, 'We have to do this now!'"

My mind was blank, I had no recollection, but I was fully aware it was now 4 a.m. and I was walking to the treadmill, taking tiny steps, crawling and screaming in pain as Sylvia supported my arm taking as much weight as she could. Turning the treadmill on, it had no such complaints, slowly waking up all my micro-muscles as they screamed back in return. I hoped it would be the last time I'd ever have to go through this torture. But knowing I was behind the record I fought on, waking my legs faster than normal. I knew this was the final push.

Just then, one of the marquee doors swung open. It was Dad. And Dad was topless. Big, bushy chest hair, everywhere. Down below he was wearing a red and green tartan kilt with a matching tartan hat with fake ginger hair flowing out the sides. He was carrying a life-size cut-out of a man.

He shouted, "It's the final day. You've made it. I've got one of your heroes here to get you to the end."

I thought I was hallucinating again.

Anna, who was sat on the floor, said, "Don, who the hell is that?!"

Dad said, "Oh come on, Anna'rrr, you all know who this is? It's Pitbull."

I looked at Anna. Anna looked at me.

"I think it's that American rapper?" she said, uncertainly.

"Anna'rrr, type 'Pitbull' into that music thing, will ya? Let's get some energy going on!" yelled Dad.

Anna did her thing on Spotify and Pitbull's "Don't Stop the Party" kicked in. I'd heard it before, but I couldn't quite get my head around what the freakin' hell was going on at 4 a.m. in the morning.

The whole tent came alive, Anna got up to dance, Dad was doing dad dancing, even the volunteers were shaking their stuff! The final day had truly begun.

I was in full stride now, running hard, and it was only right I got fully suited in my green Adventureman costume – red cape and all. By 9 a.m., Sue let me know how far I'd run – 511 miles. I was 6 miles behind the record and had 4 hours left to beat it. For the first time, I knew I was going to make it. I was back on track to beat the record and not only that, surpass it by a fair few miles, as long as nothing went wrong. Each extra mile would be stretching the record further and would turn the day into a party. I felt myself relax, slightly.

Sue placed some expensive Swiss chocolate on the treadmill and with a wink said, "Let's not worry about your nutrition any more. You've earned this."

I threw three pieces in my mouth and let them melt on my tongue. It was the first bit of "naughty" food I'd had in a month. The chocolate dissolved and slid slowly down my throat. Orgasmic.

Everything seemed to speed up, within an hour, everyone seemed to know I was going to break the record. We created a video for social media, me grimacing and grinning as I said, "Get down here for ten a.m. to watch me break the record and join the party when I get off the treadmill!"

During the seven days, we'd been reaching hundreds of thousands of people and millions more through the media and news coverage. Within 30 minutes of posting, hundreds of people had begun turning up. I could feel the excitement growing. The Attwoolls team, who had set up the marquee, began removing windows so I could see the crowd. It was something I'd imagined for months, to look everyone in the eyes, to connect and share the special moment together. This was my home town, so for me, there was no better spot on the planet than to share it with the people of Gloucester.

I turned the treadmill up, I was gunning it now, my feet on fire, a spring like Michael Jordan. I've broken records and completed life-changing challenges, but this one felt different. I wasn't craving the feeling of breaking the record, all I wanted was to feel the connection between me and everyone involved. I realised it was about the people. The people who supported. Donated. The moments you share and the connection you feel with one another. When you know you are part of something that's bigger than every single one of us. I was surrounded by well-wishers, everyone was buzzing and that's when I took my eye off the treadmill. A gasp went up as I stumbled like a drunk, just about managing to stay on my feet.

I heard Anna's voice. "Don't you dare fall off that treadmill now!"

I regained my composure and heard some relieved laughter. I looked into my support team's eyes and could see how exhausted they all were too. We were holding on together. By now, news reporters, journalists, and more and more supporters were arriving – even a DJ with his decks. He quickly got to work, the crowds swaying to his beat. I ran harder, skipping with each step. Everyone around me chatting and laughing, our guard dropping, celebration so near.

"J, in ten minutes you're going to hit five hundred and seventeen miles. You're doing to do it." Anna beamed with happiness.

I turned up the treadmill again and the crowd let out a huge cheer. Five minutes to go. I looked up and there were at least 500 people who had showed up with an hour's notice. A chant broke out: "Go Jamie! Go Jamie!" I was stretching out my legs now, striding like an athlete coming close to the finish line for gold.

Anna grabbed the microphone to let the crowd know what was happening. "Jamie's about to break the record. Let's count down. Here we go. Three... Two... One..."

As everyone said "ONE", I knew I had to keep running for a few hours more, but I turned off the treadmill to embrace the moment. I put my hands in the air and let out a huge "YEEEEEAH!" Anna handed me the microphone as all my emotions spilled out. "I can't believe I've got this far. Hats off to previous record holder Sharon Gayter. What a woman." I paused so we could show our appreciation for Sharon then said, "Right, now that's out of the way, I have to say records aren't here to be broken – they're here to be SMASHED!"

The crowd erupted, I turned the treadmill back on and went to run, but my legs had gone. When I say gone, I mean jelly legs gone.

I looked at them and said, "Come on, move, will ya!"

The crowd looked confused. I put my hands up as if to say, "I'm trying!" and slowly but surely, they started moving again, but felt like they were gone. It was like the subconscious part of my brain that's supposed to work with my legs switched off entirely and there was nothing I could do about it – it was back to gritting my teeth.

Something I hadn't shared with anyone, apart from the close team members, was that my mission was to make it to 521 miles. In 2017, Amy Hughes managed to make it to this distance, but didn't have it "officially" ratified. I felt like I wasn't going to do it and panic started to set in. I scoffed the Swiss chocolate, hoping it would get me going. I started to sing with the crowd, anything to fuel my fire, but nothing would do it.

Out of the corner of my eye I saw Dad approaching with a family, he said, "J, this family drove five hours to see you. Their ten-year-old boy Thomas has syringomyelia just like you. I said they can celebrate with us on the stage until you finish. J, let's give them some hope."

I caught Thomas' eye and we smiled at each other. I put my thumbs up at the family, turned the treadmill up and began running with all my might.

They had given me all the hope I needed. I ran faster, harder, forgetting about the distance, wanting to show Thomas what we're both made of. An hour later, Anna let me know I'd reached Amy's distance of 521 miles. Pheewww.

I asked for the microphone again and paid homage to Amy. Even though she wasn't the "official" record holder, I knew how much torture she must have gone through to reach this distance.

As I spoke, I looked to the crowds and saw Sue and Ian walking off. They didn't say goodbye. Like true Olympians they slipped away knowing their job here was done. Classy. After they left, I deteriorated even further. The chocolate was gone. I could barely stay on my feet. As the treadmill whirled around, the crowd remained magnificent. It was like they felt my pain and sang at my soul not to give up. I couldn't see anything other than a sea of people. It was a few minutes before 1 p.m. and I was on the home straight.

Anna got back on the microphone. "Jamie is about to become the new world record holder." She started the countdown. "Ten, nine, eight, seven, six, five, four... three... two... one. That's it!"

Over a thousand faces in front of me all let out a huge roar, the atmosphere changed from a slight tension to relief, joy and happiness. I'd never heard or felt anything like it. I turned off the treadmill. The record was now at 524.2 miles!

I wearily raised both arms in the air and let out a massive prolonged, "Coooooome ooooon!"

This time, I knew it really was all over. Cheers turned into chanting, "Jamie, Jamie, Jamie..." The feeling of elation was overwhelming, It was as if England had won the World Cup. Anna pushed the microphone into my hand.

I looked at the crowd and said, "I can't wait to get off this treadmill." There was a huge laugh from everyone. Every thought and emotion I'd felt spilled out. "There was one day on this record attempt I woke up and couldn't move my legs," I said. "It reminded me of being a sick kid again – not being able to move my legs. But somehow I managed to crawl back on and get moving!"

I lifted a hand into the air as applause rang out. My mind was whirring, I thought about all the families and superhero families in front of me with sick kids who now had tears running down their faces.

I continued, "No matter how hard your challenges are, just keep smashing through them!"

The crowd erupted again. I wanted to share this moment with everyone and in one last surprise Anna had chosen a song.

I said, "Anna wants to play one final song that we can share together. I don't know what it is, but it best be bloody good."

A thrash of anthemic guitar kicked in – familiar, brilliant. David Bowie's "Heroes". And now we really all could be, just for one day. My body was shutting down, someone slipped crutches under my arms so I could get to the front of the stage and be close to everyone. As Bowie sang about how we could all be heroes for ever and ever, I went arm in arm, swaying and dancing with Mum, Dad, Anna and my brother Lee. Dad popped open a bottle of champagne, poured it over my mouth, and mostly over my face. Tears of joy began rolling down my cheeks and as I looked out at all the families, kids on shoulders, friends and superhero families from the charity, everyone else was crying too.

We'd raised over £60,000 in seven days. Over £250,000 in the last year. And now, over £1 million from all my adventures. I felt drunk on all the love that was floating in the air.

In one last surge of energy to show my appreciation to the crowd, I clenched my fist, put it over my heart and let out a huge "rooooaarrr". The energy went through the roof, bursting into the sky, time slowing to a single perfect moment and all I felt was, *this is for you*.

EPILOGUE

As I hobbled from the marquee, the crowd's cheers still ringing in my ears, I was all over the place, I didn't know what planet I was on. Mum whizzed right up next to me in her car and using my crutches I propelled myself into the back seat. As we arrived back at her house, I went to get out of the car, but my legs weren't strong enough to hold me up. They'd given up. Shabir, my foster brother from Afghanistan, who's also an amateur boxing champion, picked me up like a baby, holding me in his arms, and carried me in.

As Mum ran me a bath, Shabir again hoisted me in. I hadn't said a word to anyone. Anna was soaping me down, staring at my body, which was now skin and bones – and it hit me like a freight train. I began having flashbacks from the agonising seven days that had just passed, and cried. Not just crying, but for ten whole minutes wailing ugly crying. It was dawning on me what I'd just achieved, which was both traumatic and cathartic, leaving me with a feeling that I now genuinely believed I could achieve anything. And I mean anything.

After the bath, Mum made me sausage sandwiches, smothered in butter. As soon as the butter hit the back of my tongue, my mouth filled up with saliva at the expectation that some fat was about to enter my body. I swallowed the sandwich whole, with exactly three chews.

That evening I fell into a deep sleep and didn't wake up for 14 hours, but as I took my first breath I realised immediately something wasn't right.

"Muuuum, come quick," I yelled.

She burst through the bedroom door, a worried look on her face. "What is it, J?"

"I can't breathe properly. I'm struggling to catch my breath."

Mum quickly called the doctor and, thankfully, Doctor Layzell came to see me immediately. After taking some blood tests, he said he'd have the results within a few hours.

Sure enough a few hours later, I got the call. "Hello, Jamie. We've got the results. The news isn't great, but it makes sense why you're finding it so hard to breathe. You've lost half your red blood cells. Also, your muscle enzyme, which is called creatine kinase, is three times higher than it should be."

"Sorry, Doctor Layzell, I'm not sure what that means?"

"Well, it means your body is most probably flooded with inflammation from the lack of sleep and from all the miles you ran – and because of that, unwanted enzymes have leaked out of your damaged muscles. With half your red blood cells gone, you're currently anaemic. I'd say it's best we get you to hospital, are you okay with that?"

"Yes, absolutely."

As I lay on a hospital bed in Gloucestershire Royal Hospital, on a drip, painkillered up to the max, I thought, this wasn't exactly what I had in mind after breaking the record. On my third day of recovery, I had a surprise visit from a local journalist who presented me with a "Hero of the Week" award.

As he chatted to me, he asked, "How do you feel?"

I said, "How do I feel? Well, you want to see me attempt to go to the toilet. I use that grandpa walker, over there, scream the house down as I grind out an enormous ten-metre shuffle, wondering if I'm going to get there on time – all while the nurses cheer, 'You can do it, Jamie.' So, you could say, I don't overly feel like a hero."

The journalist seemed to appreciate the humour on this shambolic state of affairs.

"I tell you what though, those nurses over there have looked after me like nothing I've ever experienced before, they're definitely the real heroes," I said proudly.

After the fancy bedside award ceremony, I kept having regular visits from doctors. As I was chatting to one of them, I explained that when I reached around 400 miles, I started to have an out-of-body experience seeing purples and greens and told her how amazing it felt.

I asked inquisitively, "Do you have a scientific reason why that would happen?"

The doctor's eyes lit up. "That's really interesting you say that," she said with utter enthusiasm. "It reminds me of a study I worked on about starving prisoners in a war camp.

We found as their bodies were put under increasing strain, they experienced what you're talking about – a huge euphoric rush, the body releasing endorphins. Only in this instance, it happened when they were getting really close to death."

My mouth was wide open as the doctor continued, "Basically, the body produces all those chemicals in one last-ditch attempt to stay alive. It's quite remarkable."

I think she could see my stunned expression and added, "That's quite a scary thought, isn't it?"

I was shocked, but not in complete disbelief.

After a few more days in hospital, I started to feel like a burden and wanted to leave. I was supposed to be supporting hospitals, not draining them.

When one of the nurses saw my frustration, she simply said, "You've spent years thanking and supporting our hospitals, so even if it's for a few days, we're so happy we get to thank you."

When I finally made it home after all the hospital shenanigans, I needed to send off the evidence to Guinness World Records for them to "officially" ratify the treadmill challenge. There was a lot of it, literally hundreds of sheets of paperwork, the records of all the volunteer shifts and a full week's worth of CCTV footage. We sent the hard drive to them just days before the first wave of coronavirus hit, when the world went to pot and into lockdown. At the time of writing, nearly a year later, the judicator is still working from home and hasn't been back into the Guinness office to watch the footage. Oh my, the craziness of the world we live in.

As the weeks and months went on, the swelling went down, but being anaemic wasn't fun. Every time I moved my body, it was all in slow motion fighting for every breath. It took my body months to recover. But recover it did, as the body always does eventually. It was around this time that while giving a talk at my old junior school, St Peter's, I had another surprise. This time it was from ITV who wanted to present me with an award – ITV's West Country Pride of Britain "Fundraiser of the Year". I was pretty blown away. What an honour.

This meant I was invited to the national televised awards, along with 19 other amazing fundraisers from around Britain, to see who would win the overall award. I knew it would be special, so I took Dad along. I was wearing my ripped, faded and quite frankly filthy Adventureman suit, while Dad scrubbed up a little better in his suit and braces, although he did look like he was out of an episode of *Peaky Blinders* – and he had a baseball cap on back to front.

As we walked on to the red carpet of Grosvenor Hotel, it felt completely surreal. Either side were lines of fans looking for autographs and selfies with the stars. As we found ourselves halfway down, I looked at Dad and said, "Shall we just stay put and milk this red carpet, or what?"

"Oh yeeeeah, son, we shall!" he shouted.

The first celeb showed up and my dad was like a kid in a sweet shop.

He screamed "Brunoooo, Brunooooo" while simultaneously fist pumping the air. With a huge grin he turned to me and said, "J, that's Frank Bruno."

He was over like a shot asking for a photo and then looking really proud said, "This is my boy, Frank. He's up for Fundraiser of the Year!"

One after another, star after star rocked up: Sir Ben Kingsley, singer Alexandra Burke, Danny Jones from McFly, England football manager Gareth Southgate, you name them, they were there! And we were on the same carpet as them! One of the stars was former Manchester United player Ryan Giggs.

Dad leaned in and said, "We gotta get a picture with Giggsy!"

As Ryan walked past, Dad excitedly asked, "Giggsy, can we get a picture together? I'd love to show my best friend, he's a huge Liverpool fan."

His face was a picture of horror as he reluctantly had his photo taken with us.

Dad looked at me and said, "He wasn't overly warm, was he?"

I replied, "Dad, you do realise Ryan Giggs was a Man United player, Liverpool's biggest rivals, don't you? I think you might have just said one of the most offensive things possible to him."

Dad just shrugged his shoulders as if to say, "Minor detail, J."

Inside, we found ourselves sat at a table where pretty much every single star had to walk past us to get to their dinner table. At one point, presenter Dermot O'Leary popped past, but before he did, he gave me a quick shoulder massage. It was actually pretty good, and I think he should consider a new profession if he ever gets bored of television work. During dinner, my nerves were really, really bad. So bad I struggled to eat. When I looked around at all the other fundraisers, they had a similar look and hadn't touched their dinners either. As each story was shown on the big screen, I had a lump in my throat for all these people who are genuinely making our world a better place.

As the show neared the end, Carol Vorderman said, "Right, now it's time to announce our national winner for Fundraiser of the Year…" All of a sudden the camera pointed at me and Carol said, "Up you come, Adventureman!"

Everyone stood up. A standing ovation. I looked at Dad in disbelief. There was a part of me that felt like it might have been me, but more like I hoped it would be me, probably just like all the other fundraisers. Walking through the crowds I felt like this should be one of these moments you cherish, but my brain couldn't comprehend what was going on. I had watched the Pride of Britain awards ceremony since I was a kid and now I had won it.

As I climbed up on stage with the amazing Carol Vorderman, she said, "I've been following you on Twitter. Let's show everyone what you've been up to."

Then a video played from all my past adventures, highlighting that we had raised more than a million for sick kids through my adventures and the Superhero Foundation. When the video finished, Carol invited me to tell people my story. I can't quite remember what I said (which is weird, I'm up on stage a lot as a motivational speaker, always keeping my cool, but on this occasion, it's fair to say that was never going to happen).

One of the first things I remember saying was, "I just want to say thank you to my mum and dad for popping me out!"

As soon as I said it, I remember thinking, did I actually just say that? Everyone laughed, including Simon Cowell right in front of me, which was pretty surreal, though I'm not sure my mum was quite as amused. It dawned on me that I was in a room with probably the most influential people in the country and all I could think of was to showcase Anna – she is my true love and partner in crime after all.

So, I said, "I'm proper in love, you know, Carol. I know I'm up here getting this award, but my wifey Anna is currently running one hundred marathons for the Girlguiding community, completely barefoot, across Britain. She makes me look like a wussy!"

Carol replied, "She's on an adventure as well? But when do you ever get to see each other?"

I replied, "Every couple of months. Actually, thinking about it, maybe that's why it works so well."

Everyone laughed again and my nerves started to settle. I managed to acknowledge the other fundraisers, which felt important as they're all as equally inspiring and deserving. And five years ago, I was sat where they were and didn't win, so I could really empathise with their disappointment.

Then Carol said, "Right, we've got two very special people to give you the award," and two Olympic heroes of mine, Greg Rutherford and Dina Asher-Smith, walked out holding the actual silver sparkly Pride of Britain award (you know, the one with the wings).

The duo said some incredible things about my achievements and at the end Greg said, "The fact you do all this and don't get any medals at the end and you raise money for sick kids is just so inspiring. For us, this is a huge honour to give you this award."

I was completely choked up, but gratefully accepted the trophy – half smiling, half welling up as I did so.

The final part of the show saw all of the Pride of Britain winners take the stage while Emeli Sandé performed her new song "Sparrow". The lyrics were beautiful, including a line about singing for all the fallen heroes. As the song reached its climax, confetti fell from above and tears rolled down my face. It couldn't have been a prouder moment – and deep down I knew it was down to every single person who had supported and donated along the way. I felt like there should have been so many people up there on stage with me.

A few months after the awards, we went into the pandemic lockdown, and Anna and I were finally getting to spend a lot of time together. And, I'm not sure how these kinds of things happen... but she fell pregnant. Nine months later, we had our first baby girl, Storm, born at home. I thought the run across America and breaking the "dreadmill" record were going to be the greatest challenges of my life, but I now have a feeling – with our daughter already running rings around us – that the adventure has only just begun.

ACKNOWLEDGEMENTS

Wow, where do I start with thank yous?! First up, the people who helped me pull this book together: Debbie Chapman for keeping me on track and off the naughty step with deadlines. James Briggs for dealing with my dyslexic brain and for correcting parts that weren't proppa' English, and Emily Kearns for your eagle eyes, spotting the things that still slipped through the net.

SPECIAL RUNNERS

Tara Lund, who flew from Canada to the US to run with me – yes, that's right, flew. Amazing support. Next up, a thank you to Richard Smith, Joe Lister and Ali Hastings from Unite Students for a big donation and all their support in bringing runners to join in on the adventure – genuinely incredible. Across America, I had a tracker where people could find me, day or night; thanks to Microsoft Partners and Ant Goddard (of course, I call him "Ant-Man") at ZeroSixZero for the tech support.

THE FINISH LINE CREW

As for the finish in Gloucester, Massachusetts, a special thanks to the Good Morning Gloucester team for helping out at the finish line: Joey Ciaramitaro, Nichole Schrafft and Pat Dalpiaz. A big thank you to Gloucester Mayor, Sefatia Romeo Theken, especially for arranging the police convoy. Another big thank you to Ray Johnston and Sheree Zizik at the fancy Beauport Hotel, and a special thank you to Loran Caputo and Brad Pierce at the amazing Cape Ann Motor Inn, who put us up for a whole week after the finish. It would be a crime if I didn't mention the famous Crow's Nest for all the beers we drank (when my run was complete, obviously). And lastly, every single person that turned up for the finish – I can't include all your names or I'd run out of space in this book – thank you.

THE TREADMILL WORLD RECORD

Up next, we have the "dreadmill" thank yous. Attempting world records is a whole different ball game, and when it comes to support, let's just say you need A LOT of help. Firstly, to Gloucester Docks for the space. A big thank you to Roger Underdown at RU Electrical, and to Pete McCrea at Production AV for the big screen outside our marquee, so people could gawp at me like I was a freak show. Thanks to Richard Lakin, for providing the treadmill itself; Chris Nyland at Nettl of Gloucester for the awesome banners, and Steve Mitchell at

Festoon Events – I knew this was an unusual event, but he nailed it. Victoria Clark, for organising all the volunteers (and my life). Raptor Security Services and All Coopers for the two cameras and 24/7 CCTV footage. Paul Montagu and his kid, Theo, for running around as the "little white van man". Dan Snowdon and Ann and Toby Wooldridge at Peppers, for all the lovely nosh. Wagamama, Cole Bar Grill and Pizza Express for supporting us. Ben Limbrick at First Aid and Trauma Training for keeping me alive, the army way. Sylvia Chrisney, for all the trigger point therapy and emotional friendship support. Sue and Ian McNuff, best mother- and father-in-law ever. Rich Leigh at Radioactive PR for all the social media support. Ermin Plant for fencing – every little helps, huh?

Big sponsors: Freemans Event Partners, for the big donation and unlimited tea and coffee. An enormous thank you to Nigel Attwooll, at, you guessed it, Attwoolls, for providing the marquee – normally for weddings but perfect for a treadmill record. James Davies from Purple Bricks, for promising that if I broke the record, they'd double their donation – that definitely helped with motivation. And a big thank you to Enzo Mora at The Mortgage Brain, a good-hearted and generous friend.

Volunteers: A final treadmill thank you is to all the volunteers, I believe over one hundred in total – all checking times and distances, abiding by GWR rules even at 4 a.m. Oh, let's not forget to say thank you to the cardboard-cut-out Pitbull – what a great celeb appearance.

I'd also like to thank the University of Gloucestershire – as an honorary fellow, they've been super-supportive.

FRIENDS AND FAM

Mont, for all the bants. Craig Joseph, for being so supportive throughout. Ed Archer from Athlete Academy, for always looking after my body and telling me when to "crack on". Mario Peters, aka "Super Mario", a good friend and mentor who's always there – you continue to give time and power me up when it matters most.

Superhero Foundation trustee thank yous are a must. Wendy Fabian, Chris Nyland, and Nigel Purveur – you really are my superheroes.

Nearly there... (promise). I'd like to include my mum and dad for producing me. Very kind of them. Of course, my brother Lee, who this book is dedicated to. And Anna and Storm – the best ladies in my life.

And finally, to YOU. For reading this, for sharing my story, for donating and for anything else that you've done to be the hero that you are – thank you!

ABOUT THE AUTHOR

Jamie has delivered motivational, inspiring and entertaining (even virtual) talks for schools, corporates, not-for-profits and after-dinner events all around the world.

"The way you tied your story to our mission statement, 'empowering people to achieve more', was outstanding. One of the best conferences we've ever had. I think the standing ovation at the end of your talk said it all"   Microsoft

"Jamie has an inspiring story to tell, using his stories to motivate others with his incredible adventures"
Sir Steve Redgrave, rower, five-time Olympic Gold medallist

"Fast-moving, inspiring and funny. You left us wanting more"
     NHS

"Your resilience and sense of adventure is another level and you delivered your talk in the most relatable and down to earth way. We'd love you back"   Sky

"You blew us away. Funny. Inspiring. One of the best talks we've seen"   Google

"We laughed, we cried. Jamie's can-do spirit that no matter what situations he faced, whether tackling −40C temperatures, or running 200 back-to-back marathons, he made it through – and shared his story in the most entertaining and inspirational way"

Amazon

To book Jamie, or find out more visit:

www.adventureman.org

Photo © Ian Baker Photography

You can also follow Jamie's adventures on Facebook, YouTube, Twitter and Instagram as "Adventureman".

ADVENTUREMAN

THE ASTONISHING TRUE STORY

Paperback
ISBN: 978-1-84953-969-2
Price: £9.99 UK / $13.99 US / $15.99 CAN

At the age of nine, Jamie's family feared he would never walk again.

Twenty years later, he set off to run 5,000 miles coast to coast across Canada.

When Jamie decides to repay the hospitals that saved his life as a child, he embarks on the biggest challenge of his life: running the equivalent of 200 marathons back-to-back, solo and unsupported, in −40 degree weather, surviving all kinds of injuries and traumas on the road and wearing through 13 pairs of trainers. And he does it all dressed as the superhero, the Flash.

Though his journey was both mentally and physically exhausting, it was the astounding acts of kindness and hospitality he encountered along the way that kept him going. Whether they gave him a bed for the night, food for the journey, a donation to his charity or companionship and encouragement during the long days of running, Jamie soon came to realise that every person who helped him towards his goal was a superhero too.

Have you enjoyed this book?

Jamie would consider you a superhero if you left an
online review wherever you bought this book.

––––––––––––

If you're interested in finding out more about our books, find
us on Facebook at **Summersdale Publishers**, on Twitter at
@Summersdale and on Instagram at **@summersdalebooks**
and get in touch. We'd love to hear from you!

Thanks very much for buying this Summersdale book.

www.summersdale.com